Early American Abolitionists

A COLLECTION OF
ANTI-SLAVERY WRITINGS
1760–1820

This book and all publications of the Gilder Lehrman Institute are made possible by the generosity of the Julienne M. Michel Trust.

Early American Abolitionists

A COLLECTION OF
ANTI-SLAVERY WRITINGS

1760–1820

GENERAL EDITOR

JAMES G. BASKER

*President, Gilder Lehrman Institute of American History
& Ann Whitney Olin Professor of English,
Barnard College, Columbia University*

ASSOCIATE EDITORS

Justine Ahlstrom · Kathleen Barry
Siobhan Phinney · Nicole Seary · Sandra Trenholm
Thorin Tritter

THE GILDER LEHRMAN INSTITUTE
OF AMERICAN HISTORY
NEW YORK · 2005

THE GILDER LEHRMAN
INSTITUTE *of* AMERICAN HISTORY

19 WEST 44TH STREET, SUITE 500
NEW YORK, NY 10036
www.gilderlehrman.org

CONTENTS

INTRODUCTION

THIS VOLUME reprints some fifteen anti-slavery texts that, with one or two exceptions, have been out of print for almost two centuries. They have been edited by an unusual editorial team, consisting of scholars at every rank from undergraduate to full professor. Our overarching purpose has been to restore to view some of the extensive anti-slavery literature—pamphlets, poems, sermons, printed speeches, and more—that flourished in early America. As the twenty-first century begins, it is easy to forget that slavery was not universally accepted during the Founding Era. Despite the failure of the founders to eradicate slavery at the national level, there were—as this literature attests—energetic and articulate opponents of slavery who attacked it relentlessly and achieved significant gains in many parts of the country over the period 1760 to 1820.

One defining element of this publishing project is its inclusion of twelve outstanding undergraduates as lead researchers and scholarly editors. These young historians are the first cohort to have been elected "Gilder Lehrman History Scholars," a new initiative designed to identify and support the top undergraduate history students across the country, with a particular eye to their potential as future professional historians. Chosen in 2003 from a national applicant pool of more than 400 nominated history majors, from over 200 colleges and universities, these twelve are a kind of "Rhodes Scholar" elite, representing the best in a rising generation of history scholars. The twelve elected for 2003 deserve specific mention:

> Kristin DeBusk, *Texas Technological University*
> Laura Ferguson, *Oregon State University*
> Sarah Gamertsfelder, *University of Maine*
> Kathryn Gin, *Stanford University*
> J. Micah Guster, *Tennessee State University*
> Rebecca Miller, *University of North Carolina, Chapel Hill*
> Raphael B. Moreen, *Princeton University*
> Nicholas Osborne, *Johns Hopkins University*

Jennifer Randazzo, *University of Notre Dame*
Sam Rosenfeld, *Columbia University*
Eric C. Steinhart, *St. Olaf College*
Thomas Wolf, *Harvard University*

These young scholars spent eight weeks in the summer of 2003 in New York City, supported by the Gilder Lehrman Institute of American History, working under the supervision of Dr. Thorin Tritter, Dr. Kathleen Barry, Justine Ahlstrom, and Nicole Seary. As the History Scholars began their research training and undertook each of their respective editorial projects, they also received behind-the-scenes visits to major archives (including Columbia's Rare Book and Manuscript Library, the Schomburg Center for Research in Black Culture, the New-York Historical Society, the New York Public Library, and others) and enjoyed small seminars with a series of leading historians that included Eric Foner, Christine Stansell, Thomas Bender, Steven Mintz, Kenneth Jackson, Catherine Clinton, and Sean Wilentz.

Beyond the training of young scholars, the aim was to publish a useful body of texts that would be of interest to scholars, college and high school teachers, and students at every level. To that end, the texts are reprinted in this volume with short editorial introductions that place them in historic context, and with essential notes that clarify the most obscure references. In addition, each of the twelve units is being published in a separate pamphlet version, to enable teachers and students to acquire inexpensively individual works from the larger collection.

Each of the titles reprinted here is potentially of interest—and perhaps surprise—to a reading public encouraged today to think of anti-slavery sentiment arising principally with Frederick Douglass, William Lloyd Garrison, and Harriet Beecher Stowe in the mid-1800s. The book begins, for example, with two works by Anthony Benezet, the Philadelphia Quaker who started a school for black children in his own home in the 1750s and, from 1759 until his death in 1784, produced a steady stream of pamphlets exposing the evils of slavery that were widely read in Britain as well as America. The first of the two (both edited by Thomas Wolf) is a reprint of Benezet's earliest anti-slavery writing, the 1759 pamphlet *Observations on the Inslaving, Importing, and Purchasing of Negroes* (here based on the 1760 second edition text), in which Benezet draws on the Bible to excoriate the immorality and sinfulness of slaveholding. The second, Benezet's *Notes on the Slave Trade* of 1781, develops a subtler indictment, implicating even those of his readers who do not own slaves but participate in the economic system that slave labor supports: "It is your money that pays the merchant, and thro' him the captain and African butchers. You therefore are guilty: Yea, principally guilty, of all these frauds, robberies, and murders."

Next is another Quaker pamphlet, *A Mite Cast into the Treasury: Or, Observations on Slave-Keeping,* by the New Jersey farmer David Cooper, who published it in 1772 in Philadelphia. Cooper attacks slavery with vehemence and profound insight, tracing the institution of African slavery, as he says in the opening lines of his introduction, back to "the power of prejudice" which leads whites "to consider people with a black skin, on a footing with domestic animals, form'd to serve and obey, whom they may kick, beat, and treat as they please." As editor Kristin DeBusk reveals, Cooper published the pamphlet anonymously and his authorship was not known until the 20th century. But he was also a man of action. On three different occasions, in 1785, 1786, and 1788, Cooper visited Congress to urge them to abolish slavery, and in 1789 he made a direct appeal to George Washington himself, the newly elected first president.

David Cooper is also the author of the third of the reprints, a 1783 pamphlet he chose this time to publish in Trenton, New Jersey. With the Revolutionary War just ended and American independence secured, Cooper's argument shifts, as editor Rebecca Miller points out, to the framework of natural rights, and the hypocrisy of Americans fighting for liberty but continuing to hold slaves. His title acknowledges the new political reality and makes clear his theme: *A Serious Address to the Rulers of America, on the Inconsistency of Their Conduct Respecting Slavery: Forming A Contrast Between the Encroachments of England on American Liberty, and American Injustice in Tolerating Slavery.* Perhaps unsurprisingly, Cooper's pamphlet was reprinted in London that same year, by the Quaker J. Phillips, who published many anti-slavery titles. With this publication, Cooper joined a rising generation of self-consciously American writers that included Joel Barlow, David Humphreys, Philip Freneau, Timothy Dwight, and Sarah Wentworth

Apthorp Morton who all regarded the founding principles of America as radically inconsistent with racial slavery.

A different kind of text altogether forms the fourth unit in the book: the published version of *The Constitution of the Pennsylvania Society, for Promoting the Abolition of Slavery*, as reprinted with revisions and supplements in 1787, here edited by Sam Rosenfeld. Originally formed in 1775, but its activities suspended for the duration of the Revolutionary War, the Pennsylvania Abolition Society was a model for abolition societies formed in other states and, because of its proximity to Congress, often took the lead on the national stage. Among the many prominent Pennsylvanians included in its membership were Benjamin Rush, James Pemberton, Benjamin Franklin, Frederick Muhlenberg, and Thomas Paine.

Next in the volume comes another piece of Pennsylvania anti-slavery writing, this time in the form of a long poem, attributed to the Quaker Joseph Sansom, entitled *A Poetical Epistle to the Enslaved Africans, in the Character of an Ancient Negro* (Philadelphia, 1790). Published by the staunchly abolitionist printer Joseph Crukshank (who published 200 other anti-slavery works), this poem is immediately striking for its white author's decision to write in the voice of a sympathetic black character. In this guise, as the editor, Raphael B. Moreen, notes in his introduction, "Sansom sought to point out to the elite white population the inherent contradiction in professing to be Christian while at the same time owning and trading slaves." To strengthen his argument and lend it the weight of historic precedent, Sansom has his black narrator cite the anti-slavery views of illustrious writers and religious authorities stretching back over most of the preceding century. As a result, the combination of Sansom's original footnotes and editor Moreen's endnotes constitutes a biographical catalogue of anti-slavery advocates from the late seventeenth and eighteenth centuries.

The sixth of the reprints comes from a New England preacher and represents yet another genre of anti-slavery writing, the sermon. Born in Massachusetts, the son of the renowned "Great Awakening" leader, Jonathan Edwards the younger had been active from his Connecticut base preaching and writing against the evils of slavery since the early 1770s. The text reprinted here, *The Injustice and Impolicy of the Slave*

Trade, and of the Slavery of the Africans (1791), was originally delivered as a sermon in New Haven on September 15, 1791. As the editor Sarah Gamertsfelder explains in her introduction, Edwards argued against slavery both on the basis of Biblical teachings and on the ideals of the successful American independence movement. Although not embracing Africans as full equals, Edwards nonetheless urged "God-fearing Christians involved in slaveholding . . . [to] recognize the error of their ways and repent." He also criticized newly independent Americans who had complained of Britain's "enslavement" but now continued to hold large numbers of black people in bondage.

Under the heading "Three Anti-Slavery Woman Writers," the seventh section reprints a collage of short abolitionist writings spanning the years 1793 to 1805 by three women, two of whom are American and the third a British visitor to the United States. Bearing a name that itself suggests her Boston society pedigree, Sarah Wentworth Apthorp Morton (known in her day as "the American Sappho") wrote against slavery in both of the poems reprinted here, including especially "The African Chief" (1793) which remained one of the most widely popular poems in nineteenth-century America. From a very different background was Isabella Oliver (later Sharp), a rural Pennsylvanian of little formal education and intense religious beliefs, whose poem "On Slavery" (1805) attacks the institution on religious, historical, and patriotic grounds. Perhaps most noteworthy, as editor Kathryn Gin stresses, the poem "debunks the 'curse of Canaan,' a common defense of slavery . . . [which argued that] Africans' black skin was taken to be the mark of this curse." Ann Tuke Alexander, the third of Gin's assembled writers, was a British Quaker who traveled around the United States for two years and was moved by what she saw in South Carolina to publish, rather bravely, her anti-slavery *Address to the Inhabitants of Charleston* before returning to Britain in 1805.

The eighth reprint opens a window on late-eighteenth-century efforts to mount a national anti-slavery campaign. Though ultimately frustrated in their hopes to pass national legislation against slavery, activists from nine abolition societies in six states (Connecticut, New York, New Jersey, Pennsylvania, Delaware, and Maryland) assembled in Philadelphia for a week in January 1794 to organize their effort. The result was this report, *Minutes of the Proceedings of a Convention of Delegates from the Abolition Societies Established in Different Parts of the United States* (1794), which attests, in the words of editor Jennifer Randazzo, "to the existence of a nationally based anti-slavery organization decades before the more widely recognized abolition movement of the nineteenth century spearheaded by William Lloyd Garrison, Frederick Douglass, and so many others." Similar conventions were to be held for several years, with limited results, though their meetings and petitions bespeak an abiding anti-slavery fervor among a significant subset of Americans at the close of the eighteenth century.

A mysterious and still unidentified author, writing in two voices, lies behind the ninth of the texts reprinted here, a long narrative poem entitled *The American in Algiers, or the Patriot of Seventy-Six in Captivity* (1797). According to the editor, J. Micah Guster, the author tells in two cantos the stories of two very different characters: a white Bostonian veteran of the Revolutionary War now held in captivity in Algiers, and a "sable bard" who tells his story of capture in Africa, the horrors of the middle passage, and a life of enslavement in America. By juxtaposing the stories of these two men, concludes Guster, the anonymous writer meant "to highlight the hypocrisy of Americans, who were outraged by the enslavement of their fellow citizens in Algeria in the late eighteenth century, while they continued to accept the slavery of blacks at home." However much the U.S. Constitution may have silently allowed the practice of slavery to continue, this text demonstrates that Americans of the time held radically different opinions about the tolerability of slavery in the nation's future.

When both the United States (in legislation signed by President Thomas Jefferson) and Britain abolished the transatlantic slave trade as of January 1, 1808, congregations of African Americans and other abolitionists from Boston to Philadelphia began to celebrate the anniversary with commemorative ceremonies every January. The tenth text in this volume captures the spirit of these celebrations, here the African American church leader Henry Sipkins' *Oration on the Abolition of the Slave Trade; Delivered in the African Church in the City of New-York, January 2, 1809*. Presented with some prefatory material reflecting the day's program, Sipkins' speech, as editor Laura Ferguson writes, "delves into the origins of the slave trade and the cruel realities of slavery, praises those who had been actively working for better conditions for free blacks, and expresses hope for a time when all people, regardless of race, will be able to enjoy liberty." The sense of jubilation at a breakthrough like the abolition of the slave trade, and the corresponding hope for continued progress toward the end of slavery expressed in such publications, would give way, as the years passed, to disappointment at opportunities missed and a deepening realization after about 1820 that universal emancipation was no nearer than before.

A black patriotic American who had served courageously in the Revolutionary War is the author of the eleventh text, a pamphlet written to protest a proposed law that would have barred the emigration of blacks into Pennsylvania and forced those already resident to register with the state. James Forten was a prosperous Philadelphia businessman, self-made and civically active, whom many immediately discerned as the anonymous author behind *Letters from a Man of Colour, on a Late Bill before the Senate of Pennsylvania* (1813). Writing in the midst of the War of 1812, Forten is self-consciously pro-American, even as he argues ardently against a racist and discriminatory piece of legislation. Editor Nicholas Osborne emphasizes that in presenting this carefully reasoned tract as being "from a Man of Colour," Forten was exemplary of the growing role of African Americans in the struggle "to defend what basic rights they had and subtly [agitate] for an expansion of them." Sometimes righteousness did prevail: to whatever degree Forten was responsible, the proposed law never even came to a vote in the Pennsylvania legislature.

The final text in this volume marks a watershed in American history. Rufus King's and John Jay's arguments against slavery—here reprinted as they appeared originally under the title *Papers Relative to the Restriction of Slavery* (1819)—emerged in the midst of the heated, complex debates of 1818–1820 that would result in what we now refer to as "the Missouri Compromise." Missouri's petition for admission as a slaveholding state, together with unexpectedly strong resistance from various northern legislators, made it clear that the long-muted competition between slaveholding and free states for ascendancy in American government was now out in the open and raging fiercely. With the prospect that a succession of new slave states from the former Louisiana Territory would tip the balance strongly against them, the so-called "free-soil states" were galvanized. Many voices rose on all sides, among whom, according to editor Eric C. Steinhart, "the true oratorical masterpiece of the debates was rendered by Senator Rufus King of New York." Shortly thereafter, longtime anti-slavery activist John Jay added his voice to the free-state cause in the epistle reprinted here, written to support the effort to restrict the legality of slavery in Missouri. Though politically aligned, King and Jay had different rationales. "King viewed slavery as politically destructive to the country," Steinhart explains, "whereas Jay objected to slavery largely on the grounds that it violated innate human rights." In the end, as the term "compromise" suggests, King, Jay, and their allies were partially successful. Slaveholding Missouri was paired with free state Maine for admission in 1820, and the precarious balance of power between free and slave states would continue on the same basis until the Kansas-Nebraska Act of 1854.

With that pamphlet, the volume ends. But of course the struggle did not. The Missouri Compromise appeared to restore peace. But discerning observers were not fooled. Having watched the free-state vs. slave-state fight very closely, Thomas Jefferson wrote: "It is hushed, indeed, for the moment. But this is a reprieve only, not a final sentence. A geographical line, coinciding with marked principle, moral and political, once conceived and held up to the angry passions of men, will never be obliterated; and every new irritation will mark it deeper and deeper." Jefferson's prescience was fully and bitterly borne out in the decades that followed, as the nation spiraled into sectarian hostility over the slavery issue and eventually into the bloodiest war in its history.

Still, the tracts, sermons, poems and other anti-slavery writings reprinted in this volume are not vestiges of a failed effort or a lost cause. They show, individually and collectively, that the mindset of the founding generation was not uniformly pro-slavery, nor even passively acquiescent in the continuance of slavery. On one level, these early American abolitionists kept the struggle alive. They kept in view the religious, political, economic, legal, social, and even national-security-based objections to racial slavery. They also, over the period 1760 to 1820, achieved real victories. Pennsylvania passed a gradual emancipation act in 1775, Vermont abolished slavery in its constitution in 1777, Massachusetts the same in 1783, and gradual emancipation acts were passed between 1784 and 1804 in Rhode Island, Connecticut, New York, and New Jersey. Though this momentum faltered and stalled in the nineteenth century, the materials in this volume teach us that the story of slavery and abolition in America is not the simple or monolithic narrative we often are given. Abolitionist ideals, though long delayed, ultimately triumphed.

And here we return to the larger significance of this project: a collective investigation by a dozen undergraduate historians who represent the next generation of historical inquiry and scholarship. It is they who have recovered and interpreted these previously forgotten historical materials, and used them to interrogate and qualify received notions. To them go our congratulations, and in them are invested our hopes for the future.

JAMES G. BASKER
Ann Whitney Olin Professor of English
Barnard College, Columbia University
President, Gilder Lehrman Institute

ACKNOWLEDGMENTS

The editors of this collection are indebted to many people and institutions for their support and help.

Thanks are due to the several historians who gave of their time and energy to work with this first cohort of Gilder Lehrman History Scholars in the summer of 2003. They include Thomas Bender, Catherine Clinton, Eric Foner, Kenneth Jackson, Steven Mintz, Christine Stansell, and Sean Wilentz. In addition, the hundreds of professors, too numerous to name, who took the time to identify and nominate the more than 400 candidates from whom the 12 Gilder Lehrman History Scholars were selected, also deserve special thanks.

The scholars and editors took advantage of several archives and libraries in doing their research and preparing these texts for publication. They wish to thank in particular Louise Mirrer, Nina Nazionale, and Mariam Touba of the New-York Historical Society; Paul LeClerc and the staff of the New York Public Library; Howard Dodson and the staff of the Schomburg Center for Research in Black Culture; James Neal, Jean Ashton, John Tofanelli, and the staff of the Columbia University Library; the staff of Wollman Library, Barnard College; the staff of Haverford College Library; Ann Gordon, editor of the Papers of Elizabeth Cady Stanton and Susan B. Anthony, Rutgers University, and the staff of Rutgers University Library; the staff of Bobst Library, New York University; and Jody Cary and the staff of the Gilder Lehrman Collection on deposit at the New-York Historical Society.

Thanks are due to Ene Sirvet, secretary of the Society of American Historians, for arranging housing and activities at Columbia University. The book designer Jerry Kelly contributed valuable advice and extraordinary help as the book went to press. All involved in the project owe thanks for the support and encouragement of the Gilder Lehrman Institute staff, headed by Executive Director Lesley Herrmann, and including Libby Garland, Pamela Mattera, Susan F. Saidenberg, and Anna Q. Zintl. The publications program of the Gilder Lehrman Institute is made possible by funds from the Julienne M. Michel Trust.

Finally, and above all, thanks are due to the co-founders of the Institute, Richard Gilder and Lewis Lehrman, for their generous financial support and their spirited encouragement of this and so many projects that promote the study of American history.

The original texts are reproduced here as printed except for the silent correction of obvious errors and the modernization of eighteenth-century typeface.

In the texts, authors' footnotes are indicated by symbols, while editorial notes are indicated by arabic numerals, and are placed after the text as endnotes.

OBSERVATIONS

On the Inflaving, importing and purchafing of

Negroes;

With fome Advice thereon, extracted from the Epiftle of the Yearly-Meeting of the People called QUAKERS, held at *London* in the Year 1748.

Anthony Benezet

When ye fpread forth your Hands, I will hide mine Eyes from you, yea when ye make many Prayers I will not hear; your Hands are full of Blood. Wafh ye, make you clean, put away the Evil of your Doings from before mine Eyes Ifai. 1, 15.

Is not this the Faft that I have chofen, to loofe the Bands of Wickednefs, to undo the heavy Burden, to let the Oppreffed go free, and that ye break every Yoke, Chap. 58, 7.

Second Edition.

GERMANTOWN:

Printed by CHRISTOPHER SOWER. 1760.

OBSERVATIONS ON THE INSLAVING, IMPORTING AND PURCHASING OF NEGROES

by Anthony Benezet

Introduction by Thomas Wolf, Harvard University

Anthony Benezet (1713–1784), Quaker educator turned pamphleteer, established himself, between 1760 and 1784, as an anti-slavery reformer of international renown. His highly popular body of writings, a distinctly Christianized synthesis of European travel literature and Enlightenment thought, targeted not simply his immediate Quaker colleagues, but also the greater American populace. In his pamphlets, he assails the flaws he perceived in both colonial Quaker mores and the American ideology of revolution. Roughly bookending Benezet's career as a pamphleteer were his short works *Observations on the Inslaving, Importing, and Purchasing of Negroes* (1760) and *Notes on the Slave Trade* (1781).

Benezet's rise to prominence followed a circuitous route, which originated far from the young republic. He early severed ties with his native Huguenot community of St. Quentin in southern France; in 1715, his father, Jean Étienne, uprooted his family to escape the rising tide of anti-Huguenot sentiment that swept through France during the reign of Louis XIV.[1] Their subsequent sixteen-year odyssey through Western Europe, over the course of which the Benezet clan converted to Quakerism, culminated in 1731 with their arrival in Philadelphia.[2] While his father and younger brothers quickly found their place amongst the shops and wharves, Benezet struggled with what he saw as the spiritual inadequacy of the mercantile life for which he thought himself destined. His unease ultimately compelled him, in 1739, to reject the lure of Philadelphia bourgeois society for a teaching position in Germantown, Pennsylvania.[3]

Benezet's three-year stint at the Germantown school represented the first chapter in his lifelong involvement with American institutional life. By 1742, Benezet had departed Germantown for William Penn's charter school. Following thirteen years at Penn's school, Benezet, in 1755, established an all-female seminary that catered to the daughters of wealthy Quakers. Benezet's foray into the service of Philadelphia's affluent, how-

ever, did little to satisfy his desire to improve the condition of the less for-
tunate; thus, in the midst of nurturing his seminary, Benezet founded a
night school in Philadelphia for African Americans.[4]

Despite his notoriously poor health, Benezet managed not only to fulfill his educational responsibilities, but also to launch a public crusade
against the manifold abuses of American society. The 1759 publication of
Observations on the Inslaving, Importing, and Purchasing of Negroes
marked Benezet's first official foray into the realm of pamphleteering. As
Benezet's first printed statement of his multifaceted anti-slavery argument, the sixteen-page *Observations* did not aspire to the length of his
future, and most famous, texts, such as *Some Historical Account of Guinea*
(1771), which was 144 pages long and was frequently reprinted in the last
three decades of the eighteenth century on both sides of the Atlantic.
Despite its highly condensed form, Benezet's *Observations,* which
includes an extract from the 1758 London Yearly Meeting of the Society
of Friends and an allegory entitled "The Uncertainty of a Death-Bed
Repentance," provides an invaluable outline of the theoretical bases of
his later writings.

The allegory that concludes *Observations* contains the main theological concept that informed Benezet's crusade: human life as a seamless
whole molded in accordance with scripture. In the allegory, the merchant Penitens, lying on his deathbed, laments that he has not been as
careful and diligent in his religious life as he has been in his business
dealings. Penitens' recognition of his folly serves as a warning to the colonial Quaker elite, who, motivated by a religious doctrine that encouraged hard work and presented with the abundant business opportunities offered in the New World, had amassed both wealth and aristocratic
privilege in the years leading up to 1760.[5] Benezet, speaking through
Penitens, implores his coreligionists to rededicate themselves to their
founding doctrines of asceticism and piety.[6]

The Yearly Meetings of the Society of Friends proved valuable forums
for anti-slavery thought, which aided Benezet's quest for reform.[7] The
extract from the epistle of the 1758 London meeting that Benezet included as an appendix to his *Observations* encapsulates a gradual effort
among leading Quakers to purge the Society of long-accumulating com-

promises with the secular world. Strikingly, the Society's warnings against the dealing or purchasing of slaves were relatively mild and contained no threat of punishment for noncompliant Quakers; indeed, the Quaker governing bodies did not explicitly couple their moral resolutions regarding slavery with institutional force until 1770, when the New York Yearly Meeting declared slave trading an offense punishable by disownment.[8]

Despite both the resistance to abolition within the Quaker community and the reluctance of the Yearly Meetings to effect radical changes, the extract Benezet cites illustrates the important role the Yearly Meetings played in developing an anti-slavery platform that included both theological and secular arguments. The epistle contains a series of arguments, intimately connected to the fundamental Quaker belief in the interpenetration of the human and divine, and its corollary, "The Golden Rule," emphasizing the effects of the slave trade upon the manners of individuals and the mechanics of secular societies, both white and black. The negative impact of the slave trade upon African societies in particular showed up as a central theme throughout Benezet's pamphlets.

Benezet originated the practice of assembling extracts of European writings on Africa into persuasive anti-slavery essays. Never having traveled to Africa himself, Benezet relied upon travelogues to portray eighteenth-century Africa under the thrall of the slave trade. First pioneered in *Observations,* Benezet's method of literary collage married images of a war-torn Africa with accounts of the vibrant culture and economics of the continent prior to the slave trade to create the sense of Africa as a paradise destroyed by European greed. Benezet's depictions offered what members of eighteenth-century Western societies considered to be reliable, scientific evidence for moral and socioeconomic positions, and proved highly influential in expanding the ranks of abolitionists. Indeed, Benezet's writings inspired many reformers of the 1760s and 1770s, including John Wesley, Granville Sharp, and Thomas Clarkson, to embrace the anti-slavery cause.[9]

In the same manner that Benezet deployed European travelogues in the interest of his crusade, he also drew upon Enlightenment thought.[10] Benezet's selective filtering of Enlightenment philosophy through the highly specific lens of Quaker abolitionism produced a unique body of thought that defies simple categorization. Since Benezet adhered, above all else, to divinely revealed law, he sought out philosophers with similar religious perspectives, from whom he borrowed arguments to support his abolitionist argument. As a consequence, the more distinctly philosophical elements of Benezet's pamphlets included the thoughts of radical, liberal, and conservative writers who, by more secularized standards, offered clashing interpretations of the political and social elements of human existence.[11]

The theologically motivated nature of Benezet's anti-slavery arguments provides insight into his negative view of the American Revolution. Whereas many Americans were willing to embrace the writings of British philosopher John Locke, whose *Second Treatise of Government* (1690) recognized popular revolt as a right of citizens abused by their political leaders, Benezet clung to a much more pacifistic ideology steeped in Quaker doctrine. As Benezet wrote to his colleague Samuel Allinson, "It is from God alone, by true faith in his promises, that deliverance must arise."[12] Believing God to be the ultimate arbiter of the fate of human societies, Benezet denounced the American Revolution as a horrible violation of the divine order and as the leading symptom of a culture of war that had corrupted the American consciousness.[13] From Benezet's perspective, the cultural values of the Revolutionary era had created in the minds of many Americans an unrealistic, romanticized image of violence, which in turn compromised abolitionist arguments that decried war as a horrid and necessary component of the slave trade.

Benezet's denunciation of the revolutionary romanticization of war coincided with his production of more graphic depictions of the evils of slavery. Emerging from Benezet's 1781 tract *Notes on the Slave Trade* (the second document reprinted here) is an image of black suffering rendered in far greater intensity than in the earlier *Observations*. As Benezet wrote, "[T]he blood of all these wretches, who die before their time, whether in their country or elsewhere, lies upon your head. The blood of thy brother . . . crieth against thee from the earth, from the ship and from the waters." Benezet sought to dispel Revolutionary rhetoric and to instill instead a popular American repudiation of war by presenting warfare as an undeniable symptom of human depravity.

4

While the revolutionary climate impeded Benezet's pacifist goals, the ongoing revolution within Quaker society benefited his efforts. As the 1738 disownment of the fiery anti-slavery rhetorician Benjamin Lay suggests, Quaker society was historically characterized by a lack of receptivity to internal dissent.[14] In the interim between the Society's shunning of Lay and Benezet's emergence, however, the Seven Years' War emerged as a full-blown morality play dramatizing the significant interest that many members of the Society, who were presumably dedicated to pacifism and asceticism, had in the forceful protection of physical assets.[15] In response to the conflict between their pacifistic beliefs and their political responsibility for the armed defense of the colony, the Quakers, in 1756, initiated a gradual withdrawal from Pennsylvania political life.

Benezet was not content to wait for the slow stream of human history to remedy human error, and thus allied himself with leading figures of the highly radical Pennsylvania press, such as Christopher Sower Jr. and Joseph Crukshank, in a grassroots reform campaign. Benezet's anti-slavery campaign relied upon the gradual circulation of his tracts through preexisting social networks, such as Quaker congregations and, in the latter decades of the eighteenth century, abolitionist organizations. Benezet, who personally distributed his pamphlets, defrayed the expenses of printing through his small teaching salary and a series of charitable donations from Philadelphia philanthropists. Benezet simultaneously maintained a far-reaching correspondence with a broad range of philosophers, politicians, and religious figures; his circle of supporters included Benjamin Franklin, Abbé Raynal, Queen Charlotte of England, and the royal houses of France and Spain.[16] By virtue of his voluminous correspondence, Benezet emerged at the nexus of an ever widening transatlantic network of anti-slavery thought. Thus, while Benezet's *Observations* and *Notes* were undoubtedly powerful syntheses of a number of diverse economic, humanitarian, philosophical, social, and theological arguments, they were also masterworks of propaganda, assuming nearly global visibility through Benezet's dogged efforts to abolish the evil of slavery.

Notes

[1] The specific pronunciation of Benezet's name is open to speculation. Benezet was baptized into the Roman Catholic Church as "Antoine Benezet" on January

31, 1713. Nevertheless, as historian George S. Brookes claims, Jean Étienne registered himself in 1726 under the anglicized name "John Stephen," and his son, through the entirety of his American existence, referred to himself as "Anthony." Consequently, the Benezet family name could have been pronounced either "ben-eh-zay" (the French form rhyming with "day") or "ben-eh-zet" (the English form rhyming with "set").

[2] George S. Brookes, ed., *Friend Anthony Benezet* (Philadelphia: University of Pennsylvania Press, 1937), 8; Roberts Vaux, *Memoirs of the Life of Anthony Benezet* (New York: Burt Franklin, 1969), 2–5.

[3] Brookes, 23–26; Vaux, 7–9.

[4] Benezet alone funded and administered the night school until 1770, when it came under the authority of the Society of Friends.

[5] Carl and Jessica Bridenbaugh, *Rebels and Gentlemen: Philadelphia in the Age of Franklin* (New York: Oxford University Press, 1962), 68.

[6] Frederick Barnes Tolles, *Meeting House and Counting House: The Quaker Merchants of Colonial Philadelphia, 1682-1763* (New York: Norton, 1948), 9–10.

[7] The Yearly Meetings were consultative bodies of Quakers that convened annually at the local, regional, national, and international levels for the purpose of reviewing policy and practice in all facets of Quaker life.

[8] Herbert Aptheker, "The Quakers and Negro Slavery," *The Journal of Negro History* 25 (July 1940): 349.

[9] Vaux, 30; David Brion Davis, "New Sidelights on Early Antislavery Radicalism," *The William and Mary Quarterly* 28 (Oct. 1971): 591.

[10] Maurice Jackson, "The Social and Intellectual Origins of Anthony Benezet's Antislavery Radicalism," *Pennsylvania History* (1999), 93.

[11] Jackson, 95.

[12] Benezet to Samuel Allinson, Philadelphia, Oct. 23, 1774, in Brookes, 322.

[13] Commenting on the education of American youth, Benezet wrote, "I might add the prodigious hurt done by those romantic & mad notions of heroism &c. which are early implanted in the tender minds from the use of those Heathen Authors Ovid, Virgil, Homer which they are generally taught in, which nourishes the spirit of War in the Youth & in other respects is so diametrically opposite to our Christian Testimony." Benezet to John Pemberton, Philadelphia, May 29, 1783, in Brookes, 389–390.

[14] Jack D. Marietta, *The Reformation of American Quakerism, 1748-1783* (Philadelphia: University of Pennsylvania Press, 1984), 113.

[15] Marietta, 103.

[16] Vaux, 102, 105, 119; Jackson, 107–108.

OBSERVATIONS

on the Inslaving, importing and purchasing of

NEGROES;

With some Advice thereon, extracted from the Epistle of the Yearly-Meeting of the People called QUAKERS held at *London* in the Year 1748.[1]

When ye spread forth your Hands, I will hide mine Eyes from you, yea when ye make many Prayers I will not hear; your Hands are full of Blood. Wash ye, make you clean, put away the Evil of your Doings from before mine Eyes ISAI. I, 15.[2]

Is not this the Feast that I have chosen, to loose the Bands of Wickedness, to undo the heavy Burden, to let the Oppressed go free, and that ye break every Yoke, CHAP. 58, 7.[3]

Second Edition.

GERMANTOWN:

Printed by CHRISTOPHER SOWER.[4] 1760.

INTRODUCTION.

C USTOMS generally approved and Opinions received by Youth from their Superiors, become like the natural Produce of a Soil, especially when they are suited to favorite Inclinations: But as the Judgments of GOD are without Partiality, by which the State of the Soul must be tried, it would be the highest Wisdom to forego Customs and popular Opinions, and try our Deeds by the infallible Standard of Truth, even the pure Spirit of Grace which leads all those who in Sincerity obey its Dictates into a Conduct consistent with their Christian Profession.

That important Injunction of our blessed Saviour, *Seek ye first the King-dom of GOD and his Righteousness, and all Things shall be added unto you,*[5] contains a short but comprehensive View of our Duty and Happiness. If then the Business of Mankind in this Life is, to first seek another; if this cannot be done, but by attending to the Means: If a Summary of the Means be, *To love the LORD our GOD with all our Heart and our Neighbor as our self:*[6] So as *never to do to another, that which* in like Circumstances *we would not have done to us;*[7] then these are Points of Moment and worthy of our most serious Consideration.

IN ancient Times it was the Practice of many Nations, when at war with each other, to sell the Prisoners they made in Battle, in order to defray the Expenses of the War. This unchristian or rather inhuman practice, after many Ages continuance, is at length generally abolished by the Christian Powers of Europe, but still continues among some of the Nations of Asia and Africa, and to our sad Experience we find it also practised by the Natives of America. In the present war,[8] how many of our poor Country Men are dragged to Bondage and sold for Slaves; how many mourn, a Husband, a Wife, a Child, a Parent or some near Rela-tion taken from them; and were we to follow them a little farther, and see them exposed to sale and bought up to be made a Gain of, what Heart so hard that would not melt with Sympathy and Sorrow: And could we hear the Purchasers, for the sake of Gain, pushing on the Savages to captivate our People, what inhuman wretches should we call them, what Punish-ment should we think their Guilt deserved! But while our Hearts are affected for our Brethren and Relations, while we feel for our own Flesh and Blood, let us extend our Thoughts to others, and allow me, gentle Reader! to recommend to thy serious Consideration, a Practice that prevails among several Nations who call themselves Christians, and I am sorry to say it, in which we as a Nation are deeply engaged, and which is of such a Nature, as that nothing can be more inconsistent with the Doctrines and Practice of our meek Lord and Master, nor stained with a deeper Dye of Injustice, Cruelty and Oppression, I mean the *Slave Trade*, the purchasing and bringing the poor Negroes from their Native Land, and subjecting them to a State of perpetual Bondage, and that often the most cruel and oppressive. And this carried on chiefly at the instigation of those to whom the Promulgation of the merciful, pure, and holy Gospel of Christ Jesus was committed. Will not the just Judge of all the Earth visit for all this? Or dare we say, that this very Practice is not one Cause of the Calamities we at present suffer; and that the Captivity of our People is not to teach us to feel for others, and to induce us to discourage a Trade, by which many Thousands are Yearly captivated? Evils do not arise out of the Dust, nor does the Almighty willingly afflict the Children of Men; but when a People offend as a Nation, or in a publick Capacity, the Justice of his moral Government requires that as a Nation they be punished, which is generally done by War, Famine or Pestilence. I know there are many Arguments offered in favour of the Purchasers, but they are all drawn from Avarice or ill founded, none will stand the Test of that divine Rule: *To do unto all Men, as we would they should do unto us.*[9] Without Purchasers, there would be no Trade; and consequently every Purchaser as he encourages the Trade, becomes partaker in the Guilt of it; and that they may see what a deep dye the Guilt is of, I beg leave to quote some Extracts from the Writings of Persons of Note, who have been long employed in the African Trade, and whose Situation and Office in the Factories[10] will not admit any to question the Truth of what they relate. By these we shall see, that in order to get Slaves, the Europeans settled at the Factories in Africa, encourage Wars, and promote the Practice of stealing Men, Women and Children, which they readily purchase without any Regard to Justice, Equity or any of the tender Ties of Nature.

William Bosman,[11] Factor for the Dutch *African* Company, at the Factory at *Delmina,*[12] who wrote an Account of that Country, now more than fifty Years past,[13] tells his Readers 'That the Booty which the Negro Soldiers aim at in their Wars, are Ornaments of Gold and Prisoners of War, in Order to sell them for Slaves at Pleasure, that many of the Inhabitants depend on Plunder and the Slave-Trade; and that when Vessels arrive, if they have no Stock of Slaves, the Factors trust the Inhabitants with Goods for the Value of one or two Hundred Slaves, which they send into the inland Country in Order to buy Slaves at all Markets, even sometimes two Hundred Miles deep in the Country, where Markets of Men were kept in the same Manner as those of Beasts with us. He farther adds: 'That, in his Time, the Europeans furnished the Negroes with an incredible Quantity of Fire-Arms and Gunpowder, which was then the Chief vendible Merchandize there. This was the State of the Negro-Trade when *Bosman* wrote his Account of *Guinea,*[14] which, as I have already said, was more than fifty Years ago; since that Time the Trade is prodigiously augmented, there being now more than ten Ships to one that was then imployed in it; and as the Demand for Slaves has augmented, so have the Negroes been the more induced not only to wage War one with another, but also to put in practice the most base and inhuman Methods, in Order to get their unhappy Countrymen into their Power, that they may sell them to the European Traders.

John Barbot,[15] Agent General of the French Royal African Company, in his Acc. printed 1732 writes as follows: 'Those Slaves sold by the Negroes, are for the most Part Prisoners of War, taken either in fight or pursuit, or in the incursions they make into their Enemies Territories; others are stolen away by their own Country-Men, and some there are who will sell their own Children, Kindred or Neighbours. This has often been seen, and to compass it, they desire the Person they intend to sell, to help them in carrying something to the Factory by Way of Trade, and when there, the Person so deluded, not understanding the Language, is sold and delivered up as a Slave, notwithstanding all his Resistance and exclaiming against the Treachery. Abundance of little Blacks of both sexes are also stolen away by their Neighbors, when found abroad on the Roads, or in the Woods; or else in the Corn Fields, at the Time of the

Year when their Parents keep them there all Day, to scare away the devouring small Birds,'

A Person of Candour and undoubted Credit now living in *Philadelphia*,[16] who was on a trading Voyage, on the Coast of *Guinea*, about seven Years ago, was an Eye-Witness of the Misery and Desolation which the Purchase of Slaves occasions in that Country, a particular Instance of which he relates in the following Manner viz. 'Being on that Coast, at a Place called *Basalia*,[17] the Commander of the Vessel according to Custom sent a Person on Shore, with a Present to the King of the Country, acquainting him with their arrival, and letting him know that they wanted a Cargo of Slaves: The King promised to furnish them with Slaves, and in Order to do it, set out to go to War against his Enemies, deigning also to surprise some Town and take all the People Prisoners. Sometime after the King sent them Word he had not yet met with the desired success, having been twice repulsed, in attempting to break up two Towns; but that he still hoped to procure a Number of Slaves for them; and in this Design he persisted, till he met his Enemies in the Field, where a Battle was fought, which lasted three Days, during which Time the Engagement was so bloody, that 4500 were slain on the spot. Think, says the Author, what a pitiable fight it was, to see the Widows weeping over their lost Husbands, and Orphans deploring the loss of their Fathers &c., What must we think of that cruel Wretch who occasioned such a Scene of Misery, or what of those who for the sake of Gain instigated him to it.

N.N. *Brue*,[18] a noted Traveler, a Narrative of whose Travels is to be met with in a new Collection of Voyages, printed by the King's Authority in the Year 1745; tells his Readers; 'That the Europeans are far from desiring to act as Peace-Makers, amongst the Negroes; which would be acting contrary to their Interest, since the greater the Wars, the more Slaves are procured.' He also gives an Account of the Manner in which the Slaves are got, in the Place where he then was, in the following Term, viz. 'When a Vessel arrives, the King of the Country sends a Troop of Guards to some Village, which they surround; then seizing as many as they have Orders for, they bind them and send them away to the Ship, where the Ship's Mark[19] being put upon them, they are hear'd of no more. They usually carry the Infants in Sacks, and gag the Men and Women for fear they should alarm the Villages, thro' which they are carried: For, says he, these Actions are never committed in the Villages near the Factories, which it is the King's Interest not to ruin, but in those up the Country.

Also, *Joseph Randal*,[20] in his Book of Geography, printed in the Year 1744, in the Account he gives of the *Guinea* Trade, after generally confirming the above Account, adds: 'That in time of full Peace nothing is more common, than for the Negroes of one Nation to steal those of another, and sell them to the Europeans. There has, says he, been Instances amongst the Negroes of Children selling their Fathers and Mothers, when they have been weary of them, and wanted to enjoy what they had; which I suppose, says that Author, gave birth to the Laws, by which the Children are not to inherit the Goods of Estates of their Fathers and Mothers. Thus, these poor Creatures are brought down to the Coast to be sold to the Merchants of Europe. When the Price is agreed upon, which for an able bodied Man, under thirty five Years of age, may be about 5 Pounds, the Women a fifth Part less, and the Children in proportion to their Age, the European Merchants brand them with hot Irons to distinguish them, and locks the poor wretches up in some Prison, till they can be sent on board; when they come to *America*, they are disposed of, some to the Spaniards to work in the Mines (for the English are obliged by the Assiento Contract,[21] to deliver thirty Thousand Slaves every Year to the Spaniards, and the rest are sold to the Planters in *America*.) It is thought that the English transport annually near fifty Thousand of those unhappy Creatures, and the other European Nations together about Two Hundred Thousand more.[22]

Let but any one reflect, that each Individual of this Number had some tender attachment which was broken by this cruel Separation; some Parent or Wife, who had not even the Opportunity of mingling Tears in a parting Embrace; or perhaps some Infant whom his Labour was to feed and Vigilance protect; or let any consider what it is to lose a Child, a Husband or any dear Relation, and then let them say what they must think of those who are engaged in, or encourage such a Trade. By the fore mentioned Accounts it appears, how by various perfidious, and cruel Methods, the unhappy Negroes are inslaved, and that mostly, by the Procurement of those called Christians, and violently rent from the tenderest

13

Ties of Nature, to toil in hard Labour, often without sufficient Supplies of Food, and under hard Taskmasters, and this mostly to uphold the Luxury or Covetousness of proud selfish Men, without any Hope of ever seeing again their native Land; or an end to their Miseries. Oh ye cruel Taskmasters! Ye hard-hearted Oppressors, will not God hear their Cry? And what shall ye do, when God riseth up, and when he visiteth; what will ye answer him? *Did not he that made you, make them? and did not one fashion you in the Womb?*

Hitherto I have considered the Trade as inconsistent with the Gospel of Christ, contrary to natural Justice, and the common feelings of Humanity, and productive of infinite Calamities to many Thousand Families, nay to many Nations, and consequently offensive to God the Father of all Mankind. Yet it must be allowed, there are some well minded Persons, into whose Hands some of the Negroes have fallen, either by Inheritance, Executorship, or even some perhaps purely from Charitable Motives, who rather desire to manage wisely for their good, than to make Gain by their Labour; these I truly sympathize with, for considering the general situation of those unhappy People, they have indeed a difficult Path to tread.

I might next consider the Trade as it is destructive of the Welfare of human Society, and inconsistent with the Peace and Prosperity of a Country, as by it the number of natural Enemies must be encreased, and the Place of those taken up who would be its support and security. Or I might shew from innumerable Examples, how it introduces Idleness, discourages Marriage, corrupts the Youth and ruins and debauches Morals. I might likewise expose the weakness of those Arguments, which are commonly advanced in Order to vindicate the Purchasers, such, as their being Slaves in their own Country, and therefore may be so to us, or that they are made acquainted with Christianity in lieu of their Liberty, or that the last Purchaser will use them better than they formerly were: But not to mention, that these are only vain pretences, that the true Motive of encouraging the Trade is selfish Avarice; to say nothing of the weakness of the Argument: That because others do ill, we may do so too; or the absurdity of recommending the Christian Religion by Injustice and disregard to the Rights and Liberties of Mankind, or the Encouragement that every new Purchaser gives to a Trade altogether unjust and iniquitous. What is already said, will I hope be sufficient to prevent any considerate Christian from being, in any Degree, defiled with a Gain so full of Horrors, and so palpably inconsistent with the Gospel of our blessed Lord and Saviour Jesus Christ, which breaths nothing but Love and Good will to all Men of every Nation, Kindred, Tongue and People.

Under the Mosaic Law Man-stealing was the only Theft punishable by Death: It is thus expressed in Exodus Chap. 21, 16. *He that stealeth a Man and selleth him, or if he be found in his Hand, he shall surely be put to death.*

Extract from the Epistle of the Yearly-Meeting of the People called QUAKERS, *held at London in the Year 1758.*

WE FERVENTLY warn all in profession with us, that they be careful to avoid being any Way concerned in reaping the unrighteous Profit arising from that iniquitous Practice of Dealing in Negroes and other Slaves; whereby in the original Purchase one Man selleth another, as he doth the Beasts that perishes, without any better Pretension to a Property in him, than that of superior Force; in direct violation of the Gospel-Rule which teacheth every one to do as they would be done by, and to do Good unto All; being the Reverse of that covetous Disposition, which furnishes Encouragement to those ignorant People to perpetuate their savage Wars, in Order to supply the Demands of this most unnatural Traffick, whereby great Numbers of Mankind, free by Nature, are subjected to inextricable Bondage; and which hath often been observed, to fill their Possessors with Haughtiness, Tyranny, Luxury and Barbarity, corrupting the Minds, and debasing the Morals of their Children, to the unspeakable Prejudice of Religion and Virtue, and the Exclusion of that holy Spirit of universal Love, Meekness and Charity, which is the unchangeable Nature & the Glory of true Christianity. We therefore can do no less than, with the greatest Earnestness, to impress it upon Friends every where, that they endeavour to keep their Hands clear of this unrighteous Gain of Oppression.

THE
UNCERTAINTY
OF A
DEATH-BED
REPENTANCE,

Illustrated under the Character of

PENITENS.

Seek ye the Lord while he may be found, call ye upon him, while he is near. Let the wicked forsake his Way, and the unrighteous Man his Thoughts: and let him return unto the Lord, and he will have Mercy upon him, and to our God; for he will abundantly pardon. ISAIAH 55, 6.

P ENITENS was a busy notable tradesman, and very prosperous in his dealings, but died in the *thirty-fifth* year of his age.

A LITTLE before his death, when the doctors had given him over, some of his Neighbours came one evening to see him; at which time, he spake thus to them:

I SEE says he, my friends, the tender concern you have for me, by the grief that appears in your countenances, and I know the thoughts that you now have about me. You think how melancholy a case it is, to see so young a man, and in such flourishing business, deliver'd up to death. And perhaps, had I visited any of you in my condition, I should have had the same thoughts of you.

BUT now, my friends, my thoughts are no more like your thoughts, than my condition is like yours.

IT is no trouble to me now to think, that I am to die young, or before I have rais'd an estate.

THESE things are now sunk into such mere *nothings*, that I have no name little enough to call them by. For if in a few days, or hours, I am to leave this carcase to be buried in the earth, and to find my self either for ever happy in the favour of God, or eternally separated from all light and peace, can any words sufficiently express the littleness of every thing else?

Is there any dream like the dream of life, in which we are amused with vain and empty things? whilst we are neglecting and disregarding that which is substantially valuable. Is there any folly like the folly of most men and women, who think themselves too wise, and are too busy to hearken to the voice of Jesus Christ calling in the heart? which, if carefully attended to, would occasion these serious reflections; but for want of attending to this divine instructor, that enemy of mankind the Devil, is suffered to fill our minds with unreasonable affections and foolish opinions; so that when we consider death as a misery, we only think of it as a miserable Separation from the enjoyments of this life. We seldom mourn over an old man that dies rich, but we lament the young, that are taken away in the progress of their fortune. You your selves look upon me with pity, not that I am going unprepar'd to meet the Judge of the quick and the dead, but that I am to leave a prosperous trade in the flower of my life.

THIS is the wisdom of our manly thoughts. And yet what folly of the silliest children is so great as this?

FOR what is there miserable or dreadful in death, but the Consequences of it? When a man is dead, what does any thing signify to him, but the state he is then in?

OUR poor friend *Lepidus*[23] dy'd, you know, as he was dressing himself for a *feast*; do you think it is now part of his trouble, that he did not live till that entertainment was over? *Feasts*, and *business*, and *pleasures*, and *enjoyments*, seem great things to us, whilst we think of nothing else; but as soon as we add death to them, they all sink into an equal littleness; and the soul, that is separated from the body, no more laments the loss of *business*, than the losing of a *feast*.

IF I am now going into the joys of GOD, could there be any reason to grieve, that this happen'd to me before I was forty years of age? Could it be a sad thing to go to heaven, before I had made a few more *bargains*, or stood a little longer behind a *counter*?

AND if I am to go amongst lost spirits, could there be any reason to be content, that this did not happen to me till I was old, and full of *riches*?

IF good Angels were ready to receive my soul, could it be any grief to me, that I was dying upon a *poor bed* in a *garret*?

AND if GOD has deliver'd me up to evil spirits, to be dragg'd by them to places of torments, could it be any comfort to me, that they found me upon a *bed of state?*[24]

WHEN you are as near death as I am, you will know, that all the different states of life, whether of youth or age, *riches,* or *poverty, greatness* or *meanness,* signify no more to you, than whether you die in a *poor* or *stately* apartment.

THE greatness of those things which follow death, makes all that goes before it, sink into *nothing.*

NOW that *judgment* is the next thing that I look for, and everlasting happiness or misery is come so near me, all the enjoyments and prosperities of life seem as vain and insignificant, and to have no more to do with my happiness, than the cloaths that I wore before I could speak.

BUT, my friends, how am I surpriz'd, that I have not always had these thoughts? How am I surpriz'd to find, that for want of yielding obedience, to that degree of light and grace, with which God hath enlightened? the words of our blessed Saviour have been fulfilled in me, darkness has been suffered to come over me, and these great things have been hid from me; for what is there in the terrors of death, in the vanities of life, or the necessities of piety, but what I might have as easily and fully seen in any part of my life?

WHAT a strange thing is it, that a little *health,* or the poor business of a *shop,* should keep us so senseless of these great things, that are coming so fast upon us!

JUST as you came into my chamber, I was thinking with my self, what numbers of souls there are now in the world, in my condition at this very time, surpriz'd with a summons to the other world; some taken from their *shops* and *farms,* others from their *sports* and *pleasures,* these at *suits at law,* those at *gaming-tables,* and all seiz'd at an hour when they thought nothing of it; frighted at the approach of death, confounded at the vanity of all their labours, designs, and projects, astonish'd at the folly of their past lives, and not knowing which way to turn their thoughts, to find any comfort: their consciences flying in their faces, bringing all their sins to their remembrance, tormenting them with the sight of the angry Judge, the worm that never dies, the fire that is never quench'd, the gates of hell, the powers of darkness, and the bitter pains of eternal death.[25]

OH my friends! bless God that you are not of this number, that you have time and strength to employ your selves in such works of piety, as may bring you peace at the last.

AND take this along with you, that there is nothing but a life of great piety, or a death of great stupidity, that can keep off these apprehensions.

HAD I now a thousand worlds, I would give them all for one year more, that I might present unto God one year of such devotion and good works, as I never before so much as intended.

YOU perhaps, when you consider that I have liv'd free from scandal and debauchery, and in the communion of the Church, wonder to see me so full of remorse and self-condemnation at the approach of death.

BUT alas! what a poor thing is it, to have liv'd only free from *murder*, *theft* and *adultery*, which is all that I can say for my self.

YOU know indeed, that I have never been reckon'd a *sot*, but you are at the same time witnesses, and have been frequent companions of my *intemperance*, *sensuality*, and great *indulgence*. And if I am now going to a judgment, where nothing will be rewarded but *good works*, I may well be concern'd, that tho' I am no *sot*, yet have no *Christian sobriety* to plead for me.

IT is true, I have liv'd in the communion of the Church and generally frequented its worship and service on *Sundays*, when I was neither too *idle*, or not otherwise dispos'd of by my *business* and *pleasures*. But then my conformity to the publick worship has been rather a thing of course, than any real intention of doing that, which the service of the Church supposes; had it not been so, I had been oftener at Church, more devout when there, and more fearful of ever neglecting it.

BUT the thing that now surprises me above all wonders, is this, that I never had so much as a *general intention* of living up to the piety of the Gospel. This never so much as enter'd into my heart. I never once in my life consider'd whether I was living as the laws of Religion direct, or whether my way of life was such, as would procure me the mercy of God at this hour.

AND can it be thought, that I have kept the Gospel terms of salvation, without ever so much as *intending* in any serious deliberate manner either to know them, or keep them? Can it be thought, that I have pleased God with such a life as he requires, tho' I have liv'd without ever considering, what he requires, or how much I have perform'd? How easy a thing would salvation be, if it could fall into my careless hands, who have never had so much serious thoughts about it, as about any one common bargain that I have made?

IN the business of life I have used prudence and reflection, I have been glad to converse with men of experience and judgment, to find out the reasons why some fail, and others succeed in any business, I have taken no step in trade but with great care and caution, considering every advantage or danger that attended it. I have always had my eye upon the main end of business, and have study'd all the ways and means of being a gainer by all that I undertook.

BUT what is the reason that I have brought none of these tempers to Religion? What is the reason that I, who have so often talk'd of the necessity of *rules* and *methods*, and *diligence* in worldly business, have all this while never once thought of any rules, or methods, or managements, to carry me on in a life of piety?

DO you think any thing can astonish, and confound a dying man, like this? What pain do you think a man must feel, when his conscience lays all this folly to his charge, when it shall shew him how regular, exact, wise he has been in small matters, that are passed away like a dream, and how stupid and senseless he has liv'd without any reflection, without any rules, in things of such eternal moment, as no heart can sufficiently conceive them.

HAD I only my *frailties* and *imperfections* to lament at this time, I should lye here humbly trusting in the mercies of God. But alas! how can I call a general disregard, and a thorough neglect of all religious improvement, a *frailty* or *imperfection*; when it was as much in my power to have been exact, and careful, and diligent in a course of piety, as in the business of my *trade*.

I COULD have call'd in as many helps, have practiced as many rules, and been taught as many certain methods of holy living, as of thriving in my shop, had I but so *intended* and *desir'd* it.

OH my friends! a careless life, unconcern'd and unattentive to the duties of Religion, is so without all excuse, so unworthy of the mercy of God, such a shame to the sense and reason of our minds, that I can hardly conceive a greater punishment, than for a man to be thrown into the state that I am in, to reflect upon it.

Penitens was here going on, but had his mouth stopp'd by a *convulsion*, which never suffer'd him to speak any more. He lay convuls'd about twelve hours, and then gave up the ghost.

NOW if every *reader* would imagine this *Penitens* to have been some particular acquaintance or relation of his, and fancy that he saw and heard all that is here describ'd, that he stood by his bed-side when his poor friend lay in such distress and agony, lamenting the folly of his past life, it would in all probability teach him such wisdom as never enter'd into his heart before. If to this, he should consider, how often he himself might have been surprised in the same state of negligence, and made an example to the rest of the world, this double reflection, both upon the distress of his friend, and the goodness of that God, who had preserv'd him from it, would in all likelihood soften his heart into holy tempers, and make him turn the remainder of his life into a regular course of piety.

FINIS.

Notes

[1] "1748" is a misprint for 1758, the year in which the Meeting of Friends in London issued this epistle.

[2] Isaiah 1:15–16. This and all subsequent Biblical references are from the Authorized (King James) Version of the Bible.

[3] Actually Isaiah 58:6, which reads, "Is not this the *fast* that I have chosen" [italics added].

[4] Christopher Sower (1721–1784): Also known as Johann Christoph Saur Jr. and Johann Christoph Sauer Jr. Espousing his father's commitment to ethnic and sectarian political activism, Sower used his Germantown press to print German-language publications.

[5] Matthew 6:33.

[6] Luke 10:27.

[7] Adapted from Matthew 7:12 and Luke 6:31.

[8] The Seven Years' War, also called the French and Indian War, in which hostilities between the French and the English actually continued from 1754 until the Treaty of Paris was signed in 1763.

[9] Matthew 7:12.

[10] The trading stations of European merchant companies, in this case as established along the coast of Africa.

[11] Willem Bosman: Dutch explorer and author of the highly popular *Description of the Coast of Guinea* (1701; English translation 1705).

[12] Also known as Elmina, a trading station located on the Gulf of Guinea in modern-day Ghana, which was first settled by the Portuguese in 1481.

[13] Bosman's travelogue *A New and Accurate Description of the Coast of Guinea* was first published in Dutch in 1701 and later translated into English in 1705. This work not only provided fodder for Benezet's writings, but also furnished the material with which the French explorer Jean Barbot expanded his French language travelogue of 1688 for an English readership (see note 15).

[14] "Guinea" was widely used in Europe, beginning in the fifteenth century, to refer to the coastal regions of West Africa between River Senegal (modern Senegal) and Cape Lopez (modern Gabon).

[15] Jean Barbot (1655–1712): French Huguenot who drew upon his recorded observations from two journeys to Africa while employed by the *Compagnie du Sénégal* (also known as the *Compagnie Royale d'Afrique*) to publish a travelogue in 1688. Barbot's posthumously published 1732 English translation enjoyed wide circulation and reigned as the authoritative history of Africa and the Atlantic slave trade for much of the eighteenth century.

[16] Possibly William Fentum, an author cited by Benezet in his *Notes on the Slave Trade* (reproduced on pages 24–28) and by "J. Philmore" in his *Two Dialogues on the Man-Trade* (1760), as reprinted in Benezet's *A Short Account of that Part of Africa Inhabited by the Negroes* (1762).

[17] Region in present-day Sudan.

[18] André Brüe: Director of the French Sanaga (or Senegal) Co. at Fort St. Louis (in modern-day Senegal) at the close of the seventeenth century. Brüe's essays and journal entries detailing his African journeys between 1697 and 1715 were incorporated into Thomas Astley's *A New General Collection of Voyages and Travels* (1745) under the title "Voyages & Travels along the Western Coast of Africa, on Account of the French Commerce."

[19] A brand impressed upon the skin of slaves by the crews of slave ships to indicate their status as merchandise owned by the company.

[20] Joseph Randall: Author of a work of geography entitled *A System of Geography; or, A Dissertation on the Creation and Various Phænomena of the Terraqueous Globe* (1744).

[21] Also known as the "Asiento Treaty," a component of the Treaty of Utrecht of 1713, which officially concluded the War of Spanish Succession (1701–1713). The terms of the Asiento Treaty required the British to provide 4,800 *piezas* (a unit of measure referring to one healthy adult male, or the equivalent) annually to Spanish New World colonies over a thirty-year period. In effect, the Asiento Treaty granted the British a monopoly on selling slaves transatlantically into the Spanish colonies.

[22] Between 1751 and 1760, the British imported an average of 23,100 slaves yearly from the western African coast. During the period between 1701 and 1810, an average of 55,000 slaves were being imported annually to the New World by all European trading powers combined.

[23] Perhaps Marcus Æmilius Lepidus (89–13 BCE), a member of the Second Roman Triumvirate (along with Antonius and Octavian) who ultimately held administrative authority over Africa.

[24] A superb and finely decorated bed for show, particularly for laying out the corpse of a distinguished person.

[25] Mark 9:48.

NOTES ON THE SLAVE TRADE.

IT may not be necessary to repeat what has been so fully declared in several modern publications, of the inconsistence of slavery with every right of mankind, with every feeling of humanity, and every precept of Christianity; nor to point out its inconsistency with the welfare, peace and prosperity of every country, in proportion as it prevails; what grievous sufferings it brings on the poor NEGROES; but more especially what a train of fatal vices it produces in their lordly oppressors and their unhappy offspring. Nevertheless for the sake of some who have not met with, or fully considered those former publications, and in hopes that some who are still active in support of slavery may be induced to consider their ways, and become more wise, the following substance of an address or expostulation made by a sensible Author,[1] to the several ranks of persons most immediately concerned in the trade, is now republished.

"And first, to the Captains employed in this trade. Most of you know the country of Guinea, perhaps now by your means, part of it is become a dreary uncultivated wilderness; the inhabitants being murdered or carried away, so that there are few left to till the ground; but you know, or have heard, how populous, how fruitful, how pleasant it was a few years ago. You know the people were not stupid, not wanting in sense, considering the few means of improvement they enjoyed. Neither did you find them savage, treacherous, or unkind to strangers. On the contrary they were in most parts a sensible and ingenious people; kind and friendly, and generally just in their dealings. Such are the men whom you hire their own countrymen to tear away from this lovely country; part by stealth, part by force, part made captives in those wars which you raise or foment on purpose. You have seen them torn away, children from their parents, parents from their children: Husbands from their wives, wives from their beloved husbands; brethren and sisters from each other. You have dragged them who had never done you any wrong, perhaps in chains, from their native shore. You have forced them into your ships, like an herd of swine,* them who had souls immortal as your own. You

---

* The following relation is inserted at the request of the author [i.e. Benezet here includes Fentum's autobiographical footnote from his text].

'That I may contribute all in my power towards the good of mankind, by inspir-

have stowed them together as close as ever they could lie, without any regard to decency or conveniency—And when many of them had been

ing any of its individuals with a suitable abhorrence for that detestable practice of trading in our fellow creatures, and in some measure atone for my neglect of duty as a christian, in engaging in a wicked traffic, I offer to their serious consideration, some few occurrences of which I was an eye witness. That being struck with the wretched and affecting scene they may foster that humane principle, which is the noble and distinguished characteristic of man.'

About the year 1749; I sailed from Liverpool to the coast of Guinea, some time after our arrival, I was ordered to go up the country a considerable distance, upon having notice from one of the Negroe Kings, that he had a parcel of slaves to dispose of, I received my instructions and went, carrying with me an account of such goods we had on board, to exchange for the slaves we intended to purchase; upon being introduced, I presented him with a small case of spirits, a gun and some trifles, which having accepted, and understood by an interpreter what goods we had, the next day was appointed for viewing the Slaves; we found about two hundred confined in one place. But here how shall I relate the affecting sight I there beheld, the silent sorrow which appeared in the countenance of the afflicted father, and the painful anguish of the tender mother, expecting to be forever separated from their tender offspring; the distressed maid wringing her hands in presage of her future wretchedness, and the general cry of the innocent, from a fearful apprehension of the perpetual Slavery to which they were doomed. I purchased eleven, who I conducted, tied two and two, to our ship. Being but a small vessel (ninety ton) we soon purchased our cargo, consisting of one hundred and seventy Slaves, whom thou may'st reader range in thy view, as they were shackled two and two together, pent up within the narrow confines of the main deck, with the complicated distress of sickness, chains and contempt; deprived of every fond and social tie and in a great measure reduced to a state of desperation. We had not been a fortnight at sea, before the fatal consequence of this despair appeared, they formed a design of recovering their natural right, Liberty, by raising and murdering every man on board; but the goodness of the Almighty rendered their scheme abortive, and his mercy spared us to have time to repent; The plot was discovered; the ring leader tied by the two thumbs over the barricado door at sun rise received a number of lashes, in this situation he remained till sun-set, exposed to the insults and barbarity of the brutal crew of sailors, with full leave to exercise their cruelty at pleasure: The consequence was, the next morning the miserable sufferer was found dead, fleed from the shoulders to the waist. The next victim was a youth, who from too strong a sense of his misery refused nourishment and died disregarded and unnoticed till the hogs had fed on part of his flesh.

25

poisoned by foul air, or had sunk under various hardships, "you have seen their remains delivered to the deep, till the sea should give up his dead." You have carried the survivors into the vilest slavery, never to end but with life: Such slavery as is not found among the Turks at Algiers, no, nor among the heathens in America.

May I speak plainly to you? I must. Love constrains me: Love to you, as well, as those you are concerned with. Is there a God? You know there is. Is he a just God? Then there must be a state of retribution: A state wherein the just God will reward every man according to his work. Then what reward will he render to you. O think betimes! before you drop into eternity: Think how, "He shall have judgment without mercy, that shewed no mercy."[2] Are you a man? Then you should have a human heart. But have you indeed? What is your heart made of? Is there no such principle as compassion there? Do you never feel another's pain? Have you no sympathy? No sense of human woe? No pity for the miserable? When you saw the flowing eyes, the heaving breast, or the bleeding sides and tortured limbs of your fellow-creatures. Was you a stone or a brute? Did you look upon them with the eyes of a tiger? When you squeezed the agonizing creatures down in the ship, or when you threw their poor mangled remains into the sea, had you no relentings? Did not one tear drop from your eye, one sigh escape from your breast? Do you feel no relenting now? If you do not, you must go on till the measure of your iniquities is full. Then will the great God deal with you, as you have dealt with them, and require all their blood at your hands. And at that day it shall be more tolerable for Sodom and Gomorrah[3] than for you: But if your heart does relent; tho' in a small degree, know it is a call from the God of Love. And to-day, if you hear his voice, harden not your heart[4]—To day resolve, God being your helper to escape for your life—Regard not money: All that a man hath will he give for his life. Whatever you lose, lose not your soul; nothing can countervail that loss. Immediately quit the horrid trade: At all events be an honest man.

This equally concerns every merchant who is engaged in the slave-trade. It is you that induce the African villain to sell his countrymen; and in order thereto, to steal, rob, murder men, women and children without number: by enabling the English villain to pay him for so doing; whom you over pay for his execrable labour. It is your money, that is the spring of all, that impowers him to go on, so that whatever he or the African does

in this matter, is all your act and deed. And is your conscience quite reconciled to this? Does it never reproach you at all? Has gold entirely blind-
ed your eyes and stupefied your heart? Can you see, can you feel no harm
therein? Is it doing as you would be done to? Make the case your own.
"Master (said a slave at Liverpool[5] to the merchant that owned him) what
if some of my countrymen were to come here, and take away my mistress,
and master Tommy and master Billy, and carry them into our country and
make them slaves, how would you like it?" His answer was worthy of a
man: "I will never buy a slave more while I live." O let his resolution be
yours! Have no more any part in this detestable business. Instantly leave it
to those unfeeling wretches, "who laugh at humanity and compassion."

And this equally concerns every person who has an estate in our American plantations: Yea all slave-holders of whatever rank and degree; seeing men-buyers are exactly on a level with men-stealers. Indeed you say, "I
pay honestly for my goods; and I am not concerned to know how they are
come by." Nay but you are: You are deeply concerned, to know that they
are not stolen: Otherwise you are partaker with a thief, and are not a jot
honester than him. But you know they are not honestly come by: You
know they are procured by means nothing near so innocent as picking of
pockets, house breaking, or robbery upon the highway. You know they
are procured by a deliberate series of more complicated villainy (of
fraud, robbery and murder) than was ever practised either by
Mahometans[6] or Pagans; in particular by murders of all kinds; by the
blood of the innocent poured upon the ground like water. Now it is your
money that pays the merchant, and thro' him the captain and African
butchers. You therefore are guilty: Yea principally guilty, of all these
frauds, robberies, and murders. You are the spring that puts all the rest in
motion; they would not stir a step without you—Therefore the blood of
all these wretches, who die before their time, whether in their country or
elsewhere, lies upon your head. The blood of thy brother, (for whether
thou wilt believe it or no, such he is in the sight of him that made him)
crieth against thee from the earth, from the ship and from the waters. O!
whatever it cost, put a stop to its cry, before it be too late. Instantly, at any
price, were it the half of thy goods, deliver thy self from blood guiltiness!
Thy hands, thy bed, thy furniture, thy house, thy land, are at present
stained with blood. Surely it is enough; accumulate no more guilt: Spill
no more the blood of the innocent! Do not hire another to shed blood!

Do not pay him for doing it! Whether thou art a Christian or no, shew thy self a man; be not more savage than a lion or a bear.

Perhaps thou wilt say, "I do not buy any NEGROES: I only use those left me by my father." But is it enough to satisfy your own conscience! Had your father, have you, has any man living, a right to use another as a Slave? It cannot be, even setting REVELATION[7] aside. It cannot be, that either war, or contract, can give any man such a property in another as he has in his sheep and oxen: Much less is it possible, that any child of man, should ever be born a Slave. Liberty is the right of every human creature, as soon as he breathes the vital air. And no human law can deprive him of that right, which he derives from the law of nature. If therefore you have any regard to justice, (to say nothing of mercy, nor of the revealed law of GOD) render unto all their due. Give Liberty to whom Liberty is due, that is to every child of man, to every partaker of human nature. Let none serve you but by his own act and deed, by his own voluntary choice, away with whips, chains, and all compulsion. Be gentle towards all men. And see that you invariably do unto every one, as you would he should do unto you.

Notes

[1] Identified by Benezet in his 1762 *Short Account of that Part of Africa Inhabited by the Negroes* as William Fentum, whose pamphlet *Two Dialogues Concerning the Man-Trade* (by "J. Philmore") is quoted in the next paragraph.

[2] James 2:13. This and all subsequent Biblical references are from the Authorized (King James) Version of the Bible.

[3] Cities destroyed by God as retribution for the inhabitants' sinfulness. See Genesis 19:24–25.

[4] Psalms 95:7–8.

[5] A port city on the west coast of England that was, together with Bristol and London, one of three leading slave-trading ports in Great Britain.

[6] Muslims.

[7] Not a reference to the book of Revelation in the Bible, but to God's overall plan for humanity—the "revealed word of God."

Garrigues Jr. to Wm Forten

A

MITE caſt into the TREASURY:

O R,

OBSERVATIONS

O N

SLAVE-KEEPING.

The Ways of Men are before the Eyes of the Lord,
and he pondereth all his goings, PROV. V. 21.

By Ben: Rush — a Phyſician at Philad?

By Anthony Benezet

PHILADELPHIA, Printed 1772.
To be had at moſt of the Bookſellers in Town*

m. K.

[2]

A MITE CAST INTO THE TREASURY
by David Cooper

Introduction by Kristin DeBusk, Texas Technological University

In 1772, a revolutionary fervor took hold in the streets of the colonies that would later become the United States. Even before the 1770 Boston Massacre, there had been boycotts, rebellions, and declarations of individual rights. The year 1772 saw the spirit of rebellion against oppression rise to new levels, moving New Jersey Quaker David Cooper (1725-1795) to speak out for the rights of slaves. In his later memoirs, he wrote, "As I have at times for many years past, felt my mind warmly affected with a sense of cruelty and wickedness of slavery, and its inconsistency with Christianity, these feelings led me in 1772 to publish a piece entitled 'A Mite into the Treasury, or Considerations on Slavery.'"[1] While this pamphlet had its origins in the American Revolution, it also had a place in another revolution taking place at the time—the Quaker movement for the abolition of slavery.

Quakers, also known as the Society of Friends, were the first organized group in the United States to fight for the abolition of slavery; however, they had not always been unified in this cause.[2] Until the 1750s, the majority of Quakers saw nothing wrong with slavery as long as slaves were treated well.[3] In Philadelphia, Quakers made up more than ten percent of the city's slave owners while representing less than ten percent of the city's population.[4] Overall, slavery had increased steadily in many Northern colonies during the eighteenth century as farmers turned from relying on indentured servants to slaves.[5] Between 1757 and 1766 approximately 1,300 slaves arrived in Philadelphia and western New Jersey,[6] and when David Cooper wrote his anti-slavery pamphlet, there was still a large number of slaves in his home state of New Jersey.

The Society of Friends as a whole, however, underwent a vital change during the eighteenth century, shifting to an abolitionist stance. Conservative, slave-owning Friends gradually became outnumbered between 1738 and 1754 with a more reform-minded group that saw slavery as an immoral practice.[7] This new generation, however, faced a significant

31

challenge in enforcing its statutes. Because the Society of Friends was established without leaders of the conventional sort, members reached a "sense of the meeting" through unanimous opinion. Decisions, especially those concerning slavery, often got postponed because of the level of opposition existing in the Society. In 1754, the Philadelphia Yearly Meeting, a Quaker business meeting consisting of members from Pennsylvania, Delaware, Maryland, Virginia, and New Jersey, finally agreed to caution its members against purchasing or owning slaves, but it took another twenty-two years before they prohibited slaveholding within the Society. Despite their slow progress, Quakers were well ahead of others in their anti-slavery efforts. The last mention of any Friends owning slaves within the Philadelphia Yearly Meeting was in the year 1781.[8] It took the rest of the United States eighty-four more years to completely rid itself of the institution.

David Cooper, one of the few Quakers who reached out to urge the wider population to abolish slavery, had a modest life. Cooper spent most of his life in Woodbury, in southern New Jersey.[9] He was a shy yet mischievous child who, although raised in the Society of Friends, was not seriously committed to his religion until after his marriage to Sibyl Matlack in 1747. Four years into his marriage he became extremely ill and, unable to work for a period of time, embraced his faith. He claimed he "now could cheerfully give up to serve my Maker, and to attend meetings."[10] From that moment on, Cooper wholeheartedly devoted his life to serving God.

Cooper's activities within the Society of Friends were quite extensive. He served as the overseer of the Woodbury Monthly Meeting after 1756 and was one of the first appointed members to the Meeting of Sufferings, a standing committee of the Philadelphia Yearly Meeting dedicated to aiding the Society with regard to political or legal dilemmas. In 1777, he was appointed elder for the Woodbury Quakers and occasionally traveled over 1,000 miles at a time visiting other Quaker meetings. He also helped to establish a Friends free school in Woodbury, worked to aid Native Americans, and participated in governmental affairs, serving as an elected member of the New Jersey General Assembly.

Cooper's concerns about the injustice of slavery emerged in 1772, when he began to correspond with Granville Sharp, a well known British abolitionist.[11] Shortly thereafter, Cooper wrote the document that follows, his first published work. Cooper later wrote and presented Quaker abolitionist bills to the United States Congress. In 1783, he joined with 535 others in signing the Quaker Anti-Slavery Petition and was one of fourteen Friends who presented it to Congress. He visited Congress again in 1785, 1786, and 1788 to call for the abolition of slavery. In his 1788 visit, Cooper presented a bill that he had drawn up himself. Although the most important pieces of the legislation were omitted before its adoption, Cooper was still optimistic. He later wrote, "I have little doubt that a law to Friends' liking may before long be obtained."[12] Unfortunately, Cooper would see no such law passed during his lifetime. However, his visits to Congress, as well as a 1789 address he made to President Washington, helped to spread the spirit of abolition to leaders of the new nation.

Cooper also reached out beyond the Quaker community, publishing the document represented here, as well as another abolitionist appeal in 1783. Both works were published anonymously, but some initially attributed *A Mite Cast Into the Treasury* to Benjamin Rush or Anthony Benezet, two of the most well known abolitionist writers of the time. Despite the fact that Cooper was a respected Quaker, no one outside of his circle of friends ever knew he wrote this text.[13] In the twentieth century the rediscovery of his papers proved he had authored this early work.

That Cooper chose to remain anonymous suggests not only his personal modesty, but also his apprehensions about the resistance that existed even within the Society of Friends in 1772. Just nineteen years earlier, the Society still prohibited the publication of material denouncing slavery.[14] When Cooper published *A Mite Cast Into the Treasury*, Quakers were able to publish abolitionist pamphlets only after receiving permission from the Quaker overseers of the press. Cooper's publisher, Joseph Crukshank of Philadelphia, had a history of publishing anti-slavery material by notable Quaker authors such as Anthony Benezet and John Woolman. Cooper decided to remain anonymous in order to guard his reputation as well as that of the Society of Friends. His anonymity assured that the Society would not be held accountable for anything he wrote and meant that he did not have to seek permission.

A Mite Cast Into the Treasury, although less well known than Cooper's other work,[15] does provide an excellent example of his views on slavery. Significantly, Cooper does not reveal himself as a Quaker in his arguments, but instead uses themes that would become common in later anti-slavery appeals. The most common feature of the work is his Biblical approach. Even the title *A Mite Cast into the Treasury* is evocative of the Biblical story of the widow's mite in Mark 12:41–44, in which Jesus considered a poor widow's offering of two mites, worth less than a penny, to be greater than the gifts of others because she gave all she had.

In the pamphlet, Cooper speaks in his own voice and that of a slaveholder, using this device to refute arguments often maintained by slaveholders. The slaveholder's arguments are preceded by the word *"object,"* meaning "objection" and are followed by Cooper's refutations. Although Cooper created the dialogue himself, the stance taken by the slaveholder in this work was typical of many slaveholders' views concerning the slave trade and slavery.

To counter the pro-slavery position, Cooper uses three main themes that are repeated throughout the document: natural law, the Golden Rule, and the concept of false balances. The first theme, natural law, was a common one in much of the Revolutionary material of the time. Cooper defines this concept, which he derived from English philosopher John Locke's *Two Treatises on Government,* as "an eternal law" inside every man whose "object is the good and happiness of mankind." Throughout his pamphlet Cooper uses Locke's concepts alongside Biblical references to argue for the immutable rights of slaves as men under God. The second theme, found in Matthew 7:12, more commonly referred to as the Golden Rule, advocates treating others as you would have them treat you. As his third theme, Cooper refers to the false balances and deceitful weights used as a metaphor in Micah 6:11. In this case, Cooper is pointing to the speciousness of the supposed benefits of slavery often given by slaveholders, including the argument that slavery exposed Africans to Christianity and that it was perfectly acceptable for slaves to work for a period of time to earn their keep before being freed. He admonishes the slaveholders for keeping fellow human beings in bondage and encourages them to do as Christ would have done and view the slaves as equal under God.

34

Although *A Mite Cast Into the Treasury* is an anti-slavery pamphlet, Cooper's life suggests some personal compromise on the subject. He kept a Dutch servant girl, most likely an indentured servant, and his diary mentions having a black boy as a helper.[16] Also, Cooper and his son-in-law, Samuel Allinson, are known to have sold a black girl to a married couple for fifteen pounds. Still, although Cooper was participating in slave ownership, the sale did contain provisions that the girl would be freed in five years and six months and that the couple would "learn the said Esther to read intelligibly, and find, provide for, and allow her sufficient meal, drink, apparel, washing, and lodging, and teach her the business of housewifery."[17] As Cooper later elaborated in his writings, he opposed slavery if individuals were not set free at an age when the law of nature gave them freedom, which he defined as eighteen for women and twenty-one for men. In this and other cases, Cooper felt servitude was not wrong if the owner provided a home and education until the servant came of age. He saw no contradiction between this view and abolitionist beliefs.

Notwithstanding Cooper's complex views on slavery, his abolitionist career was important within the Quaker anti-slavery movement. In the midst of the American Revolution, Cooper took the idea of America's "enslavement" by England to a new level and used the same Revolutionary language to speak of racial equality under God. His colorful character and fervent religious convictions shine through his writing to convey the emotional urgency that characterizes his works. His views, along with those of other anti-slavery writers of the time, exposed the American public to ideas that would influence later generations of abolitionists. For Cooper, spreading words of truth and justice was not a choice, but a God-given duty that he would attempt to fulfill for the remainder of his life.

Notes

[1] "Notices of David Cooper." *Friends' Review* (Philadelphia), 4th month 5th day, 1862.

[2] Jack D. Marietta, *The Reformation of American Quakerism, 1748–1783* (Philadelphia: University of Pennsylvania Press, 1984), 111.

[3] Jean R. Soderlund, *Quakers & Slavery: A Divided Spirit* (Princeton: Princeton University Press, 1985), 4.

[4] Marietta, 115–116.

[5] Ira Berlin, *Many Thousands Gone: The First Two Centuries of Slavery in North America* (Cambridge, Mass. and London: Harvard University Press, 1998), 180.

[6] Berlin, 182.

[7] Soderlund, 32.

[8] James Bowden, "Testimony of Friends Against Slavery," *The History of the Society of Friends in America,* vol. 2 (1854; reprint, New York: Arno Press, 1972), 215.

[9] According to the Quaker calendar, Cooper was born on the 13th of the 12th month, 1724. This date is equivalent to February 24, 1725, on the Gregorian calendar.

[10] "Notices of David Cooper."

[11] Marietta, 276.

[12] "Notices of David Cooper."

[13] Henry J. Cadbury, "Quaker Bibliographical Notes," in *Bulletin of Friends' Historical Association*, vol. 26 (Swarthmore, Pa.: Friends' Historical Association, 1937), 46.

[14] Soderlund, 17.

[15] Another work by David Cooper is *A Serious Address to the Rulers of America, on the Inconstancy of their Conduct Respecting Slavery: Forming a Contrast Between the Encroachments of England on American Liberty, and American Injustice in Tolerating Slavery.* A modern reprint is included in this volume, pages 59–74.

[16] "Notices of David Cooper."

[17] Bill of sale dated 31st day of 6th month, 1774, Allinson Family Papers, The Quaker Collection, Haverford College, Haverford, Pa. The eighteenth-century spelling has been modernized.

A

MITE cast into the TREASURY:

OR,

OBSERVATIONS

ON

SLAVE-KEEPING.

The Ways of Men are before the Eyes of the Lord,
and he pondereth all his goings, PROV. V. 21.[1]

PHILADELPHIA, Printed 1772.

To be had at most of the Booksellers in Town

INTRODUCTION.

THE POWER of prejudice over the minds of mankind is very extraordinary; hardly any extreams too distant, or absurdities too glaring for it
to unite or reconcile, if it tends to promote or justify a favorite pursuit. It
is thus we are to account for the fallacious reasonings and absurd sentiments used and entertained concerning negroes, and the lawfulness of
keeping them slaves. The low contempt with which they are generally
treated by the whites, lead children from the first dawn of reason, to
consider people with a black skin, on a footing with domestic animals,
form'd to serve and obey, whom they may kick, beat, and treat as they
please, without their having any right to complain; and when they attain
the age of maturity, can scarce be brought to believe that creatures they
have always looked upon so vastly below themselves, can stand on the
same footing in the sight of the Universal Father, or that justice requires
the same conduct to them as to whites; and those prejudices having been
generally countenanced in time past, are become so riveted, that too few
even of the sober and religious, can hear the voice of impartial justice, in
favour of that abused people, with a proper degree of patience and
attention. I therefore request all such into whose hands this may fall, to
divest themselves of every bias arising either from prejudice, or temporal
views, and coolly weigh the following hints, and, if any thing is met with,
that tends to promote christian rectitude, embrace it; without regarding
the hand from whence it comes, ever bearing in mind who it was that
declared,—"Such measure as you mete, shall be measured to you again."
Mat. vii. 2.[2]

OBSERVATIONS
ON SLAVE-KEEPING.

"Open thy mouth for the dumb, and all such as are appointed
to destruction, and plead the cause of the poor and needy."
Prov. xxxi. 8, 9.[3]

MY MIND having been frequently led to consider the inconsistency of the practice of slave-keeping, and making traffic of our fellow-men, to the precepts and doctrine of our blessed Lord and Lawgiver, which, with regard to duty one to another, is sum'd up in this short command, viz. "Whatsover ye would that men should do to you, do ye even so to them,"[4] and wishing to see an end put to this unrighteous practice among christians, felt an inclination to fling a few hints together, several of which to me appeared new on the subject, which may possibly lead some more closely to inspect their own situation, in order to discover how far they stand approved by impartial justice in this business, and as the Jewish law[5] was positive, "That whoever stealeth a man and selleth him, or if he be found in his hand, he shall surely be put to death." *Ex. xxi. 16.*[6]

The following queries may be worthy our serious attention.

Query I. Was this part of the ceremonial law intended only for the Jewish nation, or founded on universal distributive justice, adapted to the nature of things, and equally necessary to the rest of mankind?

II. Is he who encourages the thief to steal and receives the goods, more innocent than the thief?

III. As christians consider it unlawful to make slaves of their fellow-believers, does the precepts of Christ, or nature of things give a christian any stronger title to his native freedom than an African?

IV. If it was a heinous crime to take a fellow-servant by the throat and deprive him of his liberty because he could not pay a just debt, is it not much more so to deprive our fellow-servants of their freedom who owe us nothing, nor ever did us the least injury?

V. Is not the command which prohibits the coveting our neighbour's ox, servant, &c. broke with a much deeper degree of guilt, by coveting his person, and when in our power the making him our slave?

VI. Does not he, who for gain, buys, sells, or keeps in slavery the descendants of those who were unjustly deprived of their freedom, thereby justify the original act, and put himself in the place of the first agressor?

Object. But the negroes brought here are captives taken in war, and, by the custom of the country belong to the victors, who have a right to slay or otherwise dispose of them.[7]

To pass over the Europeans being the occasion of those wars by their demand for slaves, and that many of the negroes brought here, have been stole, &c. let us consider how far a custom allowed of among benighted Africans, is to be countenanced and upheld by enlightened christians, who are commanded to, "Do unto others, as they would have others do unto them," not to a part only, to those of their own religion or colour, but to all men; wherefore no christian can keep a slave or be accessary thereto, without (in some degree) incurring the guilt of breaking his Lord's command, unless he is willing himself and posterity should be slaves; and as to this custom of selling those of their own nation and colour into perpetual slavery, from parents, husbands, wives, children, and all the tender connections of life; who can think of it without the utmost abhorrence. Shall we then, shall christians plead it as an excuse for our conduct, when at the same time we are the moving cause which produce those effects, as certainly as the weights in a clock are the cause of its striking. Remove the weights and the striking ceases. Let all who bear the christian name leave buying slaves, and this infernal custom of theirs, of selling their brethren will I believe equally cease. A custom that casts the most indelible odium on the whole people, occasioning some from hence to infer that they are a different race, formed by the Creator for brutal services, to drudge for us with their brethren of the stalls.[8]—However extravagant such a supposition may appear, it is the only rational one that can fully justify the practice, and give peace of mind to a slave-keeper; for until he can persuade himself that this is the case, the above precept must continually reproach him with being a hypocrite and no christian who can thus live in a deliberate opposition to

Christ's command; and I am fully perswaded there is few to be found who justifies the practice but is more or less tinctured with this opinion. Well then if this people's custom of going to war for no other purpose than to take prisoners; stealing, kidnapping, &c. their neighbours and children, in order to sell them for slaves, cannot be thought of without raising the utmost detestation, as what the most effectually saps and destroys every social tie, on which all temporal happiness stands—is black with every guilt, and the most truly infernal of any practice that ever obtained among mankind—What excuse, what plea, will our Negro masters make at the great day of retribution, for encouraging those execrable crimes by receiving the plunder?—It will be none, I doubt, to say my Negro was born in my father's house, or in America, and therefore not obtained in that way; for I consider the person who was brought from his native country against his will and made a slave, to exist in each individual of his posterity, however distant in point of time. And the person in whose hand such posterity is found, so long as the injury is continued, to represent the original stealer or plunderer, whose right hath been conveyed down to him, and is that by which he claims property in such posterity, consequently represents him in whom this claim ultimately existed; nor can he wash his hands from this guilt by delivering such pretended property either by sale or gift to another, more than Pilot washed his from the guilt of Christ's death, whom he knew to be innocent, and had it in his power to have set at liberty.[9]

But to return to the source of this evil; if we look upon the first move so odious, so hateful, and find ourselves filled with indignation and abhorrence against the perpetrators, how can we countenance and encourage, and thereby become promoters, abetters, and accessories therein, which every one in a less or greater degree is, who buys, sells, or keeps in slavery one of these people after the age the law of nature gives each human being an equal right to freedom;[10] for can there be a greater absurdity than to say, I detest the plunderer, when I am greedily sharing the spoils, or innocent of the guilt, if I refuse to make restitution to the true owner of his property of which I am in possession, and of which he was unjustly deprived.—This opens a large field for consideration, for it really appears to me impossible for any one of their own seeking and choice, to be concerned in slave-keeping, or partake of the profits, without incurring a degree of the original guilt. For if an innocent free-man, who had no ways forfeited his freedom, was by force taken from his native country and made a slave and begets children, who by virtue of the original injury are kept slaves, and they beget others, and so on for twenty generations, the first wrong, a robbery of freedom, is continued, and exists in each of these, as much as it did in their common ancestors; nor can I defend or justify my title to one of them without defending and justifying the original injury on which my right is founded, and my refusing to restore this stolen property, of which I am possessed, to its right owner, shews that I approve the original act, and being a sharer of the spoils, become a sharer of the guilt, as also justly chargable with a repetition of the crime; for every individual of the human species by the law of nature comes into the world equally intitled to freedom at a proper age, altho' their parents may have been unjustly deprived of, or forfeited theirs. Children are not to answer for the sins of their parents;[11] and whoever having the care or possession of a child, and denys him his freedom at an age the laws of his country gives it to others, and without any act or consent of the party to justify it, commits an act of violence against the strongest of laws, the law of nature,—robs that individual of his inherent property, his freedom, a right which was never given by the universal Father to any one of his creatures over one another, without some fault on their part, not even to parents over their children.—A property more sacred, interesting, and essential to us as free agents, and accountable creatures than any other. And whoever partakes of the labour of such, or the profits arising therefrom, become sharers of the spoils of oppression.—Can we then believe the Supreme Being to be an indifferent spectator of this inhuman trade, this assumed authority of one part of his intelligent creatures levelling another part with the brute animals to drudge and toil for their will and pleasure. Buy and sell them like cattle, deprived of every rational enjoyment, with the addition of every species of human misery.—If he really is a GOD taking cognisance of the actions of men—of one flesh hath created all nations of people— is no respector of persons, but renders to every man according to his works—is particularly attentive to the cries of the poor and needy—will he not assuredly judge for those things? "Rob not the poor, because he is poor, neither oppress the afflicted in the gate. For the Lord will plead their cause, and spoil the soul, of those that spoiled them." Prov. xxii. 22, 23.[12]

The scripture mentions* the wicked balance, and bag of deceitful weights, the use of which, I believe was never more apparent than in this dark business, in excusing the keeping slaves, and in raising difficulties against setting them free, it would be endless to attempt a catalogue of the trifling and absurd reasons used on these occasions, nor have I any inclination, my intent being only just to hint at matters; to reason with those who justify slave-keeping, after its unlawfulness hath been so plainly and abundantly proved, would appear idle in me. But such who solemnly pretend to condemn the practice, yet shelter themselves under supposed difficulties in setting theirs free, or willing to free them after they have spent the prime of life in their service, or make them pay so much per year to secure their estates, &c.[13] I would beg of such to lay aside the false balance and deceitful weights, and use the true.—Weigh this matter in Christ's scales. "Do unto others, as ye would they should do to you." This will oblige you to set your negroes free at the same age your own children are, without unjustly coveting their labour till they are 25 or 30 years of age, or compelling them to pay you a yearly sum. They have as good a right to their freedom at twenty-one in the eyes of unbiased justice as your own sons, and to deny it to them, is as I said before, a repetition of the crime which brought their ancestors out of their own country, viz. a robbing them of their freedom, which if born and continued there, they would have enjoyed, nor can their being born among christians cancel this invariable law of nature, or make the seizing their freedom by force here, any less injustice than had it been done there; the injury to the individual is the same, and equally incompatible with doing as we would be done unto.—Should one of your sons be kept an apprentice by force, a year longer than his master had a right, satisfaction must be made, or a prosecution commenced and what not, for redress. But the poor Africans having no advocate but his master's conscience, may be kept year after year, and perhaps die at his drudgery like a horse at the plow, or have his freedom restored at a time of life when it is rather a punishment than favour.

---

* Mic. vi. 11.

Object. But surely thou wilt admit of some distinction between the children of white people born free, and those of our slaves who cost us great sums of money which we have not been repaid, or perhaps bought young and not earned half their cost by the time they are of age, as is my case. I have a woman bought when young, who having had children fast, hath earned very little of her purchase money, and if I should set all these free as they arrive to the age of men and women, shall be a great looser by them; thou wilt hardly say that would be reasonable.

My friend thy reasoning proceeds from the bag of deceitful weights; the true balance discovers justice to be quite another thing than thou seems to think it, here is no respect of persons. Justice to thy negroe weighs as heavy as justice to thyself, a small loss in thy interest put in this scale against the freedom of an innocent fellow-creature, weighs but as a feather against mount Atlas,[14] perhaps the barely claiming no right to them after the age of 18 and 21 may fall greatly short of christian justice in this scale; let us therefore a little investigate this matter.

Query. How came thee possessed of this woman?

Ans. I bought her of an African merchant, who brought her from Guinea[15] when a child.

Query. How came he by her?

Ans. I know not: I suppose he bought her of them who had a right to sell her.

A right to sell her! No one, not even her father could have such a right longer than till she came to the age of a woman, at which time she was pronounced free by the law of nature, the rules of equity and justice, and precepts of Christ, whether in her father's house, or a master's, in her native country, or among strangers; this inherent right she carries with her, and cannot be disseized of but by her own consent.—But it is very likely she was stolen from her parents, and then justice will say the perpetrator had not the least right to her, consequently could convey none, but that he deserved death for the act.—If this is the chain of conveyance on which thy title to these negroes stands, thou sees it is none at all, but that the life of the person thou holds under, was justly forfeited for being the means of putting them into thy power; therefore if thou had been a christian in deed and in truth, that is, been dictated in all thy conduct by the precepts of Christ, which are the perfections of justice, would sooner have cast thy money into the fire, then have made such an unchristian purchase, by doing of which, thou approved of, and made thyself a partner in all the string of crimes committed in procuring, bringing, and selling this child for a slave; but having done it, should then have acted the part of a father by her, been more earnest in giving her a christian education, than to make her earn her purchase-money, and have claimed no right to her after she came to woman's age.—This is as thou would desire a child of thine should be treated in the like circumstances; but as thou did not then discharge a christian duty by her, hath now an additional cumber, and ought to do this by her children; for being under thy care, their own father cannot do it, and by a free act of thy own, thou stands his substitute as to their education, and ought to discharge a father's duty to them in that respect.

Object. I act the part of a father by negroes! be at the cost of raising them, schooling and what not, and when they are able to earn something set them free!—I'll assure thee I'll do no such thing, it would be injustice to myself and family.—Why at that age they'll bring me near 100£[16] per head.

Do not be warm my friend, I am not about to force thee to obey the laws of God,[*] "To deal justly, and love mercy." I know thou has the laws of men on thy side. I am only endeavouring to shew thee it would be abundantly thy greatest interest so to do; and as thou calls thyself a christian, should expect much rhetorick need not be used to convince thee that to be such it is absolutely necessary to obey Christ's precepts and doctrine; to which there is nothing more diametrically opposite than the slave trade from first to last.—But if, with Dives,[17] thou art preferring this world's treasure to that which ought to be laid up in heaven,—I fear thou will share his lot in the conclusion.

Object. I am not preferring this world's treasure in that sort, but think it very just these negroes should serve me till they are 25 or 30 years of age to pay for their bringing up, and then a yearly sum for some time to secure my estate from charge.

Thou art still using the false balance, the true one will decide quite

---

[*] Mic. vi. 8.

otherwise. It hath been already shewn that by the law of nature and precepts of christianity, thou had not the least right to the mother's labour
after she was of woman's age, and thy keeping her against her will, was
robbing her of her freedom, which at that time became her own property, and in consequence of that unlawful act, now claims her children;—
but can justly have no other, or greater power over them than that of a
father until they are men and women, when having received from thee a
christian education to enable them to get a living, and be useful members of society, ought then enjoy their freedom as fully as thy own children. And as to paying a yearly sum to secure thy estate, it is the height of
injustice; this incumbrance was not brought on by any fault or act of
theirs, but by thyself, and as it was of thy own seeking, ought to bear the
burden, and not punish innocent persons for thy faults. Do the best the
present circumstances will admit of,* "Loose the bands of wickedness,
and let the oppressed go free," and thereby atone for what cannot be
recalled; for whoever attempts, to satisfy justice by setting their negroes
free by halves in that sort, will find themselves as much mistaken, I
believe, as Ananias and his wife,[18] in trying to deceive the apostles with a
part of the money their possessions sold for.—It is inflicting a penalty
upon them,—and for what?—Justice abhors punishing an innocent person; and if they are innocent why shall they not enjoy their natural rights
as fully and absolute as the rest of mankind. Or is it their being born of a
different colour from ourselves that gives us this prerogative of dealing
with them as we please; making natural justice quite another thing when
apply'd to negroes, from what it is when apply'd to those of our own
colour. However this simple circumstance may have prejudiced our
minds, it may be well for all who are concerned with this people to
remember, that they are equally the work of an Almighty hand, with a
soul to save or loose, as themselves, and being so, doubtless will avenge
their cause, altho' in his mercy he forbears long, the time of retribution
will come; justice is as much his attribute as mercy.

Object. Thou says much of doing as we would be done unto, &c. for my
part I think it a great happiness for the negroes that they are brought here,
whereby they become acquainted with the christian doctrine, which they

---

* Isa. lviii. 6

46

would have remained ignorant of, had they continued in their own country.

A hopeful argument! fabricated by the same hand as those in favour of the Spanish inquisition,[19] and with about as much sense and reason. Those murderers it is said, will with a very grave face tell an heretick at the time they are torturing him in the most exquisite manner, that they do it out of pure regard for his soul; thus for the good of their souls, destroy hereticks in a more horrible sort than a lion, or tiger, does his prey. And these make use of the most unchristian means to get and keep their fellow-men in their power, and render them the most miserable of human beings, to make them acquainted forsooth and in love with christianity, which it is well known is the least of their concern, and that few take more care to instill into their negroes than into their cattle. But this plea tho' often used, is too absurd and ridiculous to be seriously refuted, shall therefore dismiss the subject after giving another sample of like pious concern for the souls of men, which may bring it more feelingly home to ourselves. The duke of Parma on hearing of Queen Elizabeth's proclaiming a day of thanksgiving for the defeat of the Spanish Armada, exclaimed! "Mistaken woman! Blind Nation! to return thanks for the greatest misfortune that could have befallen them! for had that enterprize succeeded, they would all have been converted to the true catholic faith."[20]—Now had they obtained their ends, butchered thousands, and enslaved the rest, I suppose we should think it the greatest insult on reason, to say it would have been a real kindness to the English, tho' it might be so said with much more propriety and truth, than it can respecting negroes, who are brought from their native land, where they enjoyed freedom and independance in a more extensive degree than we do, and placed here on a footing with the brute creatures, that are generally treated with greater care and tenderness than they.* In the other case, the people of England by submitting to the conquerors, would have enjoyed their civil and natural privileges. How far that is from being the case with slaves, concerns their master's awfully to consider.

---

* In the West Indies, and some of our colonies.

POSTSCRIPT.

Having in the foregoing tract several times mentioned the law of nature; some may ask what is the law of nature. Civilians define it thus,— "The law of nature is that which God at man's creation infused into him, for his preservation and direction; is an eternal law and may not be changed; is the law of all places, persons and times without alteration, and has the same force all the world over; it's object is the good and happiness of mankind."

And John Lock,[21] that celebrated master of reason, in his treatise on government, speaks much to the present purpose: some of which is as follows, viz.

"The magistrate may remit punishment for a crime, but cannot remit satisfaction due to a private man for damage, who alone hath a right to demand, or remit the same." Page 149.[22]

"Every man has a property in his own person, this no body has any right to but himself, the labour of his body, and work of his hands are his own." Page 160.

"Man being born with a title to perfect freedom, and an uncontrouled enjoyment of all the rights and privileges of the law of nature, equally with any other man, or number of men in the world, hath by nature a power to preserve his property, that is his life, liberty, and estate, against the injuries, and attempts of other men." Page 199.

"Every man being naturally free, nothing is able to put him into subjection to any earthly power, but only his own consent." Page 223.

"The law of nature stands as an eternal rule to all men, legislators as well as others; the rules that they make for other men's actions must be conformable to this law, *i.e.* to the will of God, of which that is a declaration; and the fundamental law of nature being the good of mankind, no human sanction can be good or valid against it." P. 233.

"For one man to have an absolute arbitrary power over another, is a power which nature never gives, for it has made no such distinction between men, it can only be acquired by the individual forfeiting his life.

48

Page 259—Captives taken in a just and lawful war, and such only are subject to such a power. Page 260. But this concerns not the children who are in their minority; for since a father hath not in himself a power over the life and liberty of his child, no act of his can possibly forfeit it, so that the children whatever may have happened to the fathers, are freemen, and this absolute power reaches no farther than the men that were subdued by him, and dies with them; and tho' he governed them as slaves, he has no such right over their children. He can have no power over them but by their own consent." Page 270.

"Every man is born with a right of freedom to his person, which no other man has a power over; but the free disposal of it lies in himself." Page 271.

———

FINIS

Notes

[1] Proverbs 5:21. This and all subsequent Biblical references are from the Authorized (King James) Version of the Bible.

[2] Matthew 7:2.

[3] Proverbs 31:8–9.

[4] Matthew 7:12.

[5] Cooper refers to verses from the Old Testament as Jewish law.

[6] Exodus 21:16.

[7] An argument perhaps derived from Deuteronomy 20:14.

[8] Cooper refers to the curse of Canaan found in Genesis 9:20–25. Some apologists for slavery contended that Africans were the descendants of Canaan and, as a result, were destined to slavery.

[9] See Matthew 27:22–24.

[10] Cooper elsewhere specifies this age as eighteen for females and twenty-one for males.

[11] According to the Old Testament, children would be punished for the sins of their fathers. However, Deuteronomy 24:16 and Ezekiel 18:2 foretell a new covenant (to be fulfilled in the New Testament) under which a son will not suffer for his father's sins.

[12] Proverbs 22:22–23.

[13] Many slaveholders, including some Quakers, continued to keep slaves despite their religious and moral misgivings about the legitimacy of slaveholding. Some slaveholders, including prominent leaders such as George Washington, made provisions to have their slaves manumitted following their deaths. See David Brion Davis, "The Boundaries of Idealism," *The Problem of Slavery in the Age of Revolution 1770–1823*, (New York and Oxford: Oxford University Press, 1999).

[14] The Atlas mountain range in northwest Africa.

[15] "Guinea" was widely used in Europe, beginning in the fifteenth century, to refer to the coastal regions of West Africa between River Senegal (modern Senegal) and Cape Lopez (modern Gabon).

[16] Roughly equivalent to $9,000 in 2003.

[17] Latin for rich. Here, it refers to the unnamed wealthy man in Luke 12:16–20.

[18] See Acts of the Apostles 5:1–10.

[19] Initiated by King Ferdinand and Queen Isabella of Spain in 1478, the Spanish Inquisition was, by the eighteenth century, synonymous with religious intolerance, cruelty, and torture. The additional stigma here is that any doctrine

originating in Roman Catholic institutions was inherently suspect and probably wrong for good Protestants. The Inquisition was finally abolished in 1834.

[20] Although it is not clear from what source Cooper obtained this quotation, it is from Alessandro Farnese (1545–1592), Duke of Parma, who fought with the Spanish naval fleet, the Invincible Armada, during its 1588 invasion of England to overthrow Protestant Elizabeth I. The Spanish were famously defeated by the English.

[21] John Locke (1632–1704): English Enlightenment philosopher and author of *Two Treatises of Government* (London, 1690).

[22] Cooper here quotes from Locke's *Two Treatises of Government*. The page citation here and below are all to the 1690 London edition.

A

SERIOUS ADDRESS

TO THE

RULERS OF AMERICA,

On the Inconsistency of their Conduct respecting

SLAVERY:

FORMING A CONTRAST

Between the ENCROACHMENTS of England on American LIBERTY,

AND

American INJUSTICE in tolerating SLAVERY.

" As for me, I will assuredly contend for full and impartial
" Liberty, whether my Labour may be successful or vain."

TRENTON Printed:

LONDON, Reprinted by J. PHILLIPS, in George-Yard,
Lombard-Street. 1783.

[3]

A SERIOUS ADDRESS TO THE RULERS OF AMERICA
by David Cooper

Introduction by Rebecca Miller, University of North Carolina, Chapel Hill

As the hostilities of the American Revolution concluded in 1783, the ideology of inalienable natural rights resonated throughout the newly formed United States of America. Inspired by this rhetoric, Quaker farmer David Cooper (1725–1795) penned the pamphlet entitled, *A Serious Address to the Rulers of America, on the Inconsistency of Their Conduct Respecting Slavery: Forming a Contrast Between the Encroachments of England on American Liberty, and American Injustice in Tolerating Slavery* (1783). In this address, directed not only to the leaders of government, but also to the citizens of the burgeoning United States of America, Cooper demonstrates the marked contradiction between the professed ideals of natural rights and the actual practice of slaveholding and the slave trade. To highlight this contradiction, Cooper begins his pamphlet by juxtaposing passages concerning liberty extracted from various government documents on the left side of the page, with descriptions of slavery on the right.

In his diary, Cooper traces the origins of this anti-slavery tract: "In the First month of this year [1783], it often occurred to my mind that a use might arise from collecting and publishing some of the most striking statements of Congress in favor of liberty, with parts of the Constitutions of some of the American States on the same subject, contrasted by the idea of tolerating slavery."[1]

Cooper's anti-slavery stance was heavily influenced by the principles of the Enlightenment, particularly by the writings of political philosopher John Locke. Cooper concurred with the ideas Locke sets forth in his *Two Treatises of Government* (1690): that inviolable natural rights, namely the right to life, liberty, and property, were God-given rights, which could not be denied by government, and which in fact should be protected by government.[2]

In addition to Cooper's exposure to Enlightenment principles and the rhetoric promulgated by the War of Independence, the Quaker faith in which he grew up also played a part in forming his anti-slavery views. Born in Woodbury, New Jersey, on February 24, 1725, to John and Ann Cooper, David Cooper was raised in a devout Quaker family. Before arriving in New Jersey in 1678, his grandfather, William Cooper, served as a minister in Hertfordshire, England, and was a personal acquaintance of such influential Quaker leaders as George Fox, Isaac Pennington, and William Penn.[3] At the age of twenty-three, David Cooper married Sibyl Matlack, who bore six children before her death in 1759. A devoted husband and father, Cooper was deeply distraught for years after his wife's death. Adding to his grief, in 1762 Cooper's house was destroyed by a fire. His resolute belief in the divine goodness of God permeates his writings from this period, and it appears that he derived much of his strength from his faith.[4]

The Society of Friends, as the Quakers were formally known, began in 1650 as a small religious sect in northern England under founder George Fox. When British Quakers arrived in North America in the late 1600s, many opposed the expansion of slavery in the colonies. Finding slavery incompatible with their religious beliefs, these Quakers viewed owning a human being as prideful, ostentatious, and sinful.

Yet not all Quakers were opposed to the practice, and many, in fact, continued to own slaves, including the Quaker leadership. In the period 1681 to 1705, it is estimated that seventy percent of the leaders of the Philadelphia Yearly Meeting held slaves. George Fox had taught his parishioners that all people were equal in the sight of God and attempted to persuade the Quakers who did own slaves to limit their slaves' terms and to provide them with an education. As long as slaves were provided for in this way and well treated, many Quakers felt that there was nothing wrong with slavery.

Given the large number of slave owners among the ranks of the Quaker leadership, it's not surprising that throughout the first half of the eighteenth century abolitionist writing within the Society of Friends was not encouraged. In fact, the overseers of the Quaker press, approximately two-thirds of whom held slaves between 1681 and 1751,[5] forbad the printing of anti-slavery texts.

A remarkable change occurred in the 1750s, when the leadership of the Society was handed down to a new generation. Many of the slave-holding Quakers who had occupied leadership positions within the Society began to die or leave their meetings, and the new leaders often were adamantly opposed to the practice of slavery.[6] Cooper was one of these new leaders. In 1756, he accepted a nomination for the position of overseer at his local meetinghouse in Woodbury, New Jersey. Later that year, he was appointed as one of the representatives for the Quarterly Meeting of Gloucester and Salem, a position he would occupy for the next twenty years.

Under the auspices of the new leadership, over the next few decades Quakers became more and more intolerant toward the practice of slave-holding, eventually seeking to end the practice altogether. In 1758 they took their first step, banning the buying and selling of slaves among Quakers. Eighteen years later, in 1776, Quaker abolitionists propelled by the rhetoric of the American Revolution secured a ban on the owning of slaves within the Society of Friends. The Quakers then turned their attention outside their ranks, fighting for abolition in new states and territories, for the eradication of the African slave trade, and for the provision of relief for freed slaves.[7]

As the Quaker leadership changed their attitude toward slavery, so too did the overseers of the Quaker press. Whereas previously it had been prohibited, now the printing of pamphlets became one of the primary means through which Quakers spread their anti-slavery views. This means of dissemination was highly effective because the printing press was so useful in educating citizens in public affairs and shaping public opinion in colonial America.[8]

Quaker publisher Isaac Collins, who printed and sold Cooper's pamphlet in his shop in Trenton, New Jersey, is exemplary of this trend. In addition to printing government volumes and a newspaper (the *New Jersey Gazette*), Collins published an assortment of pamphlets, books, and broadsides. He also printed a remarkable number of anti-slavery texts. As one historian notes, "by issuing these publications [anti-slavery pamphlets by Anthony Benezet, John Woolman, and Granville Sharp], Collins probably did as much as, or more than, most Quaker printers in the colonies toward the dissemination of information about the iniquitous practice of buying, selling or keeping slaves."[9] On May 14, 1783, an advertisement for Cooper's pamphlet appeared in Collins' newspaper. Ironically placed next to notices announcing rewards for the return of runaway slaves, the advertisement informed the public of its nine-pence cost and its availability at Isaac Collins' shop.

Cooper, in keeping with the Quaker practice of humility, had chosen to publish his pamphlet anonymously so as not to draw attention to himself. In a letter to his dear friend and son-in-law, Samuel Allinson, he expresses his contentment with remaining anonymous in his writings: "As to my situation in life, it comes so near my humble wishes, that I think myself more happy in this obscure sphere than most of my fellow men who are making a noise in the world; who sacrifice all true happiness in pursuit of the bubble, honour—a happiness that depends on the breath of variable mortals."[10]

Within the Quaker abolitionist community, Cooper's *A Serious Address* was positively received and widely disseminated. In his diary Cooper noted that "Anthony Benezet interested himself in its circulation."[11] Benezet demonstrated this interest by delivering thirty copies to the president of Congress for distribution to each member and also by furnishing every member of the New Jersey Assembly with a copy.[12] After reading the document, a Philadelphian signing himself as "I.P."[13] sent a letter to John Pemberton, living in London: "A fresh publication on the subject is lately come out here entitled 'A Serious Address to the Rulers of America.' . . . It is a performance which merits attention being close and pointed, and the arguments which have been published by the professing advocates for Liberty turned upon themselves."[14] Cooper's pamphlet also made its way into the hands of George Washington; the copy of *A Serious Address* housed in the Boston Athenaeum is from Washington's library and bears his signature.

Shortly after the printing of *A Serious Address* in the United States, British publisher James Phillips reprinted the pamphlet in London. Phillips, an influential and well known Quaker publisher, was among a committee of twenty-three Quakers who, in the 1780s, were launching a campaign against the African slave trade. Throughout the 1780s, Phillips published numerous anti-slavery tracts, including works by Anthony

Benezet, Ottobah Cugoano, and Thomas Clarkson, which were disseminated throughout the Anglophone world.[15] The pivotal years were
1787–1788, when Phillips joined eleven other anti-slavery advocates to
form the London Committee for the Abolition of the Slave Trade. In the
span of fifteen months, the Committee distributed 79,733 abolitionist
pamphlets, most of which were printed at Phillips's printing house in
London, and prompted the introduction in Parliament of William
Wilberforce's bill to abolish the transatlantic British slave trade.[16]

Cooper remained active throughout the 1780s in his campaign
against slavery in America. In 1783, the year he published *A Serious
Address,* he traveled with thirteen Friends to Princeton to present an
address to Congress on the subject of slavery.[17] Two years later, Cooper
journeyed to Trenton to deliver to the New Jersey Assembly eight petitions for the gradual abolition of slavery. At the Quakers' Yearly Meeting
of 1786, the decision was made to call upon Congress to revive their consideration of the abolitionist petition delivered to them by the Friends in
1783. In 1788, Cooper and seven other Friends presented to the delegates of the New Jersey Legislature an address on behalf of the enslaved
Africans of the United States, along with a bill regarding the abolition of
slavery, which Cooper authored.[18]

Throughout his life, Cooper was tireless in his efforts and firm in his
commitment to eradicate slavery and the slave trade in the newly
formed United States of America. After his death, a member of Cooper's
own Woodbury Monthly Meeting praised "this dedicated friend" for the
"vital principle of *action* that was shown by its fruits in the general tenor of
his life."[19] Cooper left an indelible mark on the course of American abolitionism. He presaged the anti-slavery arguments used by such notable
Republican abolitionists as Salmon Chase and Abraham Lincoln, who
based their ultimately successful efforts to end slavery on the natural
rights strain of reasoning that Cooper had brought forth in the 1780s.

Notes

[1] *Friends' Review* (Philadelphia), Sept. 12, 1862.

[2] Bernard Bailyn, *The Ideological Origins of the American Revolution* (Cambridge:
Harvard University Press, 1967), 77.

[3] *Friends' Review* (Philadelphia), June 15, 1862.

[4] *Friends' Review* (Philadelphia), June 26, 1862.

[5] Jean R. Soderlund, *Quakers and Slavery: A Divided Spirit* (Princeton: Princeton University Press, 1985), 35.

[6] In the period from 1706 to 1730 slave ownership among leaders was approximately 58.6 percent, between 1731 and 1753 that number dropped to 34.2 percent, and finally, from 1754 to 1780, the figure drops to 10.2 percent.

[7] Jack D. Marietta, *The Reformation of American Quakerism, 1748-1783* (Philadelphia: University of Pennsylvania Press, 1984), 276.

[8] Richard F. Hixson, *The Press in Revolutionary New Jersey* (Trenton: New Jersey Historical Commission, 1975), 6.

[9] Richard F. Hixson, *Isaac Collins, A Quaker Printer in 18th Century America* (New Brunswick: Rutgers University Press, 1968), 41.

[10] Samuel Allinson, "Allinson Family Papers, 1761-1812," Special Collections, Alexander Library, Rutgers, The State University of New Jersey, New Brunswick.

[11] Although the pamphlet was signed "A Farmer," *A Serious Address* was attributed to Philadelphia Quaker Anthony Benezet as recently as 1998.

[12] *Friends' Review* (Philadelphia), Jan. 1, 1862.

[13] Israel Pemberton, a Quaker from Philadelphia, was a member of the eminent Pemberton family and was brother to John Pemberton, the addressee of this letter.

[14] David J. Cadbury, "Quaker Bibliographical Notes," *Bulletin of Friends' Historical Association*, vol. 26 (Swarthmore, Pa.: Friends' Historical Association, 1937), 46.

[15] Judith Jennings, *The Business of Abolishing the British Slave Trade: 1783-1807* (London: Frank Cass & Co. Ltd., 1997), 127.

[16] J. R. Oldfield, "The London Committee and Mobilization of Public Opinion Against the Slave Trade," *The Historical Journal* 35, no. 2 (1992), 331-333.

[17] *Friends' Review* (Philadelphia), Oct. 26, 1862.

[18] *Friends' Review* (Philadelphia), Jan. 1, 1862.

[19] John Comley, ed., *Friends' Miscellany* 8 (Philadelphia: William Sharpless, 1831), 342.

A

SERIOUS ADDRESS

TO THE

RULERS OF AMERICA,

On the Inconsistency of their Conduct respecting

SLAVERY:

FORMING A CONTRAST

Between the ENCROACHMENTS of England on
American LIBERTY,

AND

American INJUSTICE in tolerating SLAVERY.

"As for me, I will assuredly contend for full and impartial
Liberty, whether my Labour may be successful or vain."

TRENTON Printed:

LONDON, Reprinted by J. PHILLIPS, in George-Yard,
Lombard-Street. 1783.

A
SERIOUS ADDRESS, &c.

A Sound mind in a sound body, is said to be a state of the highest human happiness individually; when these blessings are separate, a sound mind, wise and prudent conduct, tend much to support and preserve an unsound body. On the other hand, where the body is sound, the constitution strong and healthy, if the mind is unsound, the governing principle weak and feeble, the body feels the injuries which ensue, the health and constitution often become enfeebled and sickly, and untimely death closes the scene.[1] This reasoning holds good politically, being sometimes realized in bodies politick, and perhaps never more so than in the conduct lately exhibited to mankind by Great Britain. Her constitution was sound, strong, and firm, in a degree that drew admiration from the whole world; but, for want of a sound mind, her directing and governing powers being imprudent and unwise, to such a debilitated and sickly state is this fine constitution reduced, that, without a change of regimen, her decease may not be far remote. America is a child of this parent, who long since, with many severe pangs, struggled into birth, and is now arrived to the state of manhood, and thrown off the restraints of an unwise parent, is become master of his own will, and, like a lovely youth, hath stepped upon the stage of action. State physicians pronounce his constitution strong and sound: the eyes of the world are singularly attentive to his conduct, in order to determine with certainty on the soundness of his mind. It is the general Congress, as the head, that must give the colouring, and stamp wisdom or folly on the counsels of America. May they demonstrate to the world, that these blessings, a sound mind in a sound body, are in America politically united!

IT was a claim of freedom unfettered from the arbitrary control of others, so essential to free agents, and equally the gift of our beneficent Creator to all his rational children, which put fleets and armies into motion, covered earth and seas with rapine and carnage, disturbed the repose of Europe, and exhausted the treasure of nations. Now is the time to demonstrate to Europe, to the whole world, that America was in earnest, and meant what she said, when, with peculiar energy, and unanswerable reasoning, she plead the cause of human nature, and with undaunted firmness insisted, that *all mankind* came from the hand of their Creator *equally free*. Let not the world have an opportunity to charge her conduct with a contradiction to her solemn and often repeated declarations; or to say that her sons are not real friends to freedom; that they have been actuated in this awful contest by no higher motive than selfishness and interest, like the wicked servant in the gospel, who, after his Lord had forgiven his debt, which he was utterly unable to pay, shewed the most cruel severity to a fellow servant for a trifling demand, and thereby brought on himself a punishment which his conduct justly merited.[2] Ye rulers of America beware! Let it appear to future ages, from the records of this day, that you not only professed to be advocates for freedom, but really were inspired by the love of mankind, and wished to secure the invaluable blessing to all; that, as you disdained to submit to the unlimited control of others, you equally abhorred the crying crime of holding your fellow men, as much entitled to freedom as yourselves, the subjects of your undisputed will and pleasure.

HOWEVER habit and custom may have rendered familiar the degrading and ignominious distinctions, which are made between people with a black skin and ourselves, I am not ashamed to declare myself an advocate for the rights of that highly injured and abused people; and, were I master of all the resistless persuasion of Tully[3] and Demosthenes,[4] could not employ it better, than in vindicating their rights as men, and forcing a blush on every American slaveholder, who has complained of the treatment we have received from Britain; which is no more to be equaled, with ours to negroes, than a barley corn is to the globe we inhabit. Must not every generous foreigner feel a secret indignation rise in his breast, when he hears the language of Americans upon any of their own rights as freemen being in the least infringed, and reflects that these very people are holding thousands and tens of thousands of their innocent fellow men in the most debasing and abject slavery, deprived of every right of freemen, except light and air? How similar to an atrocious pirate setting in all the solemn pomp of a judge, passing sentence of death on a petty thief. Let us try the likeness by the standard of facts.

THE first settlers of these colonies emigrated from England, under the sanction of royal charters, held all their lands under the crown, and were protected and defended by the parent state, who claimed and exercised a control over their internal police, and at length attempted to levy taxes upon them, and, by statute, declared the colonies to be under their jurisdiction, and that they had, and ought to have, a right to make laws to bind them in all cases whatsoever.

THE American Congress in their declaration, July 1775,[5] say,

"IF it were *possible* for men who exercise their reason to believe that the Divine Author of our existence intended a *part* of the human race to hold an absolute property in, and an unbounded power over others, marked out by infinite goodness and wisdom, as the objects of a legal domination never rightly resistible, however severe and oppressive; the inhabitants of these colonies might at least require from the parliament of Great Britain some evidence, that this *dreadful authority* over

AFRICA lies many thousand miles distant, its inhabitants as independent of us, as we are of them; we sail there, and foment wars among them, in order that we may purchase the prisoners, and encourage the stealing one another to sell them to us; we bring them to America, and consider them and their posterity for ever, our slaves, subject to our arbitrary will and pleasure; and if they imitate our example, and offer by force to assert their native freedom, they are condemned as traitors, and a hasty gibbet strikes terror on their survivors, and rivets their chains more secure.

DOES not this forcible reasoning apply equally to Africans? Have we a better right to enslave them and their posterity, than Great Britain had to demand Three-pence per pound for an article of luxury we could do very well without?[6] And Oh! America, will not a *reverence* for our *great Creator*, *principles* of *humanity*, nor the *dictates* of *common sense*, awaken thee to *reflect*, how far thy government falls short of impartially *promoting* the *welfare* of *mankind*, when its laws suffer, yea, justify men in murdering, torturing, and abusing their fellow men, in a

them has been granted to that body. But a *reverence* for our *great Creator, principles of humanity,* and the dictates of *common sense,* must convince all those who reflect upon the subject, that government was instituted to promote the welfare of mankind, and ought to be administered for the attainment of that end."

AGAIN they say,—"By this perfidy (Howe's conduct in Boston)[7] *wives* are *separated* from their *husbands, children* from their *parents,* the aged and sick from their *relations* and *friends,* who wish to attend and *comfort* them."

"WE most solemnly before GOD and the world declare, that exerting the utmost energy of those powers which our beneficent Creator hath graciously bestowed upon us, the arms we have been compelled by our enemies to assume, we will in defiance of every *hazard,* with unabated firmness and perseverance, em-

manner shocking to humanity?"

HOW abundantly more aggravated is our conduct in these respects to Africans, in bringing them from their own country, and separating by sale these near connections, never more to see each other, or afford the least *comfort* or tender endearment of social life. But they are black, and ought to obey; we are white, and ought to rule.—Can a better reason be given for the distinction, that Howe's conduct is *perfidy,*[8] and ours innocent and blameless, and justified by our *laws?*

THOU wicked servant, out of thine own mouth shalt thou be judged.—Is a claim to take thy property without thy consent so galling, that thou wilt defy every hazard, rather than submit to it? And at the same time hold untold numbers of thy fellow men in slavery, (which robs them of every thing valuable in life) as *firmly riv-*

ploy for the preservation of our liberties, being with one mind resolved to die freemen rather than live *slaves.*"

"WE exhibit to mankind the remarkable spectacle of a people attacked by *unprovoked enemies,* without any imputation, or even suspicion, of offence.—They boast of their privileges and civilization, and yet proffer no milder conditions than servitude or death."

"IN our own native land, in defence of the freedom that is our birthright, and which we ever enjoyed till the late violation of it; for the protection of our property acquired solely by the honest industry of our forefathers and ourselves; against violence actually offered, we have taken up arms."

IN a resolve of Congress, October 1774,[9] they say,

"THAT the inhabitants of the English colonies in North-America, by the *immutable laws* of *nature,* are entitled to life, liberty and property; and they have never ceded to any sovereign power whatever a right to dispose of either without their consent."

To the People of Great Britain.[10]

"KNOW then that we consider ourselves, and do insist, that we are and ought to be, as free as our fel-

etted by *thee,* as thou art resolved to use the utmost energy of thy power, to preserve thy own freedom?

HAVE the Africans offered us the least *provocation* to make us their *enemies?*—Have their infants committed, or are they even *suspected* of any offence? And yet we leave them no alternative, but *servitude* or *death.*

THE unenlightened Africans, in their own native land, enjoyed freedom, which was their birthright, until the more savage Christians transported them by thousands, and sold them for slaves in the wilds of America, to cultivate it for their lordly oppressors.

WITH equal justice may negroes say, By the *immutable laws of nature,* we are equally entitled to life, liberty and property with our lordly masters, and have never *ceded* to any power whatever, a *right* to deprive us thereof.

DOES this reasoning apply more forcibly in favour of a white skin than a black one? Why ought a negro to be less free than the

low-subjects in Britain, and that no power on earth has a right to take our property from us without our consent."

"ARE the proprietors of the soil of America less lords of their property than you are of yours? &c.—Reason looks with indignation on such distinctions, and freemen can never perceive their propriety; and yet, however, chimerical and unjust such discriminations are; the Parliament assert, that they have a right to bind us in all cases without exception, whether we consent or not; that they may take and use our property when and in what manner they please; that we are pensioners on their bounty for all we possess, and can hold it no longer than they vouchsafe to permit."

"IF neither the *voice of justice*, the dictates of the law, the principles of the constitution, or the *suggestions* of *humanity*, can restrain your hands from shedding human blood in such an *impious* cause, we must then tell you, that we never will submit to be hewers of wood or drawers of water for any ministry or nation on earth. And in future, let *justice* and *humanity* cease to be the boast of your nation?"

subjects of Britain, or a white face in America? Have we not all one Father? Hath not one God created us? Why do we deal treacherously every man against his brother? *Mal. ii. 10.*[11]

DO Americans reprobate this doctrine when applied to themselves? And at the same time enforce it with tenfold rigor upon others, who are indeed *pensioners* on their *bounty* for all they *possess*, nor can they *hold* a single enjoyment of life longer than they *vouchsafe* to *permit*?

YOU who have read a description of the inhuman scenes occasioned by the slave-trade, in *obtaining*, *branding*, *transporting*, *selling*, and keeping in *subjection* millions of human creatures; reflect a moment, and then determine which is the most *impious cause*: and after this, if neither the *voice of justice*, nor suggestions of *humanity*, can *restrain* your *hands* from being contaminat-

To the inhabitants of the colonies.[13]

"WEIGH in the opposite balance, the endless miseries you and your descendants must endure, from an established arbitrary power."

Declaration of Independence in Congress, 4th July, 1776.

"WE hold these truths to be self-evident, that *all men* are created *equal*, that they are endowed by their Creator with certain *unalienable rights*; that among these are *life*, *liberty*, and the *pursuit of happiness*."

Declaration of rights of Pennsylvania, July 15, 1776.[14]

"THAT *all men* are born *equally free* and *independent*, and have certain natural inherent and *unalienable rights*, among which are, the enjoying and defending *life* and *liberty*, acquiring, possessing and protecting *property*, and pursuing and obtaining happiness and safety."

Declaration of rights of Massachusetts, Sept. 1, 1779.[16]

"*All men* are born *free* and *equal*,

ed with the practice; cease to *boast* the Christian name from him, who commanded his followers "to do unto others as they would others should do unto them."[12]

WHO would believe the same persons, whose feelings are so exquisitely sensible respecting themselves, could be so callous toward negroes, and the *miseries* which, by their *arbitrary power*, they wantonly inflict.

IF these solemn *truths*, uttered at such an awful crisis, are *self-evident*: unless we can shew that the African race are not *men*, words can hardly express the amazement which naturally arises on reflecting, that the very people who make these pompous declarations are slave-holders, and, by their legislative, tell us, that these blessings were only meant to be the *rights* of *white men*, not of *all men*: and would seem to verify the observation of an eminent writer; "When men talk of liberty, they mean their own liberty, and seldom suffer their thoughts on that point to stray to their neighbours."[15]

and have certain natural, essential, and *unalienable rights*; among which may be reckoned the right of enjoying and defending their *lives* and *liberties*; that of acquiring, possessing and protecting *property*; in fine, of seeking and obtaining *safety* and *happiness*."

THIS was the voice, the language of the supreme council of America, in vindication of their rights as men, against imposition and unjust control: Yes, it was the voice of all America, through her representatives in solemn Congress uttered. How clear, full, and conclusive! "We hold these truths to be self-evident, that all men are created equal, and endowed by their Creator with the unalienable rights of life, liberty, and the pursuit of happiness." "By the immutable laws of nature *all men* are entitled to life and liberty." We need not now turn over the libraries of Europe for authorities to prove, that blacks are born equally free with whites; it is declared and recorded as the sense of America: Cease then ye cruel task-masters, ye petty tyrants, from attempting to vindicate your having the same interest in your fellow men as in your cattle, and let blushing and confusion of face strike every American, who henceforth shall behold advertisements offering their brethren to sale, on a footing with brute beasts.

BUT what shall I say! Forgive it, Oh Heaven, but give ear, Oh earth! While we are execrating our parent state with all the bitterness of invective, for attempting to abridge our freedom, and invade our property; we are holding our brethren in the most servile bondage, cast out from the *benefit* of our *laws*, and subjected to the cruel treatment of the most imperious and savage tempers, without *redress*, without advocate or friend.

OUR rulers have appointed days for humiliation, and offering up of prayer to our common Father to deliver us from *our* oppressors, when sighs and groans are piercing his holy ears from oppressions which we commit a thousand fold more grievous: pouring forth blood and treasure year after year in defense of our own *rights*; exerting the most assiduous attention and care to secure them by laws and sanctions, while the poor Africans are continued in chains of slavery, as creatures unworthy of notice in these high concerns, and left subject to laws disgraceful to humanity, and opposite to every precept of Christianity. One of these in effect gives fifteen pounds for the murder of a slave; that is, after a slave has absconded a certain time, twenty pounds is given to any one who shall bring his head, and but five pounds if he is brought alive. Another, which empowers certain officers to seize negroes set free, and sell them for the benefit of government: And, even during the present contest, negroes have been seized with the estates of persons who had gone over to the British, and sold by publick auction into *perpetual slavery*, and the proceeds cast into the stock for the *defence* of American *liberty*. Of the same complexion is an instance in New-Jersey: A female Quaker, about seven years since, manumitted her negroes; the times having reduced her so, as to be unable fully to discharge a debt for which she was only surety; the creditor, a great declaimer in behalf of *American freedom*, although he was offered his principal money, obtains a judgment, levies on these free negroes, who, by the assistance of some real friends of freedom, procured a *habeas corpus*, and removed their case before the justices of the supreme court. How many such mock patriots hath this day discovered, whose flinty hearts are as impervious to the tender feelings of humanity and commiseration as the nether millstone; can sport with the rights of men; wallow and riot in the plunder, which their unhallowed hands have squeezed from others! But only touch *their* immaculate interests, and what an unceasing outcry invades every ear. A love for my country, a regard for the honour of America, raises an ardent wish, that this picture may never be realized in her rulers.

IT may be objected that there are many difficulties to be guarded against in setting of negroes free, and that, were they all to be freed at once, they would be in a worse condition than at present. I admit that there is some weight in these objections; but are not these difficulties of our own creating? And must the innocent continue to suffer, because we have involved ourselves in difficulties? Let us do justice as far as circumstances will admit, give such measure as we ask, if we expect Heaven to favour us with the continuance of our hard earned liberty. The work must be begun, or it can never be completed. "It is begun, and many negroes are set free." True, it is begun, but not in a manner likely to produce the desired *end*, the entire *abolition* of *slavery*. This is the business of the superintending authority, the main spring which gives motion to the whole political machine; which, were they to undertake in good earnest, I have no doubt but we should soon see a period fixed, when our land should no longer be polluted with slave-holders, nor give forth her increase to feed slaves: and indeed it hath been a matter of wonder to many, that that body, who have been so much employed in the study and defence of the *rights* of *humanity*, should suffer so many years to elapse without any effectual movement in this business. Had they, with the declaration of independence, recommended it to the different Legislatures to provide laws, declaring, that no person imported into, or born in America after that date, should be held in slavery; it would have been a step correspondent with our own *claims*, and, in time, have completed the work, nor can I see any impropriety, but what the nature of the case will justify, to have it still take place.

To shew the necessity of this matter taking its rise at the head, if any thing effectual is done, I may instance the Quakers. Some among them, it is said, always bore a testimony against slavery from its first introduction, and the uneasiness increasing, advices were given forth, cautioning their members against being concerned in importing slaves, to use those well whom they were possessed of, school their children, &c. but some of the foremost of that society having experienced the profits of their labour, no effectual stop could be put to the practice, though many became uneasy, and set their negroes free, until the difficulties attending the late French and Indian war,[17] brought the rights of men into a more close inspection, when a rule was agreed upon, prohibiting their members from being concerned with importing, buying, or selling of slaves; and some years after a further rule was made, enjoining all those who held slaves to set them free, otherwise to be separated from religious membership.—The work was then soon accomplished, and they now say there are very few members belonging to the yearly meeting of Philadelphia who hold a slave.[18]

WHEN a grievance is general, it is but trifling to apply partial means; it is like attempting to destroy a great tree by nibbling at its branches. It is only the supreme power, which pervades the whole, that can take it up by the roots. The disquisitions and reasonings of the present day on the rights of men, have opened the eyes of multitudes, who clearly see, that, in advocating the rights of humanity, their slaves are equally included with themselves, and that the arguments which they advance to convict others, rebounds with redoubled force back on themselves, so that few among us are now hardy enough to justify slavery, and yet will not release their slaves; like hardened sinners, acknowledge their guilt, but discover no inclination to reform. It is true these convictions have occasioned the release of many slaves, and two or three states to make some feeble efforts looking that way;[19] but I fear, after the sunshine of peace takes place, we have little more to expect, unless the sovereign power is exerted to finish this sin, and put an end to this crying transgression.

LET me now address that august body, who are by their brethren clothed with sovereign power, to sit at the helm, and give a direction to the important concerns of the American union. You, gentlemen, have, in behalf of America, *declared* to Europe, to the world, "That all men are born *equal*, and, by the *immutable laws* of *nature*, are *equally* entitled to liberty."[20] We expect, mankind expects, you to demonstrate your *faith* by your *works*; the sincerity of your *words* by your *actions*, in giving the *power*, with which you are invested, its utmost *energy* in promoting *equal* and *impartial* liberty to *all* whose lots are cast within the reach of its influence; then will you be revered as the real friends of mankind, and escape the execrations which pursue human tyrants, who shew no remorse at sacrificing the ease and happiness of any number of their fellow-men to the increase and advancement of their own, are wholly regardless of others rights, if theirs are but safe and secure. We are encouraged in this expectation by the second article of your non-importation agreement in behalf of America, October 1774, *viz.* "That we will neither import nor purchase any slave imported after the first day of December next, after which time we will wholly discontinue the slave-trade, and will neither be concerned in it ourselves, nor will we hire our vessels, nor sell our commodities or manufactures to those who are concerned in it."[21] And much would it have been for the honour of America, had it been added and confirmed by laws in each state (nor will we suffer such a stigma to remain on our land, as that it can produce slaves, therefore no child, born in any of the United States after this date, shall be held in slavery).—But the children of slaves are private property, and cannot be taken from their masters without a compensation. What! After it hath so often been echoed from America, "All men are born equally free."[22] "No man or body of men can have a legitimate property in, or control over their fellow-men, but by their own consent expressed or implied." Shall we now disown it, in order to hold our slaves? Forbid it all honest men; it is treason against the rights of humanity, against the principles upon which the American Revolution stands, and by which the present contest can only be justified; to deny it, is to justify Britain in her claims, and declare ourselves rebels. Wherefore our rulers undoubtedly ought to give these principles, these laws which themselves have declared *immutable*, a due force and efficacy. This every well-wisher to their country, either in a religious or political sense, have a right to ask and expect. But we have laws that will maintain us in the possession of our slaves: "The fundamental law of nature being the good of mankind, no human sanctions can be good, or valid against it, but are of themselves void, and ought to be resisted." LOCK[23]

Therefore none can have just cause of complaint, should so desirable an event take place, as that no person brought into, or born within any of the United States after the declaration of independence, shall be held a slave.

WHEN I read the constitutions of the different states, they afford a mournful idea of the partiality and selfishness of man; the extraordinary care, and wise precautions they manifest to guard and secure our own rights and privileges, without the least notice of the injured Africans, or gleam of expectation afforded them, of being sharers of the golden fruitage, except in that of the Delaware state, who, to their lasting honour, while they were hedging in their own, provided against the invasion of the rights of others. By the twenty-sixth article of their constitution they resolve, that "No person hereafter imported into this state from Africa, ought to be held in slavery under any pretence whatever; and no negro, Indian or mulatto slave, ought to be brought into this state for sale from any part of the world."[24] Had they went further, and made provision, by which slavery must at length have terminated within their jurisdiction, it would have been doing something to the purpose; and, as this is the only constitution in which posterity will see any regard paid to that abused people, I hope the same human considerations which led them so far, will induce them to take the lead in doing their part toward putting an effectual end to this crying evil, which will ever remain a stain to the annals of America.*

AND you who in the several states are clothed with legislative authority, and have now an opportunity of displaying your wisdom and virtue by your laws freed from every foreign control, although this people were below notice, and their rights and interest thought unworthy of a sanction in your constitutions; let me beseech you, if you wish your country to escape the reproach and lasting infamy of denying to others what *she* hath so often, and in the most conclusive language, declared were the rights of *all*; if you wish to retain the name of Christians, of friends to human nature, and of looking up acceptably in prayer to the common Father of men, to deal with you in the same tenderness and mercy as you deal with others; that you would even now regard the rigorous oppressions of his other children, and your brethren, which they suffer under laws, which you only can abrogate. View your negro laws calculated not to protect and defend them, but to augment and heighten their calamitous situation! Cast out and rejected by the regulations formed for the defence and security of the rights and privileges, and to guard and improve the morals and virtue of the whites: Left open to the gratification of every passion and criminal commerce with one another, as though they were brutes, and

---

* When this was written, I had, by information, been led to believe, that the late Pennsylvania slave law was very partial and inadequate; but have since learned, that it is a judicious and well constructed law, which provides for the entire abolition of slavery in that state.

not men; fornication, adultery, and all the rights of marriage union among blacks, considered beneath the notice of those rules and sanctions formed to humanize and restrain corrupt nature, or the regard of those whose duty it is to enforce them. Yes, blush Americans! Ye have laws, with severe penalties annexed, against these crimes when committed between whites; but, if committed by blacks, or by white men with black women, with the aggravated circumstances of force and violence, they pass as subjects of mirth, not within the cognizance of law, or magistrates inquiry, and lose the very name of crimes. Hence children often become familiar with these scenes of corruption and wickedness, before they are capable of distinguishing between the duties of Christianity, and the appetites of unrestrained nature. No marvel then if slave-holders are often scourged by the vices of their own offspring, which their untutored slaves have been a means of inflicting—children who, instead of being educated in the nurture and admonition of the Lord, are too often nurtured in pride, idleness, lewdness, and the indulgence of every natural appetite; that, were there no other inducement, this singly is sufficient to cause every real Christian to lift a hand against, and exert their utmost influence in, bringing this hydra mischief to a period. But when we consider the accumulated guilt, in other respects, abundantly set forth by other writers on this subject, brought on this land through the introduction of this infernal traffick, at a time when we were denied the privilege of making laws to check the mighty evil; and that near ten years have now elapsed since this restraint hath been removed, and no effectual advance yet made towards loosing the bands of wickedness, and letting the oppressed go free, or even of putting it in a train whereby it may at length come to an end; I say, it is a matter of anxious sorrow, and affords a gloomy presage to the true friends of America. Have we reason to expect, or dare we ask of him, whose *ways* are all *equal*, the continuance of his blessings to us, whilst our *ways* are so *unequal*.

I shall now conclude with the words of Congress to the people of England, a little varied to suit the present subject.

"IF neither the voice of *justice*, the dictates of *humanity*, the *rights* of *human nature*, and establishment of *impartial liberty now in your power*, the good of your *country*, nor the fear of an *avenging God*, can restrain your hands from this *impious practice* of holding your fellow-men in *slavery*: making traffick of, and advertising in your publick prints for sale as common merchandize, *your brethren* possessed of immortal souls equal with yourselves; then let *justice, humanity, advocates for liberty,* and the sacred name of *Christians,* cease to be the *boast* of *American rulers.*"[25]

A FARMER.

February, 1783

———

FINIS.

Notes

[1] In opening his address, Cooper draws from John Locke's *Some Thoughts Concerning Education* (1693), which originated from a series of letters Locke wrote to Edward Clarke regarding the upbringing of his children.

[2] See Matthew 18:21–35. This and all subsequent Biblical references are from the Authorized (King James) Version of the Bible.

[3] Marcus Tullius Cicero (106 BCE–43 BCE): Rome's most famous orator, lawyer, and statesman, who served as consul in 63 BCE and authored several influential essays and speeches including *De amicitia, De oratore, Brutus,* and the *Phillipics.*

[4] Demosthenes (382 BCE–322 BCE): Generally regarded as the greatest of the official Athenian orators and noted by historians for crafting distinctly convincing arguments using plain language, Demosthenes is best known for his orations against Philip of Macedon.

[5] *The Declaration of the Causes and Necessity of Taking Up Arms,* written by John Dickinson and Thomas Jefferson on July 6, 1775, during the meeting of the second Continental Congress in Philadelphia. After the battles of Lexington and Concord, Congress believed it necessary to publish an explanation of why the colonics had taken up arms against England.

[6] In accordance with the Sugar Act (1764), a three-pence tax was placed on foreign goods including sugar, molasses, and coffee—one of several British taxes that the American colonists resented and protested as being an oppression comparable to enslavement.

[7] British commander General William Howe and his troops occupied Boston from April 1775 to March 1776. The Boston colonists agreed to deposit their arms with the magistrates of the town for safe-keeping upon their exit from Boston. When the colonists handed over their weapons, Howe, in violation of a prior agreement, seized the arms and detained a large number of Boston inhabitants.

[8] See note 7 above.

[9] *The Declaration and Resolves of the First Continental Congress* (Philadelphia, Oct. 14, 1774) was written in response to the Coercive (Intolerable) Acts, which imposed various restrictions on colonists, including forbidding town meetings and closing Boston Harbor.

[10] From John Jay's *Address to the People of Great Britain* (Philadelphia, 1774), written shortly after his election to the First Continental Congress.

[11] Malachi 2:10.

[12] Matthew 7:12.

[13] From William Livingston's *To the Inhabitants of the Several Anglo-American*

Colonies (Oct. 1774). Two years after writing this address, Livingston, a representative at the First Continental Congress, was elected first governor of New Jersey.

[14] From article 1 of the Pennsylvania Constitution of 1776. Framed by a convention in Philadelphia on July 15, 1776, the Constitution was completed on September 8, 1776, and was principally authored by Benjamin Franklin, George Bryan, and James Cannon.

[15] Source unknown, but possibly inspired by Samuel Johnson's *Rambler*, no. 146 (Aug. 10, 1751).

[16] From *A Declaration of the Rights of the Inhabitants of the Commonwealth of Massachusetts* (a section within the Massachusetts Constitution), written in 1779 by John Adams, who modeled it after the Virginia Declaration of Rights, composed by George Mason.

[17] Also known as the Seven Years' War, in which hostilities between the French and English, prompted by their competition to gain control of North America, actually continued from 1754 until the Treaty of Paris was signed in 1763. Battles were fought at Fort Duquesne, Fort Necessity, Fort Frontenac, and Ticonderoga as Britain sought to seize control of French forts in the West. Both sides were allied with various Native American tribes.

[18] In 1758, the process of abolishing slavery within the Society of Friends was initiated when the Philadelphia Yearly Meeting deemed that any slave-owning Friends who held leadership positions within the Society would be dismissed. Slaveholding was completely banned in the Society in 1776.

[19] Cooper is referring to Vermont, Pennsylvania, and Massachusetts, which abolished slavery in 1777, 1780, and 1783, respectively. In Massachusetts, the judicial sanctioning of slavery was removed in the state supreme court case *Commonwealth vs. Jennison,* while in Vermont and Pennsylvania it was abolished in the state constitutions.

[20] Apparently an amalgamation composed by Cooper from various phrases of Revolutionary rhetoric.

[21] In response to the growing anti-slavery sentiment of the times, the First Continental Congress drafted a set of *Declarations and Resolves,* which included a non-importation agreement. The drafting of the agreement commenced on October 14, 1774, and was completed and adopted eight days later.

[22] A phrase that occurs in various texts of the period including the 1776 Constitution of Pennsylvania and George Mason's *Virginia Declaration of Rights* (June 12, 1776).

[23] English philosopher John Locke (1632–1704) is considered the founding theorist of classical liberalism. Locke's views on the separation of church and

state, the basing of government on the consent of the governed, among others of his ideas, profoundly shaped the thought of America's founding generation, and helped mold American democracy.

[24] The General Assembly of Delaware had sought to prohibit both the importation and exportation of African slaves, but their attempt had been vetoed by Governor John Penn in 1775. This passage is from article 26 of the Delaware Constitution, drafted in September 1776.

[25] Cooper's adaptation of a passage from John Jay's *An Address to the People of Great Britain* (1774).

THE
CONSTITUTION

OF THE

Pennſylvania Society,

FOR PROMOTING THE

ABOLITION OF SLAVERY,

AND THE RELIEF OF

FREE NEGROES,

UNLAWFULLY HELD IN

BONDAGE.

BEGUN IN THE YEAR 1774, AND ENLAGRED ON THE

TWENTY-THIRD OF APRIL, 1787.

TO WHICH ARE ADDED,

THE ACTS OF THE

General Aſſembly of Pennſylvania,

FOR THE

Gradual Abolition of Slavery.

" *All Things whatſoever ye would that Men ſhould do to you, do ye even ſo to them; for this is the Law and the Prophets.*" Mat. vii. 12.

PHILADELPHIA:

PRINTED BY JOSEPH JAMES, IN CHESNUT-STREET.

M.DCC.LXXXVII.

[4]
THE CONSTITUTION OF THE
PENNSYLVANIA ABOLITION SOCIETY

Introduction by Sam Rosenfeld, Columbia University

If, as an increasing number of scholars attest, the decades preceding the American Revolution comprised the first great era of anti-slavery sentiment and agitation in the Anglo-American world, then the embodiment of that spirit can be found in the first organization established anywhere dedicated to the abolitionist cause. Begun unassumingly by a handful of activist Quakers in the spring of 1775 under the title "The Society for the Relief of Free Negroes Unlawfully Kept in Bondage," the Pennsylvania Abolition Society (PAS) came to dominate and to typify Revolutionary-era abolitionism in much the same way the Massachusetts Anti-Slavery Society did for the movement of the 1830s and 1840s.[1] Elite in its leadership and Quaker-dominated, the organization pioneered the basic tenets of late-eighteenth-century abolitionism, chief among them gradualism, a focus on legal activism, and a preoccupation with respectability and moderation. Although the American Revolution disrupted the functioning of the Society for nine years, the group was reactivated in 1784, and then greatly enlarged and reconstituted in 1787. In the spring of 1787, the PAS released the pamphlet entitled *The Constitution of the Pennsylvania Society, for Promoting the Abolition of Slavery, and the Relief of Free Negroes, Unlawfully Held in Bondage. Begun in the Year 1774,[2] and Enlarged on the Twenty-Third of April, 1787. To Which Are Added, the Acts of the General Assembly of Pennsylvania, for the General Abolition of Slavery.* The pamphlet served as a public declaration of the Society's resurgent vigor and expanded purpose, and inaugurated what would turn out to be more than two decades of the group's predominance in the broader Anglo-American anti-slavery struggle.

To be sure, the group's formal launch in 1775 was inauspicious. Ten Quakers met at the Sun Tavern in Philadelphia on April 14 to form an organization with the limited mandate of providing legal representation and aid to free blacks who remained illegally enslaved. The impetus driving the formation of this group stemmed from anti-slavery Quaker doctrine going back to the previous century, but even with deep philosophical origins, the PAS, in practice, experienced a tentative early life. Under the presidency of John Baldwin and the active leadership of Thomas Harrison, the group managed to meet only four times in 1775, before the outbreak of war pushed it into a nine-year hiatus. But in those four meetings, the PAS brought six cases of wrongful enslavement up for investigation and legal action under the guidance of the group's esteemed counselor, Miers Fisher.[3] The contingent of high-powered litigators in the Society would continue to expand after the reorganization in the 1780s, and legal agitation would remain a fundamental component of the PAS method for decades to come.

During the Society's resuscitation in 1784, the PAS drafted its first constitution and expanded its membership significantly to include prominent and non-Quaker Pennsylvania figures like Benjamin Rush. The Society remained a predominantly legal organization with an ever-growing corps of eminent legal activists working in the state's courts, and over the next three years, the PAS's efforts helped free nearly one hundred African Americans in Pennsylvania.[4]

This was all, in a way, merely a prelude to the reorganization of 1787, which included a new constitution and an expansion in the Society's size and scope. Membership tripled that year, and the group changed its name from the "Society for the Relief of Free Negroes Unlawfully Kept in Bondage" to the "Pennsylvania Society for Promoting the Abolition of Slavery and for the Relief of Free Negroes Unlawfully Held in Bondage," reflecting a more expansive and far-reaching vision of what might be accomplished.[5] Still more influential figures joined the Society. Tench Coxe, soon to be the assistant secretary of the treasury under Alexander Hamilton, had become a member in December of 1786; he quickly persuaded Benjamin Franklin and James Pemberton to join the group and to assume the presidency and vice-presidency, respectively, thereby catapulting the organization to a new level of influence and respect.

The sudden expansion of the group may have been brought about, in part, by the debates surrounding the imminent national convention to forge a constitution.[6] The debate over slavery certainly did loom large at the Constitutional Convention, which took place in Philadelphia in the summer of 1787. The sectional compromise that would emerge out of that debate—with its three-fifths clause that provided legal sanction to the institution of slavery and its postponement of any proposals to abolish the slave trade for twenty years—established the ambiguous legal and political context in which the PAS would do its work for the coming decades.

There was also a more concrete reason for the 1787 expansion. Pennsylvania's 1780 state law, calling for gradual abolition, had provided an opportunity for African Americans throughout the North and upper South to seek redress in the state. Throughout the following decade, even PAS members were startled by the numbers flooding across the Quaker State's borders to agitate for their own freedom. Thus, the PAS's 1787 expansion in resources and scope was as much a product of the practical demands placed on the organization by blacks themselves as it was a reflection of broader contemporary political and intellectual currents.[7]

The effect the political ferment and public pressure had on the PAS is evident in its new 1787 Constitution. The revitalized Society placed much more emphasis on reaching across state and national boundaries to coordinate with fellow abolitionist organizations, which had sprouted up in the preceding few years, and on disseminating appeals to the literate public. As drafted by a committee consisting of Coxe, Rush, Harrison, Jonathan Penrose, and William Jackson, the constitution is broader in scope than the version from just three years earlier. Whereas the preamble of 1784 included a plea to relieve the suffering of slaves and freedmen "either in this city or its Neighborhood,"[8] the new one speaks of "a desire to diffuse" the blessings of liberty "wherever the miseries and vices of slavery exist."[9] This would translate into major petition and memorial drives across the country, at both the state and federal levels, and the distribution of 1,000 copies of the PAS constitution in pamphlet form in the spring of 1787 (reprinted here).[10]

Though clearly the PAS was seeking to make its existence and agenda popularly known through such dissemination, it must be stressed that the PAS's top-down, work-within-the-system approach did not change significantly with the 1787 expansions. Far from tapping into any kind of mass base of support, the organization remained, in one scholar's words, a group of "deferential petitioners" who pressed gentlemen in power "to devise legislation that would attack slavery without upsetting the American political order."[11] One need look no further than Franklin's refusal in 1787 to present his own organization's memorial to the Constitutional Convention, for fear of it being too controversial, to discern the group's fundamental outlook of moderation and compromise.[12] Typical recipients of this pamphlet included the British abolitionist Richard Price, who wrote to thank Franklin personally for sending it, and the notable Granville Sharp, president of the Society for the Abolition of the Slave Trade in London.[13] It was clear the new PAS would spread the word farther out, but not necessarily farther down. Moreover, despite the growing numbers of blacks who had come to Pennsylvania in the 1780s, the Society still refused to admit black members, and would continue to exclude them until the 1830s.

After 1787, the PAS continued to take its legalistic approach to activism, even as petitions and propaganda campaigns came to the fore as major components of the PAS program. The other two documents included in this pamphlet, the two acts that comprise Pennsylvania's 1780 gradual abolition law, underscore the continued emphasis on legislative and judicial means to pursue the Society's mission.

Ironically, the 1780 act came about during a period when the long-standing stalwarts of abolitionism in Pennsylvania, the Quakers, were most excluded from power. During the Revolution, Quakers found themselves branded as loyalist traitors for their pacifism and were shut out of politics as they never had been before. But the spirit of enlightened reform and natural rights philosophy that pervaded the Revolutionary atmosphere found expression in the Quakers' ostensible opponents, a group of radical, largely secular assemblymen who came to power in the wake of Pennsylvania's progressive state constitution of 1776. The gradual abolition act stood as the crown jewel of these secularists' wide-ranging reform agenda, which came to fruition in a wave of legislation between 1779 and 1781. George Bryan, a leading light within the Assembly's radical wing, served as the act's architect and most vocal proponent. He found common cause with the Quaker elite whose power he had supplanted, using their moral authority to bolster the case for abolition. For the act's preamble, which linked American slavery to the British despotism that had provoked the Revolution, Bryan likely benefited from the editorial input, if not the actual prose contributions, of the great Republican propagandist Thomas Paine, then employed as a clerk for the Pennsylvania General Assembly.[14]

Opposition to anti-slavery legislation in Pennsylvania proved tenacious. Slaveholding interests managed to force extensive compromises in the act, most importantly in extending the age when children born to slaves would gain their freedom from 18 for females and 21 for males to 28 for both. Though the bill passed by a vote of thirty-four to twenty-one in January of 1780, the pro-slavery forces did not relent in their efforts to undermine it. The 1781 amendment to the act, also included in the pamphlet, represented both losses and gains for Bryan's allies. It rendered out-of-state slaveholders exempt from the act as long as their slaves were registered within six months. However, a proposed amendment from opponents of abolition that would have allowed owners of unregistered slaves to retain them for an unspecified amount of time was soundly defeated.[15]

This issue of registration proved to be the nexus upon which most PAS legal agitation turned in the 1780s and 1790s. Sections V and VI of the 1780 act, requiring freedom for all slaves and indentured servants not registered within six months of either the passage of the law or the birth of the servant, gave rise to particularly ambiguous legal statuses for many African Americans—and thus created the fertile ground on which the PAS's advocates would press for individual blacks' freedom.[16] Weaknesses in the registration provisions of the act would also prompt the PAS to petition for a 1788 amendment that, among other things, delineated more clearly the requirements for slave registration and strengthened protections for blacks against kidnapping and out-of-state transport.[17] In short, Pennsylvania's gradual emancipation law stood as the major springboard and central referent for the PAS's legal advocacy throughout the late eighteenth and early nineteenth centuries.

Publicists within the Society were able to make explicit the link between the 1780 act and their organization's agenda by distributing this pamphlet. The man to whom they turned for publishing was Philadelphia printer Joseph James, who, from at least 1789 on, was a member of the PAS.[18] His career as a printer began in 1777 and lasted into the late

1790s. His own religious affiliation is unclear, but James frequently published work by Quaker writers, among them Robert Barclay, Anthony Benezet, and London Quaker Stephen Crisp. James also published numerous anti-slavery works by such poets as Hannah More, William Roscoe, and Phillis Wheatley. As a printer, James stood among a whole contingent of publicizers and disseminators working to spread the PAS's message across the Anglo-American world.

After the expansion of 1787, the PAS continued to grow and, for two more decades, to thrive. Between 1787 and 1830 the PAS drafted more than twenty petitions to Congress and more than forty to the Pennsylvania legislature.[19] And, following yet another expansion of the organization's agenda in 1789 to include resources dedicated to "Negro improvement," the PAS augmented its direct legal aid to hundreds of African Americans in Pennsylvania with new social services and educational assistance.

But in the first three decades of the nineteenth century the group's membership atrophied, and the legalistic, moderate approach to abolitionist politics that it so perfectly characterized floundered in the face of entrenched establishment opposition. The Society's moderation, which bespoke an Enlightenment-era optimism in the powers of rational persuasion to bring about fundamental social change, eventually proved no match for the tenacity of pro-slavery interests among the elite in both the free North and the slaveholding South, particularly following the rapid expansion and entrenchment of "King Cotton" in the first decades of the new century. At the same time, longstanding black traditions of direct action and grassroots political agitation, combined with the sweeping moral and reformist fervor that transformed the country during the Second Great Awakening, eventually gave rise to a radically different kind of abolitionism in the 1830s and 1840s. PAS-style deference to the status quo had come to be seen by these new reformers as tantamount to capitulation; they discarded the gradualism of their forerunners and replaced it with a popular-based immediatism.

This transformation is an oft told story, and an important one. But perhaps just as important is the notion conveyed by James Pemberton in a 1787 letter to the Society for the Abolition of the Slave Trade in London, in which he sizes up the prospects for the first wave of anti-slavery agitation in the Western world, agitation that he and his organization had done so much to spearhead: "There is the same variety in truths that there is in certain seeds and plants. Some of them are of a hasty growth and soon offer their fruits to the hand that cultivates them, while others, like the trees of the forest, require many years to bring them to maturity. . . . You are perhaps planting seeds for the next generation, but your labor is absolutely necessary to secure a harvest to your posterity."[20]

Notes

[1] Richard S. Newman, *The Transformation of American Abolitionism: Fighting Slavery in the Early Republic* (Chapel Hill: University of North Carolina Press, 2002), 4.

[2] It is unclear why the title cites 1774 as the year of the PAS's founding. All available records, including the Society's own minutes, date the founding to April, 1775.

[3] Wayne J. Eberly, "The Pennsylvania Abolition Society, 1775–1830" (PhD diss., Pennsylvania State University, 1973), 56.

[4] Eberly, 27.

[5] Eberly, 29.

[6] Eberly, 27.

[7] Newman, 61–85.

[8] Manuscript Collection of the PAS (vol. 1, 1784), Butler Library, Columbia University.

[9] Eberly, 46.

[10] PAS Minutes: 1787–1916, Apr. 1787, Butler Library, Columbia University.

[11] Newman, 41.

[12] That perennial pragmatist and dealmaker Tench Coxe was the key figure to advise Franklin to table the petition at the Constitutional Convention in 1787. Franklin took this suggestion to heart, agreeing that submitting the petition would "alarm some of the Southern states, and thereby defeat the wishes of the enemies of the African trade." See John P. Kaminski, ed., *A Necessary Evil? Slavery and the Debate Over the Constitution* (Madison: Madison House, 1995), 42.

[13] John Bigelow, ed., *The Collected Works of Benjamin Franklin*, vol. 9 (New York: J. P. Putnam's Sons, 1888), 412.

[14] For further discussion of the debate over Paine's purported authorship of the preamble see John Keane, *Tom Paine: A Political Life* (London: Bloomsbury, 1995), 572–573.

[15] Arthur Zilversmit, *The First Emancipation: The Abolition of Slavery in the North* (Chicago: University of Chicago Press, 1967), 136.

[16] Eberly, 58. See also Robert M. Cover, *Justice Accused: Anti-slavery and the Judicial Process* (New Haven: Yale University Press, 1975), 62–67.

[17] Eberly, 63.

[18] Eberly, 223. James' name is listed among the 270 members documented in the Society's 1789 Act of Incorporation.

[19] Newman, 5.

[20] PAS Minutes: 1787–1916, James Pemberton letter to the London Abolition Society, Oct. 1787.

THE
CONSTITUTION

OF THE

Pennsylvania Society,

FOR PROMOTING THE

ABOLITION OF SLAVERY,

AND THE RELIEF OF

FREE NEGROES,

UNLAWFULLY HELD IN

BONDAGE.

BEGUN IN THE YEAR 1774,[1] AND ENLARGED ON THE
TWENTY-THIRD OF APRIL, 1787.
TO WHICH ARE ADDED,

THE ACTS OF THE

General Assembly of Pennsylvania,

FOR THE

Gradual Abolition of Slavery.

---

*"All Things whatsoever ye would that Men should do to you,
do ye even so to them; for this is the Law and the Prophets."*
Mat. vii. 12.[2]

PHILADELPHIA:

PRINTED BY JOSEPH JAMES, IN CHESNUT-STREET.

M.DCC.LXXXVII.

THE CONSTITUTION

OF THE

Pennsylvania Society,

FOR PROMOTING THE

ABOLITION OF SLAVERY,

AND THE RELIEF OF

FREE NEGROES,

UNLAWFULLY HELD IN

BONDAGE;

ENLARGED AT PHILADELPHIA, APRIL 23d, 1787.

Introduction

IT having pleased the Creator of the world, to make of one flesh, all the children of men—it becomes them to consult and promote each other's happiness, as members of the same family, however diversified they may be, by colour, situation, religion, or different states of society. It is more especially the duty of those persons, who profess to maintain for themselves the rights of human nature, and who acknowledge the obligations of Christianity, to use such means as are in their power, to extend the blessings of freedom to every part of the human race; and in a more particular manner, to such of their fellow-creatures, as are entitled to freedom by the laws and constitutions of any of the United States, and who, notwithstanding, are detained in bondage, by fraud or violence.—From a full conviction of the truth and obligation of these principles—from a desire to diffuse them, wherever the miseries and vices of slavery exist, and in humble confidence of the favour and support of the Father of Mankind, the subscribers have associated themselves under the title of the "Pennsylvania Society for promoting the abolition of slavery, and the relief of free Negroes unlawfully held in bondage."

For effecting these purposes, they have adopted the following constitution:

The Officers of the society.

I. The officers of the society shall consist of a president, two vice-presidents, two secretaries, a treasurer, four counsellors, an electing committee of twelve, and an acting committee of six members; all of whom, except the last named committee, shall be chosen annually by ballot, on the first SECOND-DAY called Monday, in the month called January.

Duty of the presidents and vice-presidents.

II. The president, and in his absence one of the vice-presidents, shall preside in all the meetings, and subscribe all the public acts of the society. The president, or in his absence, either of the vice-presidents, shall moreover have the power of calling a special meeting of the society whenever he shall judge proper. A special meeting shall likewise be called at any time, when six members of the society shall concur in requesting it.

Of the secretaries.

III. The secretaries shall keep fair records of the proceedings of the society, and shall correspond with such persons and societies, as may be judged necessary to promote the views and objects of the institution.

Of the treasurer.

IV. The treasurer shall keep all the monies and securities belonging to the society, and shall pay all orders signed by the president or one of the vice-presidents—which orders shall be his vouchers for his expenditures. He shall, before he enters upon his office, give a bond of not less than two hundred pounds, for the faithful discharge of the duties of it.

Of the counsellors.

V. The business of the counsellors shall be to explain the laws and constitutions of the states, which relate to emancipation of slaves, and to urge their claims to freedom, when legal, before such persons or courts as are authorized to decide, upon them.

Of the electing committee.

VI. The electing committee shall have the sole power of admitting new members. Two-thirds of them shall be a quorum for this purpose—and the concurrence of a majority of them by ballot, when met, shall be necessary for the admission of a member. No member shall be admitted, who has not been proposed at a general meeting of the society, nor shall an election for a member take place in less than one month after the time of his being proposed. Foreigners or persons who do not reside in this state, may be elected corresponding members of the society, without being subject to any annual payment, and shall be admitted to the meetings of the society during their residence in the state.

VII. The acting committee shall transact such business as shall occur in the recess of the society, and report the same at each quarterly meeting.—They shall have a right, with the concurrence of the president or one of the vice-presidents, to draw upon the treasurer for such sums of money as shall be necessary to carry on the business of their appointment. Four of them shall be a quorum. After their first election, two of their number shall be relieved from duty at each quarterly meeting, and two members shall be appointed to succeed them.

Duty of the acting committee.

VIII. Every member upon his admission, shall subscribe the constitution of the society, and contribute ten shillings annually in quarterly payments, towards defraying its contingent expenses. If he neglects to pay the same for more than two years, he shall, upon due notice being given him of his delinquency, cease to be a member.

Sum to be paid annually.

IX. The society shall meet on the first SECOND-DAY called Monday, in the months called January, April, July and October, at such place as shall be agreed to by a majority of the society.

Days of meeting.

X. No person holding a slave shall be admitted a member of this society.

No slave-holder to be a member.

XI. No law or regulation shall contradict any part of the constitution of the society, nor shall any law or alteration in the constitution be made, without being proposed at a previous meeting. All questions shall be decided, where there is a division, by a majority of votes. In those cases where the society is equally divided, the presiding officer shall have a casting vote.

Manner of altering the constitution, and making laws, and of deciding questions

OFFICERS

The Present Officers of the Society.

PRESIDENT:

BENJAMIN FRANKLIN.[3]

VICE-PRESIDENTS:

JAMES PEMBERTON,[4]

JONATHAN PENROSE.[5]

SECRETARIES:

BENJAMIN RUSH,[6]

TENCH COXE.[7]

TREASURER:

JAMES STARR.[8]

COUNSELLORS:[9]

WILLIAM LEWIS,

JOHN D. COXE,

MIERS FISHER,

WILLIAM RAWLE.

ELECTING COMMITTEE:[10]

THOMAS HARRISON,	NORRIS JONES,
NATHAN BOYS,	SAMUEL RICHARDS,
JAMES WHITEALL,	FRANCIS BAILEY,
JAMES READ,	ANDREW CARSON,
JOHN TODD,	JOHN WARNER,
THOMAS ARMATT,	JACOB SHOEMAKER, jun.

ACTING COMMITTEE:[11]

THOMAS SHIELDS,	WILLIAM ZANE,
THOMAS PARKER,	JOHN WARNER,
JOHN OLDDEN,	WILLIAM M'ELHENNEY.

An ACT *for the gradual Abolition of Slavery.*[12]

Section 1. WHEN we contemplate our abhorrence of that condition, to which the arms and tyranny of Great Britain were exerted to reduce us—when we look back on the variety of dangers to which we have been exposed, and how miraculously our wants in many instances have been supplied, and our deliverances wrought, when even hope and human fortitude have become unequal to the conflict—we are unavoidably led to a serious and grateful sense of the manifold blessings which we have undeservedly received from the hand of that Being, from whom every good and perfect gift cometh. Impressed with these ideas, we conceive that it is our duty, and we rejoice that it is in our power, to extend a portion of that freedom to others, which hath been extended to us; and a release from that state of thraldom, to which we ourselves were tyrannically doomed, and from which we have now every prospect of being delivered. It is not for us to enquire why, in the creation of mankind, the inhabitants of the several parts of the earth were distinguished by a difference in feature or complexion. It is sufficient to know that all are the work of an Almighty Hand. We find in the distribution of the human species, that the most fertile as well as the most barren parts of the earth are inhabited by men of complexions different from ours, and from each other; from whence we may reasonably, as well as religiously, infer, that he who placed them in their various situations, hath extended equally his care and protection to all, and that it becometh not us to counteract his mercies. We esteem it a peculiar blessing granted to us, that we are enabled this day to add one more step to universal civilization, by removing, as much as possible, the sorrows of those who have lived in undeserved bondage, and from which, by the assumed authority of the kings of Great Britain, no effectual, legal, relief could be obtained. Weaned by a long course of experience from those narrow prejudices and partialities we had imbibed, we find our hearts enlarged with kindness and benevolence towards men of all conditions and nations; and we conceive ourselves at this particular period extraordinarily called upon, by the blessings which we have received, to manifest the sincerity of our profession, and to give a substantial proof of our gratitude.

Section II. AND WHEREAS the condition of those persons who have heretofore been denominated Negro and Mulatto slaves, has been attended with circumstances which not only deprived them of the common blessings that they were by nature entitled to, but has cast them into the deepest afflictions by an unnatural separation and sale of husband and wife from each other and from their children—an injury, the greatness of which can only be conceived by supposing that we were in the same unhappy case. In justice, therefore, to persons so unhappily circumstanced, and who, having no prospect before them whereon they may rest their sorrows and their hopes, have no reasonable inducement to render their service to society, which otherwise they might; and also in grateful commemoration of our own happy deliverance from that state of unconditional submission to which we were doomed by the tyranny of Britain.

No child born hereafter to be a slave.

Section III. Be it enacted, and it is hereby enacted, by the representatives of the freemen of the commonwealth of Pennsylvania, in general assembly met, and by the authority of the same, That all persons, as well Negroes and Mulattoes and others, who shall be born within this state from and after the passing of this act, shall not be deemed and considered as servants for life, or slaves; and that all servitude for life, or slavery of children, in consequence of the slavery of their mothers, in the case of all children born within this state, from and after the passing of this act as aforesaid, shall be, and hereby is utterly taken away, extinguished and forever abolished.

Negro and Mulatto children to be servants till 28 years of age.

Section IV. Provided always, and be it further enacted, by the authority aforesaid, That every Negro and Mulatto child born within this state after the passing of this act as aforesaid (who would, in case this act had not been made, have been born a servant for years, or life, or a slave) shall be deemed to be, and shall be, by virtue of this act, the servant of such person or his or her assigns, who would, in such case, have been entitled to the service of such child, until such child shall attain unto the age of twenty-eight years, in the manner and on the conditions whereon servants bound by indenture for four years are or may be retained and holden; and shall be liable to like correction and punishment, and enti-

94

tled to like relief in case he or she be evilly treated by his or her master or mistress, and to like freedom dues and other privileges as servants bound by indenture for four years are or may be entitled, unless the person to whom the service of any such child shall belong shall abandon his or her claim to the same; in which case the overseers of the poor of the city, township or district respectively, where such child shall be so abandoned, shall by indenture bind out every child, so abandoned, as an apprentice for a time not exceeding the age herein before limited for the service of such children.

Section V. And be it further enacted by the authority aforesaid, That every person, who is or shall be the owner of any Negro or Mulatto slave or servant for life, or till the age of thirty-one years, now within this state, or his lawful attorney, shall on or before the said first day of November next, deliver or cause to be delivered in writing to the clerk of the peace of the county, or to the clerk of the court of record of the city of Philadelphia, in which he or she shall respectively inhabit, the name, and surname, and occupation or profession of such owner, and the name of the county and township, district or ward wherein he or she resideth; and also the name and names of any such slave and slaves, and servant and servants for life or till the age of thirty-one years, together with their ages and sexes severally and respectively set forth and annexed, by such person owned or stately employed and their being within this state, in order to ascertain and distinguish the slaves and servants for life and till the age of thirty-one years, within this state, who shall be such, on the said first day of November next, from all other persons; which particulars shall by said clerk of the sessions and clerk of the said court be entered in books to be provided for that purpose by the said clerks; and that no Negro or Mulatto, now within this state, shall from and after the said first day of November, be deemed a slave or servant for life, or till the age of thirty-one years, unless his or her name shall be entered as aforesaid on such record, except such Negro and Mulatto slaves and servants as are herein after excepted; the same clerk to be entitled to a fee of two dollars for each slave or servant so entered as aforesaid from the treasurer of the county, to be allowed to him in his accounts.

All slaves to be registered before the 1st of November next.

95

Owners of
slaves, though
not registered,
to be liable for
their support,
unless, &c.

Section VI. Provided always, That any person in whom the ownership or right to the service of any Negro or Mulatto shall be vested at the passing of this act, other than such as are herein before excepted, his or her heirs, executors, administrators and assigns, and all and every of them severally shall be liable to the overseers of the poor of the city, township or district to which any such Negro or Mulatto shall become chargeable, for such necessary expense, with costs of suit thereon, as such overseers may be put to, through the neglect of the owner, master or mistress of such Negro or Mulatto; notwithstanding the name and other descriptions of such Negro or Mulatto shall not be entered and recorded as aforesaid; unless his or her master or owner shall before such slave or servant attain his or her twenty-eighth year, execute and record in the proper county, a deed or instrument, securing to such slave or servant, his or her freedom.

Negroes, &c. to
be tried like oth-
er inhabitants.

Section VII. And be it further enacted by the authority aforesaid, That the offences and crimes of Negroes and Mulattoes, as well slaves and servants as freemen, shall be enquired of, adjusted, corrected and punished in like manner as the offences and crimes of the other inhabitants of this state are and shall be enquired of, adjudged, corrected and punished, and not otherwise; except that a slave shall not be admitted to bear witness against a freeman.

Jury to value in
case of sentence
of death.

Section VIII. And be it further enacted by the authority aforesaid, That in all cases, wherein sentence of death shall be pronounced against a slave, the jury before whom he or she shall be tried, shall appraise and declare the value of such slaves; and in case such sentence be executed, the court shall make an order on the state treasurer, payable to the owner for the same and for the costs of prosecution; but in case of remission or mitigation, for the costs only.

Reward for tak-
ing up runaways,
same as for
white servants.

Section IX. And be it further enacted by the authority aforesaid, That the reward for taking up runaway and absconding Negro and Mulatto slaves and servants, and the penalties for enticing away, dealing with, or harbouring, concealing or employing Negro and Mulatto slaves and servants, shall be the same, and shall be recovered in like manner as in case of servants bound for four years.

Section X. And be it further enacted by the authority aforesaid, That no man or woman of any nation or colour, except the Negroes or Mulattoes who shall be registered as aforesaid, shall at any time hereafter be deemed, adjudged, or holden within the territories of this commonwealth as slaves or servants for life, but as free-men and free-women; except the domestic slaves attending upon delegates in congress from the other American states, foreign ministers and consuls, and persons passing through or sojourning in this state and not becoming resident therein, and seamen employed in ships not belonging to any inhabitant of this state, nor employed in any ship owned by any such inhabitant. Provided such domestic slaves be not aliened or sold to any inhabitant, nor (except in the case of members of congress, foreign ministers and consuls) retained in this state longer than six months.

> None to be deemed slaves, but those registered.

Section XI. Provided always, and be it further enacted by the authority aforesaid, That this act or any thing in it contained, shall not give any relief or shelter to any absconding or run-away Negro or Mulatto slave or servant, who has absented himself, or shall absent himself from his or her owner, master or mistress residing in any other state or country, but such owner, master or mistress shall have like right and aid to demand, claim and take away his slave or servant, as he might have had in case this act had not been made: And that all Negro and Mulatto slaves now owned and heretofore resident in this state, who have absented themselves, or been clandestinely carried away, or who may be employed abroad as seamen and have not returned or been brought back to their owners, masters or mistresses, before the passing of this act, may within five years be registered as effectually as is ordered by this act concerning those who are now within the state, on producing such slave before any two justices of the peace, and satisfying the said justices by due proof of the former residence, absconding, taking away, or absence of such slaves as aforesaid; who thereupon shall direct and order the said slave to be entered on the record as aforesaid.

> Except runaways from other states.

> Slaves carried away, &c. from this state may be brought back and registered.

Preamble.

Section XII. AND WHEREAS attempts may be made to evade this act, by introducing into this state Negroes and Mulattoes bound by covenant, to serve for long and unreasonable terms of years, if the same be not prevented:

No Negroes or Mulattoes, other than infants, to be bound for longer than seven years.

Section XIII. Be it therefore enacted by the authority aforesaid, That no covenant of personal servitude or apprenticeship whatsoever, shall be valid or binding on a Negro or Mulatto, for a longer time than seven years, unless such servant or apprentice were, at the commencement of such servitude or apprenticeship, under the age of twenty-one years; in which case such Negro or Mulatto may be holden as a servant or apprentice respectively, according to the covenant, as the case shall be, until he or she shall attain the age of twenty-eight years, but no longer.

Repeal of former acts.

Section XIV. And be it further enacted by the authority aforesaid, That an act of assembly of the province of Pennsylvania, passed in the year one thousand seven hundred and five, entitled, "An act for the trial of Negroes;"[13] and another act of assembly of the said province, passed in the year one thousand seven hundred and twenty-five, entitled, "An act for the better regulating of Negroes in this province;"[14] and another act of assembly of the said province, passed in the year one thousand seven hundred and sixty-one, entitled, "An act for laying a duty on Negro and Mulatto slaves imported into this province;"[15] and also another act of assembly of the said province, passed in the year one thousand seven hundred and seventy-three, entitled, "An act for making perpetual an act for laying a duty on Negro and Mulatto slaves imported into this province; and for laying an additional duty on said slaves," shall be, and are hereby repealed, annulled and made void.

JOHN BAYARD,[16] *Speaker.*

Enacted into a Law at Philadelphia, on Wednesday, the first Day of March, Anno Domini, 1780.

THOMAS PAINE,[17]
Clerk of the General Assembly.

98

An ACT *to give Relief to certain Persons taking Refuge in this State, with Respect to their Slaves.*[18]

Section I. WHEREAS many virtuous citizens of America, and inhabitants of states that have been invaded, are obliged by the power of the enemy, to take refuge in this state. AND WHEREAS it is just and necessary that the property of such persons should be protected.

Preamble.

Section II. Be it therefore enacted, and it is hereby enacted, by the representatives of the freemen of the commonwealth of Pennsylvania, in general assembly met, and by the authority of the same, That all and every person and persons, under the above description, now residing in this state, or who hereafter may be in like circumstances, shall retain, possess and hold their slaves; any thing in the "Act for the gradual abolition of slavery," passed the first day of March, one thousand seven hundred and eighty, to the contrary notwithstanding.

Persons taking refuge, may retain their slaves, &c.

Section III. Provided always, That the owner or owners of such slaves, his or their lawful attorney, shall, in six months from the passing of this act, or in six months after their arrival in this state, as the case may be, register said slaves in manner and form directed in the fifth section of the act above mentioned, for the gradual abolition of slavery. And be it further provided, That such slaves shall not be aliened or sold to any inhabitant, nor retained in this state as slaves longer than six months after the conclusion of the present war with Great Britain.

Provided they are registered within six months.

And not sold or retained in the state longer than six months after the war.

Section IV. And be it also provided, and declared, That nothing herein contained, shall be deemed, construed, or taken to enslave any person or persons, who have been emancipated or freed under or by virtue of the act aforesaid.

Proviso.

Signed by order of the House,
FREDERICK A. MUHLENBERG,[19] *Speaker.*
Enacted into a Law at Philadelphia, on Monday, the first Day of October, Anno Domini, 1781.
SAMUEL STERRETT,[20]
Clerk of the General Assembly.

99

Notes

[1] It is unclear why the title cites 1774 as the year of the PAS's founding. All available records, including the Society's own minutes, date the founding to April, 1775.

[2] Matthew 7:12. The Golden Rule featured prominently in eighteenth-century anti-slavery appeals on both sides of the Atlantic, appearing in the writings of such major figures as the British abolitionist statesman William Wilberforce and the Pennsylvania Quaker Anthony Benezet. This and all subsequent Biblical references are from the Authorized (King James) Version of the Bible.

[3] Benjamin Franklin (1706–1790): Statesman, inventor, diplomat, publisher, and writer, Franklin was one of the most renowned figures in eighteenth-century America. He became president of the PAS in 1787, at age 81, and served until his death three years later. Although more of a figurehead than a hands-on leader of the organization (those duties fell to Pemberton), Franklin did sign his name to some of the PAS's most important petitions in this period, including a 1789 address to the public inaugurating the Society's new "Plan for Improving the Condition of the Free Blacks." His final written work, published in 1790, was a satirical letter to the *Federal Gazette* that parodied the arguments of a pro-slavery congressman by expressing them in the guise of a North African prince enslaving Christians.

[4] James Pemberton (1723–1808): An eminent Quaker merchant in Philadelphia, Pemberton would succeed Franklin as President of the PAS in 1790 and serve in that capacity until 1803. His leadership role in the anti-slavery movement allowed him to rehabilitate his public career following his high-profile resignation from the Pennsylvania General Assembly during the Seven Years' War and his arrest during the Revolution, both on account of his "suspicious" pacifist beliefs.

[5] Jonathan Penrose (1735/6–1797?): From a large wealthy Philadelphia shipbuilding family, Penrose was a founding member of the Society in 1775 and served as its President from 1785 until the group's 1787 enlargement brought Franklin to the top post.

[6] Benjamin Rush (1745–1813): A doctor and professor (the author of the first chemistry textbook in the United States), Rush was Pennsylvania's representative to the Second Continental Congress, at which he signed the Declaration of Independence in 1776; a delegate to the Constitutional Convention in 1787; and a key figure behind Pennsylvania's revamping of the state constitution in 1789. He joined the PAS in 1784 and later served as its President from 1803 to 1813.

[7] Tench Coxe (1755–1824): An early proponent of a nationalist and industrial

economic policy, Coxe served under Alexander Hamilton as the assistant secretary of the treasury from 1790 to 1792. From 1792 to 1797 he served as commissioner of revenue and, from 1803 to 1812, purveyor of public supplies. He joined the PAS in 1786.

[8] James Starr: A 1775 founding member, Starr served as the PAS's treasurer from 1784 to 1793.

[9] The four men listed under this heading all seem to be lawyers. As Richard S. Newman has put it, "Of the PAS's influential figures, none stood out more than the lawyers. They dominated committees, policy decisions, and the very definition of PAS strategy. . . . Perhaps no single law firm or organization in antebellum America could boast such an impressive group of legal minds." The most notable of the lawyers listed here is William Rawle, who offered legal counsel and labor to the PAS for forty years (until the 1830s) while simultaneously holding such posts as the presidency of the Pennsylvania bar in the 1810s and 1820s. See Richard S. Newman, *The Transformation of American Abolitionism: Fighting Slavery in the New Republic* (Chapel Hill: University of North Carolina Press, 2002), 28–29.

[10] The Electing Committee was an innovation of the 1787 reorganization, and consisted of twelve members elected annually. Of those listed here, Harrison, Boys, Whiteall, Todd, Armatt, Bailey, and Warner were all founding members in 1775.

[11] Originally known as the Standing Committee, the Acting Committee succeeded in helping nearly one hundred African Americans regain their freedom between 1784 and 1787. Following the group's enlargement in 1787, the Committee took on a more firmly entrenched executive role as the center of activity during the out-of-session periods between the Society's quarterly meetings.

[12] The bill came up for debate at the behest of the state's Executive Council in September of 1779, when President Joseph Reed sent a message to the General Assembly calling for action on the proposal: "See you give the compleat sanction of Law to this noble and generous purpose, and adorn the annals of Pennsylvania with this bright display of Justice and publick Virtue."

[13] The law set out loose regulations for quick trials for blacks; the array of punishments it sanctioned included lashings, brandings, and confinement.

[14] This act, which came about in part as a result of growing fears about slave insurrections, comprised a harsh and extensive set of regulations for "slothful" free blacks (including taxes and duties, and measures prohibiting miscegenation), as well as a written sanction for the death penalty to be used for slaves, with compensation provided for the owner.

[15] This act, instigated by Quaker pressure, dramatically reduced the extent of slaveholding in Pennsylvania in the 1760s and 1770s.

[16] John Bayard (1738–1807): A successful merchant, originally from Maryland, who served as a delegate to the Continental Congress in 1785.

[17] The famed radical republican and intellectual, and author of such classic works as *Common Sense* and *The Age of Reason*, had fallen on hard financial times in the late 1770s, and so took a clerking position for the General Assembly. Paine was a longstanding opponent of slavery; a fiery anti-slavery essay he wrote and published in March of 1775 entitled "To Americans" may have helped spur the founders of the PAS to organize in the month following its publication.

[18] According to William M. Wiecek, this "sojourner's provision," which passed in the wake of the abolition act, came about as a result of Philadelphia's hopes for becoming the new national capital; this created the need to accommodate visiting diplomats, federal officials, and congressmen who owned slaves and who wanted protection from abolition laws. William M. Wiecek, *The Sources of Antislavery Constitutionalism in America, 1760–1848* (Ithaca: Cornell University Press, 1977), 50.

[19] Frederick A. Muhlenberg (1750–1801): Leading Pennsylvania politician (of the radical "constitutionalist" persuasion) and former Lutheran minister, Muhlenberg was elected as one of the state's three delegates to the Continental Congress in 1779 and served as Speaker of the Pennsylvania General Assembly from 1780 to 1783. Always bolstered by his base support in the Pennsylvania German community, he became an influential Federalist over the next decade and served as the first ever Speaker of the House for the new national government in 1789.

[20] Samuel Sterrett: Assistant clerk of the Pennsylvania General Assembly before succeeding Paine in the top post in 1780, where he worked until November of 1781. In 1788 he was one of Maryland's delegates to the Constitutional Convention, and it appears that he served as a U.S. representative from Maryland in the 1790s.

A

POETICAL EPISTLE

TO THE

ENSLAVED AFRICANS,

IN THE CHARACTER OF AN ANCIENT

NEGRO,

BORN A SLAVE IN

PENNSYLVANIA;

But liberated fome Years fince, and inftructed in ufeful Learning, and the great Truths of Chriftianity.

WITH

A brief hiftorical Introduction, and biographical Notices of fome of the earlieft Advocates for that oppreffed Clafs of our Fellow-Creatures.

Princes fhall come out of Egypt. Ethiopia fhall foon ftretch out her hands unto GOD. Pfalm lxviii. 31.

[5]

A POETICAL EPISTLE TO THE ENSLAVED AFRICANS
by Joseph Sansom

Introduction by Raphael B. Moreen, Princeton University

Just three years after the Pennsylvania Abolition Society's publication of its constitution (1787), the young Joseph Sansom (1767–1826) plunged into the abolitionist campaign with his 1790 poem *A Poetical Epistle to the Enslaved Africans*. While most other anti-slavery writers turned to prose, Sansom drew on the eloquence of poetry to give his subject a poignancy not often found in such works. Even more noteworthy, Sansom, a white Quaker, chose to express his ideas in the voice of a free black. While the poem itself was published anonymously, perhaps because of the controversial character the author was adopting, scholars over the years have attributed it to Sansom.[1] *A Poetical Epistle to the Enslaved Africans* offers a glimpse into the driving force behind abolitionist societies of the late eighteenth century and into the roots of Quaker anti-slavery sentiment.

Born in Philadelphia to Quaker parents Hannah Callendar and Samuel Sansom Jr., Joseph Sansom matured into a man of many talents.[2] From advertisements in the *Pennsylvania Gazette,* we know that Sansom was employed as a merchant with his older brother William.[3] Sansom ultimately made his mark, however, as a man of letters and philosophy— a colonial "Renaissance man" of sorts. As one periodical notes, he was a merchant merely in name; his life was instead "devoted to travel, literature, and the arts."[4] Elected to the American Philosophical Society, Sansom was also an officer of the Pennsylvania Society for Promoting the Abolition of Slavery—one of the largest and most influential abolitionist organizations in the young nation.[5]

As the text of this poem suggests, religion played an important role in Sansom's life. His earliest surviving piece of writing, as a young man of nineteen in 1786, was a series of notes, taken in shorthand, for what would become a collection of published sermons by William Savery.[6] The sermons are notable for what may have attracted Sansom's interest: their heavy emphasis on placing one's faith and trust in heaven, a theme clearly evident in Sansom's poem, published four years later. Following the publication of his poem in 1790, Sansom cultivated a greater interest in the arts. While he was drawn to painting, his concern with its vanity and his religious convictions instead compelled him to create silhouettes.[7] He produced a series of thirty-four silhouettes, the subjects including members of his family, leading Philadelphians, and famous personages of the world at large. Sansom published this collection in 1792 as *An Occasional Collection of Physiognomical Sketches Chiefly North Americans*.[8] Included were such figures as George Washington, James Madison, Robert Morris, and Sansom's successful mercantile brother, William.

Sansom's later publications focused on other interests. He seems not to have published any other pieces expressing his anti-slavery opinions, nor any other poetry. Nor did he work again with the printer who published this poem, Joseph Crukshank, a Philadelphia printer who published other anti-slavery texts—more than two hundred works including abolitionist tracts by such noted authors as Anthony Benezet and John Wesley. Crukshank was born in Philadelphia and was a member of the Society of Friends.[9] Sansom's chief later works, *Letters from Europe during a Tour through Switzerland and Italy in the Years 1801 and 1802* and *Sketches of Lower Canada, Historical and Descriptive,* both published in the early nineteenth century, deal exclusively with the less controversial material of the travelogue. Sansom also wrote other pieces about a variety of subjects: a trip to an Indian council in 1791, a biography of William Penn in 1809, and a brief sketch of Nantucket, Massachusetts, in 1811.[10]

Sansom was better known for a series of medals he created between 1805 and 1807 entitled *History of the American Revolution in a Series of Medals*.[11] These medals would be his most enduring legacy and the design of the medals, not his poetical epistle, are what prompted his election to the American Philosophical Society and earned a place for his portrait by Charles Willson Peale in the Philadelphia Museum. In fact, Sansom's authorship of the poetical epistle was likely not well known and generated him little acclaim—Sansom's contemporaries seemed to be aware of his other works without connecting him to *A Poetical Epistle*.[12]

Nevertheless, at least one contemporaneous review of Sansom's poem reveals its reception, that in the short-lived *Universal Asylum and Columbian Magazine*. The review praises the author for: "having rescued from oblivion, or at least brought into more general notice, the names of several of those friends of humanity, both in America and Great Britain, who first asserted the equal rights of their fellow-men, and opposed the iniquitous traffick in human flesh."[13] While the author of the review raves that "much information may be obtained" through the epistle, he laments the general lack of spirit in Sansom's writing, calling the composition "rather languid."[14] Critics and scholars have had similarly mixed responses to Sansom's other literary works. For example, one commentator described Sansom's *Letters from Europe* as "rare but arid."[15] Meanwhile, *Sketches of Lower Canada* led one nineteenth-century reviewer to remark, "My readers must pardon me for having occupied so much of their time, upon a volume so unworthy of their notice."[16]

Despite Sansom's uneven literary talent, his *Poetical Epistle* warrants our attention in the twenty-first century for its extraordinary choice of narrator and point of view. The poem's speaker, as Sansom notes in the title, was born a slave, but had been free for some years and was fully familiar with the precepts of Christianity. Indeed, it would not have been a rare occurrence to find such a person in 1790 Philadelphia. Pennsylvania had passed a gradual manumission law in 1780, and by 1800 most of Philadelphia's 4,000 African Americans were free.[17] At first glance, Sansom's appeal—through his black speaker—might be seen as directed to slaves. More likely, however, Sansom was actually trying to reach elite, powerful whites who could influence policies of emancipation.

The Quaker attachment to moderation and patience led them to favor gradual over immediate abolition. Slavery ran contrary to their religious beliefs, but at the same time Quakers tended to feel a responsibility to prepare their slaves for freedom by providing them with both religious and general education.[18] Quakers had first moved against slavery in a petition in 1688, presented by the Germantown Friends.[19] In 1696, the Pennsylvania Society of Friends recommended that its members disassociate themselves from the slave trade. Finally, the Society, led by John Woolman and Anthony Benezet, moved against the institution of slavery itself in 1758.[20] And Quakers set up schools for education following manumission and even compensated former slaves for back wages.[21]

Sansom's poem must be read against his Quaker background, which seems to have moved him, in the words of one scholar, to "distinguish between the sinfulness of nominal Christians who participate in the slave trade and the ideals of true Christianity."[22] The true Christian tradition, according to Sansom's narrator, preached respect and love for fellow creatures and viewed slavery as a sin. Sansom sought to point out to the elite white population the inherent contradiction in professing to be Christian while at the same time owning and trading slaves. Addressing those in power in the voice of a free black man was perhaps easier than making the statements directly. By arguing against slavery on religious grounds, Sansom positions himself at one end of an increasingly variegated spectrum. At the time Sansom's poem was published, abolitionism was moving from strictly religious arguments against slavery to include rationales against slavery based on humanitarianism and sentimentality, sensibilities that highlighted the sufferings of slaves over the religious contradictions inherent in slavery.[23]

Despite the fact that Sansom uses a black narrator to articulate objections to slavery, the poem does not advocate slaves taking action to ameliorate their position. This reflects the ideal of working within existing laws, promoted by the Pennsylvania Abolition Society, which had been formed in 1775 and, like the Quakers, favored gradualism. Instead of taking action, the narrator urges slaves to be patient, and in the meantime to devote themselves to industry and honest labor. Eventually, the narrator believes, white men of good conscience will free those slaves still in bondage. Sansom, taking into account the slaveholding population's fear of slave rebellions, carefully chooses not to radically attack the wrongs of slavery, but instead gently chastises those in power about the religious hypocrisy of slaveholding. This method would have spoken most effectively to the white men of good conscience who were in a position to steer policy first toward the abolition of the slave trade, and then to emancipation, Sansom's ultimate objective.

Notes

[1] See Winthrop D. Jordan, *White over Black: American Attitudes Toward the Negro, 1550–1812* (Chapel Hill: University of North Carolina Press, 1968), 496, note 17. Jordan attributes *A Poetical Epistle* to Joseph Sansom. See also James G. Basker,

Amazing Grace: An Anthology of Poems About Slavery, 1660–1810 (New Haven: Yale University Press, 2002), 415.

[2] See Randolph C. Randall, "Authors of the Port Folio Revealed by the Hall Files," *American Literature* 11 (1940): 407, note 91 for Sansom's genealogical background and some other interesting facts about him.

[3] Advertisement, *Pennsylvania Gazette*, Apr. 27, 1791. Both William and Joseph are mentioned as being located on "Second, below Arch street, No. 67," selling such items as ". . . Ravens duck, Florentines, Ticklenburgh, Sattinets and Lastings . . ." See also Randall, 407. Randall notes that in the Philadelphia city directories from 1802 through 1805, Sansom is officially listed as a merchant.

[4] Charles Coleman Sellers, "Joseph Sansom, Philadelphia Silhouettist," *Pennsylvania Magazine of History and Biography* 88 (1964): 398.

[5] *Pennsylvania Gazette*, Jan. 4, 1792. Sansom is listed along with six others under the title of "Corresponding Committee."

[6] William Savery, *Two Sermons: Delivered at the Bank Meeting-House* (Burlington, N.J.: Allinson, 1805).

[7] Sellers, "Joseph Samson," 397.

[8] Sellers, "Joseph Samson," 396. See pages 399–400 and 407–438 for reproductions of Sansom's silhouettes.

[9] Isaiah Thomas, *The History of Printing in America* (New York: Weathervane Books, 1970), 396.

[10] Sansom also attended "a Quaker-sponsored conference with the Five Nations in 1796." The account of this conference can be found in "A Series of Letters Written on a Journey to the Oneida, Onondago, and Cayuga Tribes of the Five Nations . . . undertaken by Isaiah Rowland, James Cooper, John Price, and Joseph Sansom . . ." (Sellers, *Pennsylvania Magazine of History and Biography*, 401). Joseph Sansom, "Outlines of the Life and Character of William Penn," *Port Folio* 1 (1809): 189–194. Sansom's sketch of Nantucket is entitled "A Description of Nantucket."

[11] Charles Coleman Sellers, *Benjamin Franklin in Portraiture* (New Haven: Yale University Press, 1962), 362. The medals commemorated three events: "The Declaration of Independence," "The Recognition of Sovereignty," and "The Retirement of Washington."

[12] See Henry D. Biddle, *Extracts from the Journal of Elizabeth Drinker, from 1759 to 1807, A.D.* (Philadelphia: J.B. Lippincott, 1889), 340. Drinker's personal journal mentions Sansom's silhouettes being enjoyed, but is quiet on the subject of his poetical epistle.

[13] "A Poetical Epistle," *Universal Asylum and Columbian Magazine* 5 (1790): 403. The magazine lasted only two years, from 1790 through 1792.

[14] "A Poetical Epistle," *Universal Asylum and Columbian Magazine* 5 (1790): 403.

[15] Joseph G. Fucilla, "An American Diplomat in Settecento Italy," *Italica* 26 (1949): 99.

[16] "Sketches of Lower Canada," *The Portico, a Repository of Science* 4 (1817): 357.

[17] Randall M. Miller and John David Smith, *Dictionary of Afro-American Slavery* (Westport: Greenwood Press, 1988), 570.

[18] Sydney V. James, *A People Among Peoples: Quaker Benevolence in Eighteenth-Century America* (Cambridge: Harvard University Press, 1963), 111.

[19] The petition invoked divine law: "There is a saying, that we shall doe to all men like as we will be done ourselves; making no difference of what generation, descent or colour they are." See Roger Bruns, *Am I Not a Man and a Brother: The Anti-Slavery Crusade of Revolutionary America, 1688-1788* (New York: Chelsea House Publishers, 1977), 3.

[20] Arthur Zilversmit, *The First Emancipation: The Abolition of Slavery in the North* (Chicago: University of Chicago Press, 1967), 74.

[21] Jordan, 357.

[22] Basker, 415.

[23] Jordan, 365–372.

A

POETICAL EPISTLE

TO THE

ENSLAVED AFRICANS,

IN THE CHARACTER OF AN ANCIENT

NEGRO,

BORN A SLAVE IN

PENNSYLVANIA;

But liberated some Years since, and instructed in
useful Learning, and the great Truths of Christianity.

WITH

A brief historical Introduction, and biographical
Notices of some of the earliest Advocates for
that oppressed Class of our Fellow-Creatures.

*Princes shall come out of Egypt. Ethiopia shall soon stretch out her
hands unto GOD.* Psalm lxviii. 31.

PHILADELPHIA:

PRINTED BY *JOSEPH CRUKSHANK*, IN MARKET-STREET,
BETWEEN SECOND AND THIRD-STREETS. M DCC XC.

INTRODUCTION.

THE cruel and unnatural Practice of stealing and enslaving the inoffensive Natives of Africa, which has so long prevailed among Christians, to the dishonour of our holy Profession, originated with the Portugueze, soon after their discoveries in that part of the Globe, during the fifteenth and sixteenth centuries.[1] In 1481 they built the castle of Del Mina,[2] on the Gold Coast,[3] from whence they barbarously ravaged the neighbouring country, and carried off its Inhabitants, who were afterward sold in Portugal, with as little remorse as the plundered productions of their native land.

The Spaniards began to trade with the Portugueze Settlements for Negro Slaves, in the year 1508, so early had their inhuman Colonists, in the West Indies, sacrificed the harmless Natives of the Carribbees,[4] to avarice and cruelty: but some English Adventurers first encroached upon their fancied right of discovery, about the middle of the sixteenth century.

In 1562 capt. Hawkins,[5] afterward knighted by queen Elizabeth[6] for his successful enterprizes, made a descent upon the western coast of Guinea, seized on the defenceless Natives, sailed away with his booty, and afterward sold them to the Spanish Settlers at Hispaniola.[7] It is said that the Queen expressed great abhorrence of this detestable conduct, on the Captain's return to England, laden with the spoil of the unhappy Negroes: but it is certain that she never prohibited the Trade, and that the Royal patent was granted to some of the principal Slave Merchants in 1585.

The Dutch attacked the Potugueze fortifications on the coast of Guinea,[8] and possessed themselves of some of the most important in 1637, under pretence of the war with Spain. Most of these were afterward ceded to them by treaty; and continued under their new Masters, not ports of beneficial interchange between Man and Man, but marts of slavery and blood.

The French[9] and Danes[10] fell into the Negro Trade about the same period, to promote the settlement of their Colonies; although Lewis XIII.[11] reluctantly subscribed the laws that consigned Mankind to perpetual slavery in his American Dominions; and cardinal Cibo,[12] a minister of the Papal See, had early instructed the Missionaries in Congo to prevent, if possible, the unchristian practice of stealing and selling Men.

Negro Slaves were probably introduced into North America by the Dutch. In 1619 one of their Guinea ships touched at James-Town in Virginia, and a part of the unnatural Cargo was purchased by the Settlers.[13] A few years afterward they brought great numbers of Slaves into their Colony called the New-Netherlands, now New-York,[14] and sold them into different parts of the Continent.

In 1656, many zealous Christians of the Society then first distinguished by the name of Quakers (because, like the Prophets and Apostles, they sometimes trembled at the Word of the LORD) came over to America, to preach the Gospel and disseminate their peaceable principles. They were then prosecuted by the Government as disturbers of the Public peace: but no severities could check their perseverance in religious duty, or daunt their resolution to protest, in the name of GOD, against every species of cruelty and oppression. The People commiserated their sufferings, and some of the Settlers of all ranks and professions embraced their doctrine; many of whom were possessed of Slaves. They were exhorted by their new Teachers to the exercise of love and charity toward them as Fellow-Creatures, equally favoured with the illuminating grace of GOD; and most of them became more like Fathers than Masters, setting an example of christian moderation and personal industry, to their idle and oppressive Neighbours. This was the dawn of emancipation from those chains of ignorance and slavery, which Avarice had forged, and Cruelty had endeavoured to rivet upon the Negro Race.

Toward the close of the century several benevolent Individuals successively laboured to soften the extreme rigour of the American Planters, and to instruct the Victims of their unprincipled barbarity, in the moral and religious duties of Men: but the West India Planters rejected their pious arguments as the instigations of fanaticism, and their attempts to humanize the Negroes were construed into treason and conspiracy.

In 1688, some Followers of our venerable Proprietor, who had lately emigrated from Kriesheim in Germany, and were therefore free from the fascinating effects of custom and interest, conscientiously represented to the Yearly Meeting of Pennsylvania, the unlawfulness of stealing, buying, or holding Mankind as Slaves, in the christian System of fellowship and brotherly love.[15] The subject was then referred, but in 1696 that Body advised its Members to discourage the future importation of Negroes, and gave general directions for the benefit of those already imported.[16]

In 1704, the British Society for the Propagation of the Gospel,[17] founded a Catechising School in the city of New-York for the instruction of the enslaved Negroes in the principles of Christianity; and a few years afterward they recommended the institution of similar Establishments to all their Missionaries in America, as a christian duty.

In 1711, the situation of the Negroes was again represented to the Yearly Meeting of Pennsylvania, and from that time was seldom off its Journals, until the united efforts of the Pious and the Benevolent procured the first public restoration of their rights about the middle of the present century.[18]

The Moravian Brethren sent Missions about this time to several of the West India Islands for the conversion of the Negroes to the christian faith.[19]

At this period the Trade to Guinea for Negro Slaves was eagerly pursued by the European Nations, who had unfeelingly engaged in it, and more than an hundred thousand Human Beings were now annually exported from Africa, like beasts of burthen, destined to cultivate the European Colonies, or moisten them with blood and tears. One eighth part was usually consigned to destruction on the fatal passage; of the remainder the British West India Islands consumed about 50,000, their North American Colonies 6000, the French Settlements 26,000, the Portugueze 9000, the Spanish 4000, and the Danish 1000. This shocking robbery was then principally perpetrated by English and French Traders, and it has since decreased very considerably.

In 1758, the People called Quakers, in Pennsylvania, came to a final resolution to deny the rights of membership in their religious Society, to all such of their Members as should persist in detaining their Fellow-Creatures in bondage, after Gospel admonition against the unjust practice. Many strenuous Advocates for the oppressed Negroes appeared

about this time among the different Professors of Christianity, whose
pious endeavours for their relief were at length blessed with considerable success: but of late the generous ardour for liberty, which characterizes the present age, has spread with unexampled rapidity. Where soli-
tary Individuals lately wept over the suffering Negroes, numerous Societies are now established to befriend the Enslaved, and to protect the
Free.[20] They have solemnly represented the horrours of the Slave Trade
to the Legislatures of Great Britain, France, and the United States of
America; and unless the clamours of Self-interest and mistaken Policy
can stifle the groans of Distress, and obliterate the dictates of Humanity,
decisive measures will soon be adopted for the abolition of a TRADE
that has deeply stained the annals of the eighteenth century with robbery and murder.

May the just and merciful CREATOR of Men, e'er long dispose the
Oppressors themselves *to loose the bands of wickedness, to undo the heavy burdens, and to let the Oppressed go free.*[21]

POETICAL EPISTLE

TO THE
ENSLAVED AFRICANS.

Whose Oppressors slay them, and hold themselves not guilty.[22]

BRETHREN by birth, and Partners in distress,
You may the CHRISTIAN'S GOD with patience bless.
May resignation calm your Souls to peace
While your wrongs lessen, and your rights increase.

   Hark! An indignant *MARON thus replies:
"Is not †ORIFA pow'rful, good, and wise?
Must wretched OTTOWAH *that God* adore
Whose Followers dragg'd him from his native shore,
And still (inhuman, tyger-hearted Brood)
Prowl over Africa for Human Blood?
Is't not by his command, proud Christians say,
They Negroes kidnap, whip, torment, and slay,
As Executioners of wrath DIVINE
Commission'd to destroy our fated Line?

---

* In several of the West India Islands large bodies of the abused Negroes have occasionally fled from their Oppressors, and taken refuge in the woods and mountains. They are called Marons, and defend themselves from the Usurpers of their rights, with the unconquerable fierceness of desperation.

† In the kingdom of Benin, on the coast of Guinea, the Negroes believe in an infinitely great and good Being, whom they call Orifa, affirming him to be the Creator of Heaven and Earth; and those of Cambea and Cassan acknowledge the existence of ONE supreme GOD, without adoring him under any corporeal representation. How long will pseudo Philosophers persist in classing the Negro of Africa with the Ourang Outang of Borneo? – and not rather consider the People of Benin as brethren and fellow-believers? [Editor's note: Modern-day Benin is located on the coast of West Africa, between Nigeria and Togo. Borneo is a large island in the South Pacific.]

Say, do their boasted Testaments contain
Exclusive rights to wrong their Fellow-Men?"

Not so—Who good reject, and cherish evil,
Are of their father and their lord the Devil.
GOD, for the Father, chargeth not the Son:
Each shall account for what himself hath done.*
And the New-Testament commandeth, †"Do
To others as ye would 'twere done to you."

Whatever Pow'r within the mind bears sway,
Whatever Principle our hearts obey,
Is there supreme. 'Tis thus St. PAUL[23] records,
§"On earth are many Gods and many Lords."
Some idolize what Some abominate,
These love themselves, and Those their Brethren hate.
Yet ONE all-pow'rful, over-ruling GOD
Hath spread the glowing firmament abroad,
And hung the earth on nought, whose sun-beams greet
The Evil and the Good with light and heat,
Whose clouds with blessings fraught in rain descend,
And Just and Unjust equally befriend—
All Nations own him, in all Lands the Same,
Known to the Faithful by whatever name—
'Twas He who taught our Fathers to believe
That good Men please him, and that bad Men grieve,
By the eternal SPIRIT of his SON,
Who did in Jewry *once* for sins atone:
But through all ages, unto all Mankind,
Hath *ever* been *a* GOD *within the Mind,*
Teaching Men all ungodliness to flee,
And in the present World live righteously.

---

* *The Son shall not bear the iniquity of the Father, neither shall the Father bear the iniquity of the Son: the righteousness of the Righteous shall be upon him, and the wickedness of the Wicked shall be upon him.* Ezek. xviii. 20.

† See Matt. vii. 12.

§ See I Cor. viii. 5.

When by a secret influence DIVINE,
My heart becomes its great CREATOR's shrine
(In faith and humble reverence beheld,
By whom the world was made, by whom upheld)
Then doubting kindles into hope and love,
No selfish views my swelling bosom move,
Unenvied then the Proud in grandeur roll,
And all my wishes centre in the SOUL.
Though *humbled by Oppression's iron hand,*
I feel myself a Man almost unman'd,
Hard Task-Men, from my weeping Mother's breast
To manhood and old age, my strength opprest,
Nor taught me duties social or DIVINE;
Nay, in such tasks as those forbade to join.

If colour (the imagin'd mark of CAIN)[24]
Condemn our Race to glut the thirst of Gain
(Doubtful criterion at best of right—
Self gives the casting vote for *black* or *white*)
A *sun burnt skin* was sure a slender plea
To rob our Sires of life or liberty,
Though *still* deny'd to breathe their native air
Their wretched Offspring languish in despair.

Yet *early* in the awful name of GOD,
FOX* testified against the unnat'ral fraud.
In forms divided, but in substance one,

---

* GEORGE FOX, of Drayton in Great Britain, one of the most remarkable of those Professors of spiritual Christianity, who, in the words of their historian Sewel, "Began to take heed to a Divine Conviction in the conscience, and accordingly preached to others the doctrine of an inward Light wherewith CHRIST had enlightened Men, in the latter end of the time of king Charles I." He visited Barbados in the year 1671, and then advised his Brethren on that Island *to train up their Negroes in the fear of GOD, that all might come to the knowledge of the LORD; and to cause their Overseers to deal mildly and gently with them, and not to use cruelty toward them, and that after certain years of servitude they should set them free.* See his Journal, pag. 431, 36, & 37.

BAXTER[*] and GODWYN[†] wrote in unison.
Bondage must not be endless, neither cruel,
Said they, and pious BURLING,[§] and learn'd SEWALL,[‡]
And [¶]MANY more of grateful memory,
Whose gentle use prepared US to be free.

---

[*] RICHARD BAXTER, an eminent dissenting minister of the last century, some of whose Discourses are now extant. His Directions to Slave-Holders contain a great deal of christian admonition respecting their treatment of the Negroes, and were first published at London in 1673. "They are reasonable creatures as well as you," says he, "and born to as much natural liberty; they have immortal souls, and are equally capable of salvation with yourselves; equally under the government and laws of God;" exhorting them to consider "how cursed a crime it is to equal Men to beasts."

[†] MORGAN GODWYN, probably a British clergyman, undoubtedly a humane and benevolent man. He published a book entitled the Negroe's and Indian's Advocate, in the year 1680, with a dedication to the then Archbishop of Canterbury. It is principally addressed to the Planters of Barbados, earnestly pleading with them on behalf of the Negroes held by them, to use his own words, "In a Soul-murthering and brutifying state of bondage. Whereas," continues he, "a brute may in some sense have a right to divers things according to the Scripture (which is a book of reason and of justice too) the Slave must be divested of all. For by Moses's law, the ass sinking under his burden had a right to be relieved by the next Traveller, Exod. xxiii. 5; nor was the ox to be muzzled which did tread out the corn, Deut. xxv. 4, his labour meriting better usage; and one of the reasons for the Sabbath rest was, That the ox and ass might have respite from toil as well as their Owners, Exod. xxiii. 12. (We see here no working them to death was allowed.) So that here is a plain right belonging unto brutes, whilst by us it is denied unto Men *whose flesh is as our own,* a thing greatly deserving *to be laid to heart.*"

[§] WILLIAM BURLING, of Long Island, wrote several humane and animated Tracts against Slave-Holding, about the year 1718. Some of them were printed, but they are now very scarce. In one of these he mentions his having been sensible of its injustice before he was twelve years of age. He was a man well respected among the People called Quakers, some of whom remember to have heard that he used annually to represent to his Brethren in their Yearly Meetings about that time, the gross iniquity of compelling a certain description of our Fellow-Creatures, and their Posterity, to serve others during life, without any reward for their labour; entreating them not to shield it from *the judgment of truth,* but to suffer the censure of the Church to pass upon this *unjust Practice.*

[‡] Judge SEWALL, a New-Englander of the Presbyterian Communion. He reprobated Slave-Holding, as a lawyer and a christian, early in the present century, in a

Memorial entitled the Selling of Joseph, which was probably presented to the General Court on behalf of the injured Negroes. The following extracts are additional proofs that the Conscientious and the Humane of our own age are neither peculiar nor enthusiastic in their serious protest against the complicated iniquity of Negro Slavery, but *harmonious, orthodox, and just.*

"It is most certain that all Men as they are the Sons of Adam are co-heirs, and have equal right unto liberty, and all other comforts of life. GOD *hath given the earth* (with all its commodities) *unto the Sons of Adam.* Psal. cxv. 16. *And hath made of one blood all Nations of Men, for to dwell on all the face of the earth, and hath determined the times before appointed, and the bounds of their habitations, that they should seek the Lord. Forasmuch then as we are the offspring of God,* &c. Acts xvii. 26, 27, & 29. Now although the title given by the last ADAM doth infinitely better Men's estates respecting GOD and themselves, and grants *them* a most beneficial and inviolable lease under the broad seal of Heaven, who were before only Tenants at will: yet through the indulgence of God to our first Parents after the Fall, the outward estate of all and every of their Children remained the same as to one another, so that originally and naturally there was no such thing as Slavery. Joseph was rightfully no more a Slave to his Brethren than they were to him, and they had no more authority to *sell* him than they had to *slay* him; and if they had nothing to do to sell him, the Ishmaelites bargaining with them, and paying down twenty pieces of silver, could not make a title, neither could Potiphar have any better interest in him than the Ishmaelites had. Gen. xxxvii. 20 & 28. For he that shall in this case plead *alteration of property* seems to have forfeited a great part of his own claim to humanity. *There is no proportion between twenty pieces of silver and liberty.*"

To the argument that *our ships bring lawful Captives taken in the African Wars,* the Judge replies: "For aught is known, their wars are much such as were between Jacob's Sons and their brother Joseph. Every War is upon one side unjust. An unlawful war cannot make lawful Captives; and by receiving we are in danger to promote, and partake in their barbarous cruelties. I am sure if some Gentlemen should go down to the Brewsters to take the air, or to catch fish; and a stronger Party from Hull should surprise them and sell them for Slaves, to a ship outward bound, *they would think themselves unjustly dealt with, both by Sellers and Buyers.* It is observable that the Israelites were strictly forbidden the buying or selling one another for Slaves. Levit. xxv 39. and Jer. xxxiv. 8–17. And GOD gaged his blessing in lieu of any loss they might conceit they suffered thereby. Deut. xv. 18. Christians should carry it to all the World, as the Israelites were to carry it one toward another. These Ethiopians, as black as they are, are the sons and daughters of the first Adam, the brethren and sisters of the last ADAM, and the OFF-SPRING of GOD."

1 "It is observable in the history of the Reformation from Popery, that it had a gradual progress from age to age. The uprightness of the first Reformers, in

Long, long remember'd, from my earliest years,
Prophetic sounds still tingle in my ears,
Still gentle *SANDIFORD methinks I see,

---

attending to the light and understanding given them, opened the way for sincere hearted People to proceed further afterward; and thus each one truly fearing GOD, and labouring in those works of righteousness appointed for them in their day, findeth acceptance with him; though, through the darkness of the times, and the corruptness of manners and customs, some upright Men may have had little more for their day's work than to attend to the righteous Principle in their minds, as it related to their own conduct in life, without pointing out to others the whole extent of that which the same Principle would lead succeeding ages into. Thus, for instance, amongst an imperious, warlike People, supported by oppressed Slaves, some of these Masters I suppose are awakened to feel and see their errour; and, through sincere repentance, cease from oppression, and become like fathers to their servants, shewing by their example a pattern of humility in living, and moderation in governing, for the instruction and admonition of their oppressive Neighbours. Those, without carrying the reformation further, I believe have found acceptance with the Lord. Such was the beginning, and those who succeeded them, and have faithfully attended to the nature and spirit of the reformation, have seen the necessity of proceeding forward; and not only to instruct others, by their example, in governing well, but also to use means to prevent their Successors from having so much power to oppress others." WOOLMAN.

* RALPH SANDIFORD, a merchant of Philadelphia, descended of a respectable Family of that name in the Island of Barbados. He received a religious education in the Episcopal Church, under the care of a pious Tutor, probably in some part of Great Britain, by whom he was so successfully instructed in the principles of charity and justice, that he could not but perceive the inconsistency of Slave-Holding, with the dictates of religion and morality, on his first landing in Pennsylvania. Here he joined the Society called Quakers, and became very earnest in his endeavours to prevail with them to oblige all their Members to liberate their Slaves. But the Fore-Runners of Negro-Freedom appear to have been only commissioned to declare their violated rights, and to announce the approach of liberty. The sun itself never breaks in upon the gloom of night, but with reflected rays. – His Brief Examination of the Practice of the Times [Slave-Holding] was printed at Philadelphia in 1729. It is written with becoming energy, except a few reflections on the conduct of his Brethren, who foresaw that the emancipation of the Negroes must be a gradual and progressive work. These however he excuses to the Reader, as having been wrung from him by *the exasper-*

Proclaiming Blacks by GOD and nature free.
To wasting zeal and sympathy a prey,
Methinks I hear the venerable *LAY,
Now, at distress and wrong for pity sigh,
And now, "All Slave-Keepers, Apostates," cry;
But, if no *human* sword our blood avenge,
Invoke on *legal* murders GOD's revenge.
Or, when remember'd pangs his bosom swell,
Brand the vile TRADE with every stamp of HELL.
But vain his tears—his imprecations vain,

---

ation of oppression, which he describes to have affected his mind, at particular times, *as if the rod had been upon his own back.*

* BENJAMIN LAY, an Englishman by birth, was brought up to the Sea, and sailed some years in the West India Trade. About the year 1710 he married and settled in Barbados; but the wretched situation of the poor Negroes on that Island so preyed upon his benevolent temper, that he removed to Pennsylvania a few years afterward, to avoid the painful sight of their misery. But it had been so strongly painted upon his imagination, that it was still present in idea, and the horrours of Slavery were seldom out of his mind. At this period Slave-Holding had become very common, even in Pennsylvania, and among the People called Quakers: yet the Negroes were there generally as well provided for as common bound Servants, and moderately used. Lay, notwithstanding, exclaimed against the Practice, as if he had been still among the Negro Drivers of Barbados, and thus lost the force of conviction by the warmth that was meant to excite it. He published his Treatise on Slave-Keeping in 1737, which abounds with genuine effusions of intemperate zeal, forming an incoherent medley of sympathetic descriptions, angry exclamations, pious rhapsodies, and unjustifiable surmizes respecting the conduct of his own Friends, and the Ministers of Religion. Yet those who knew him, believe him to have been an honest, well-meaning man, whose ardent opposition to the African Trade, and the Slavery of the Negroes, has tended to accelerate the period of their sufferings. In person he was rather under size, but remarkable for the simplicity of his dress, which was principally of his own manufacture, and for his animated manner, especially when declaiming against Slavery. He died about the year 1760, a few miles from Philadelphia, having attained his eightieth year, in habits of extreme temperance and solitude. The print we have of him is said to be a striking likeness. He is drawn, reading in the mouth of a cave, from the circumstance of his frequenting such a retirement, for the sake of privacy and meditation.

123

Our long-lost freedom *then* or *thus* to gain.
COLUMBIA[25] *use* had sear'd to Negro-groans,
And distant EUROPE heard not AFRIC's moans,
Until thy meeker spirit, *WOOLMAN, rose,
Aiming to soften rather than oppose;
And thou, lov'd †BENEZET, of kindred mind,
The World thy country, and thy Friends MANKIND.
Heav'n-born (now Heav'n return'd) awhile they strove,
Subduing enmity by faith and love.

------

*JOHN WOOLMAN was born in West Jersey, anno 1720, of reputable parents in religious profession with the People called Quakers, among whom he was a minister from the twenty-second year of his age. He travelled a great deal in the service of the Gospel, and sometimes undertook his religious journies upon this Continent, like the primitive Apostles, on foot, not from necessity, but with the pious view of assimilating himself to the low circumstances of some among whom he laboured, to increase his fellow feeling for the Distressed, and qualify him to administer suitable advice, as well as spiritual consolation. He was a man of good natural parts and great personal industry, yet temperate in all respects; and so scrupulously careful not to partake of the gain of oppression, in any degree, that he denied himself the use of those conveniencies of life which are furnished by the labour of Slaves. Their cause, as he sometimes mentioned to his Friends, *lay almost continually upon him*, and he strove for their relief, both in public and private, until a few days before his death, the last sermon he preached in public being on this subject. In the beginning of the year 1772 he embarked for Great Britain, on a religious visit to those of his Persuasion in that Kingdom. He was there taken with the small-pox, and died of that disorder in the city of York, toward the end of the same year.

The I. Part of his Considerations on keeping Negroes, was written in 1746, but first published in 1754.

The II. Part of the same Work in 1762.

Various other religious Tracts in 1768, 1770 & 1773.

All which are bound up together at the end of his Journal, printed at Philadelphia in 1775.

† ANTHONY BENEZET, a native of France, was born at St. Quintin, in Picardy, anno 1712. His Parents were zealous Protestants, who having suffered greatly under the long and oppressive reign of Lewis XIV. withdrew into Great Britain a short time before the death of that prince. They resided some years in the city of London, where the elder BENEZET embraced the religious principles of the People called Quakers. In 1731 he again removed with his Family,

and finally settled in Pennsylvania. ANTHONY, the eldest Son, had been brought up to business; but becoming dissatisfied with mercantile concerns, he accepted the offer of a place in the Society's Academy in Philadelphia, as English Master, soon after his marriage, in 1736. This useful employment was congenial to his diligent habit, and benevolent temper. The vivacity of his Nation was happily tempered in his composition, by the sober and exemplary conduct observable in the christian Society of which he was a Member; indeed so uniform was his assiduous attention to the duties of life, even in old age, that he conscientiously denied himself the unnecessary part of those hours usually allotted to rest; having been heard to say that *he could not reconcile a habit of such slothful indulgence with the activity of Christian fervour.* He occasionally interested himself on behalf of all his distressed Fellow-Creatures, from his first arrival in America, spending a great part of his time and estate in unremitted endeavours to serve the Poor and the Friendless. He considered himself as a citizen of the world, and regarded all Mankind as friends and countrymen, *on principles of reason and humanity,* which he believed to *describe a wider circle for the operation of charity and benevolence, than that which is limited by parentage, or native country.* The few hours unappropriated to his school, and other necessary engagements, were generally employed in all the compilation of instructive passages from pious Authors of all Denominations, and publishing their united testimonies in favour of piety, virtue, and particularly justice, with respect to the injured Africans; the last of which he put into the hands of his Executors for publication, within three hours of his peaceful and happy departure. He also wrote several Tracts upon the Slave-Trade, &c. with other moral Treatises, and a short Account of the People called Quakers, principally intended for the use of his own Countrymen, which he published both in French and English. His first Publications against the flagrant injustice of Negro-Slavery appeared about the year 1760, and being written in a truly christian spirit, his arguments then gained candid attention even in the breasts of the Interested. The two last years of this revered Philanthropist were wholly applied to the tuition of the Negroes, at the Free-School, founded in Philadelphia about the year 1770, by the voluntary contributions of his Brethren*, which he endowed with his whole estate, excepting a few legacies and charitable bequests, at his lamented death in 1784, to be appropriated to the use of that benevolent Institution, on the decease of his widow. [Editor's note]: Louis XIV (1639–1715) was the symbol of absolute monarchy during his age. He felt that French Protestants were his enemies. Thus, he revoked the Edict of Nantes in 1685, which had ensured freedom of worship to all French Protestants.

*Their Friends in England have likewise contributed very liberally to the support of this School.—Unsolicited they lately wrote to the Trustees to draw on their Donation Fund for £500 Sterling, which Sum, and Anthony Benezet's Legacy have been since vested in ground-rents to the value of £200 per annum.

Then mitred *GLOUCESTER declar'd our Race,
Equals by Nature, and co-heirs of GRACE;
Which came by Christ *to every name and state.*
Can these one Father's Children separate!
No—the gall'd Slave, born under whip and chain,
May wear his fetters, and be GOD's *Free-Man,*
Free from the worst of earthly tyrants, Sin,
Who rules bad Masters, and bad Slaves within;
Nay—*rich* tow'rd GOD *in faith and in good works,*
Treasure in Heav'n—*where* no Man Stealer lurks.

   Tho', variously dispens'd, GOD's bounteous store
Enrich the Worthless, leave the Worthy poor,
Know, Brethren, that the FATHER of Mankind
His choicer gifts hath never so confin'd;
Those envied blessings, health and happiness,
The Poor, in common with the Rich, possess.
Think ye the Proud are happy in their pride?
You little know how oft 'tis mortify'd:
Think ye the Rich amidst their riches blest?
Care follows riches—enemy to rest.
Think ye superior bliss annex'd to pow'r?
Alas!—the Great scarce know a quiet hour.
No *human* pleasures are unmix'd with pain;
Yet, *with contentment, godliness is gain.*
Oh! That my Brethren for themselves could read—
The Scriptures shew what's happiness indeed:
The ONE *true* GOD *for ever blefs'd to know,*
And in his love abide, with Friend and Foe.
Yet there's †*a surer way* true bliss to gain,

---

* The Bishop of Gloucester, in a Sermon preached before the Society for the Propagation of the Gospel, at their annual meeting in 1766, and since published, denominates the atrocious act of stealing the poor Negroes from their native land, and slowly murdering them by cruel usage in the European Colonies, *a sacrifice to their great Idol the God of Gain.*

† 2 Pet. i. 19.

126

Free to the Wise, and to the Simple plain,
Taught *the Observant* by that Guide within,
Who trod the path himself, and bids us, *Walk therein.*

   *The Apostles PAUL and PETER both command,
"Servants, obey your Masters, heart and hand,
Not with eye-service—but with free good-will,
In singleness of heart, your tasks fulfil:
One is your Master, even CHRIST, and HE
Alike rewardeth both the Bond and Free.
If any suffer, having done amiss,
'Tis duty to be patient, and submiss:
But if for doing well ye *bear* the rod,
Fear not—this is acceptable with GOD."
For conscience' sake *thus* in obedience free,
You'll come to know *the Christian liberty.*

   But my glad Soul anticipates the day,
When Men no more on Fellow-Men shall prey,
Or dare—pretending *policy* and *fate,*
Divine and human laws to violate.
Three centuries our groans have pierc'd the Skies—
But bright'ning visions light my clouded eyes:
Religion and Philosophy unite
Our Minds t' enlighten, and our wrongs to right.
And much, my Countrymen, depends on you;
Be patient, humble, diligent, and true,
In hope of coming freedom, as you can—
Commend your righteous cause to GOD and Man.
You see the efforts of the Good and Wise,
Think not to right yourselves—let GOD arise,
Fit you for freedom, and then make you free,
As he defign'd his creature MAN to be.

   Shun Cities then, unwieldy haunts of Trade,
Industry beckons to the rural shade:

---

* See Eph. vi. 5–8. & I Pet. ii. 18–20.

There honest Labour earns two-fold reward,
First health, then plenty from the well-turn'd sward.
Where oft at eve, far round to th' list'ning Swain,
Thund'ring Niagara bodes the coming rain,
Or *westward* where Ohio's winding tide
Darts o'er the rocks, or rounds the mountains' side,
Adventrous Settlers friendly welcome give,
And teach the Needy how to work—and live.

Meanwhile—in silence let us wait the hour
That shall to civil-life our Race restore—
And Oh! When Liberty's enchanting smile
Height'neth enjoyment and endeareth toil,
If we remember whence the blessing flows,
To GOD 'twill lead us, as from GOD it rose—
Who solemn inquisition makes for Blood,
And turns the rod o'th' Wicked from the Good.
To him let AFRIC's dusky Sons sing praise,
His works are marvellous and just his ways.
May Time's swift course the pleasing theme prolong,
And Children's Children still repeat the Song.
Nor be their names forgot (in free estate)
Whom Love first urg'd our cause to advocate;
Or theirs who now the generous plea inforce,
SHARP,[26] RAYNAL,[27] DE WARVILLE,[28] and WILBER-
FORCE,[29]
CLARKSON,[30] who lives and labours but for us,
Sage NECKAR,[31] PINKNEY,[32] MIFFLIN,[33] PORTEUS,[34]
MADISON,[35] PARRY,[36] aged FRANKLIN,[37] SCOT,[38]
LA FAYETTE,[39] MARSILLAC,[40] and BOUDINOT[41]—
Illustrious groupe—[*]yet these are but a part
Of those engraven on my grateful heart,
In distant Climes, whom wond'ring Nations see

---

[*] On this occasion it were injustice not to mention the late James Ramsay, vicar of
Teston in Great Britain, who wrote largely in vindication of the Negroes. He died
in 1789.

128

Bound in thy seraph-band, Philanthropy.
May philosophic Minds no more embrace
Those endless feuds which martyr half the Race,
But rather Concord and her train restore—
Echo the Rights of Men from shore to shore,
Strengthen the Weak—illuminate the Blind,
Reform—convert—and humanize Mankind;
Till CHRIST proclaim the CHRISTIAN JUBILEE,
Break every yoke, and set the Oppressed free—
Sheathe up, or to a ploughshare turn the sword,
Take to himself the pow'r, and reign king, priest,
and LORD.

   And now to GOD I ONE and ALL commend
As to a common Father, Guide, and Friend,
To whom belongeth filial love and fear;
Call on him, *he is gracious and will hear,*
Draw nigh to him with hearts contrite and true,
And then, doubt not, he will draw nigh to you,
Teach you to live as Men who once must die,
To judgment rise—then live eternally.
How rise?—(*As the tree falls, 'tis writ, it lies**)
Foolish the Wicked, and the Virtuous wise.
With all his virtues—vices on his head,
Man once must meet the JUDGE of Quick and Dead.
There where the Slave's long servitude is o'er,
And the Oppressor's voice is heard no more,
Where Sin and Death shall never more destroy,
And *all the Sons of* GOD *for ever shout for joy.*

———

FINIS.

———

* Eccles. xi. 3.

Notes

[1] The Portuguese established their first outpost in Africa in 1415 at the seaport of Ceuta (located in modern-day Morocco). Slaves were first brought back to Portugal from Africa in 1444. By 1500 the Portuguese had explored and established forts along four thousand miles of the African coastline, from which the slave trade would flourish for the next 375 years.

[2] Usually referred to as "Elmina," meaning "the mine," a trading post established by the Portuguese and later conquered by the Dutch in the seventeenth century.

[3] Part of coastal West Africa, first explored by the Portuguese, which corresponds roughly to present-day Ghana. It is named for the quantities of gold found in the area that were brought to the coast for sale.

[4] Spain imported slaves to its New World holdings in the sixteenth century because the native population had declined dramatically as a result of Spanish cruelty and the introduction of deadly European diseases.

[5] John Hawkins (1532–1595): The first Englishman to venture on a slave-trading voyage. Between 1562 and 1567, he made three expeditions to the coast of Africa, operating as an unofficial agent of the English Crown, under Queen Elizabeth.

[6] Elizabeth (1533–1603): Daughter of Henry VIII, who reigned as queen of England from 1558 to 1603.

[7] The Caribbean island that is divided between present-day Haiti and the Dominican Republic, where the Spanish first landed in the New World and created one of the original Spanish settlements.

[8] In 1637, the Dutch captured the Portuguese trading port of Elmina. Conquering this and other Portuguese possessions significantly increased the Dutch share in the slave trade.

[9] Although authorized under Louis XIII (see note 11 below), French involvement in the slave trade was not substantial until the reign of Louis XIV (1661–1715). The French interest in the slave trade arose at the same time that sugar cane, a crop requiring large amounts of slave labor, became the staple of French West Indies' agriculture.

[10] The Danes were a relatively small presence in the slave trade, most active during the eighteenth century. In 1792, Denmark outlawed the slave trade by royal decree, to take effect January 1, 1803.

[11] Louis XIII (1601–1643), King of France from 1610 until 1643, and his principal advisor, Cardinal Richelieu, brought France into the Atlantic slave trade by royal authority in 1642.

[12] Giovanni Battista Cibo (1432–1492) became Pope Innocent VIII (1484–1492).

[13] Here Sansom refers to a Dutch ship in Jamestown in 1619, although modern scholars dispute whether or not these Africans were slaves at the time.

[14] Although the Dutch did import slaves into what is now New York, the volume of the trade never rose to a level that would justify Sansom's term "great numbers."

[15] The first protest by members of the Society of Friends against slaveholding was the Germantown Friends' Protest Against Slavery issued by the Germantown Monthly Meeting of Friends, Pennsylvania, 1688. See Roger Bruns, *Am I Not a Man and a Brother: The Anti-Slavery Crusade of Revolutionary America, 1688-1788* (New York: Chelsea House Publishers, 1977), 3.

[16] In 1696, the Philadelphia Yearly Meeting not only advised its members not to encourage the importation of any more blacks, but also stipulated that those slaves already in Pennsylvania must receive a religious education. See Arthur Zilversmit, *The First Emancipation: The Abolition of Slavery in the North* (Chicago: University of Chicago Press, 1967).

[17] Organization that worked to educate, convert, and baptize non-Christians in the New World, Africa, and Asia.

[18] As Sansom later notes, it was not until 1758 that the Philadelphia Yearly Meeting made it illegal for Quakers to own slaves, carrying with it the possible punishment of expulsion from the sect.

[19] These missions to the West Indies were the first ventures in the New World for the Moravian Church. In 1735, however, the Moravians left for Georgia and later Pennsylvania, where they founded the towns of Nazareth and Bethlehem.

[20] Many abolition societies had sprung up in the latter decades of the eighteenth century. They included the Pennsylvania Society for Promoting the Abolition of Slavery (PAS), of which Sansom was an active member, and the Connecticut Abolition Society, founded in 1790.

[21] Isaiah 58:6. This and all subsequent Biblical references are from the Authorized (King James) Version of the Bible.

[22] Zechariah 11:5. The verse should read "possessors," not "oppressors."

[23] Saul of Tarsus: Important figure in early Christianity and the leading apostle in the first century CE.

[24] Defenders of slavery supported the idea that black people were descendants of Cain, and thus biblically ordained to be slaves. See Genesis 4:15. As early as the 1770s, however, writers such as John Wesley and Phillis Wheatley were successfully refuting this racist and scripturally unfounded claim. See James G. Basker, *Amazing Grace: An Anthology of Poems About Slavery 1610–1810.* (New Haven: Yale University Press, 2002), 177–178, 219.

[25] The United States of America.

[26] Granville Sharp (1735–1813): Noted British scholar and abolitionist. The most important of Sharp's efforts on behalf of abolition was his involvement in the case of the slave James Somersett, resulting in Justice Mansfield's decision of 1772, which held that no slave could be compelled to leave Britain by his master. In effect, it meant that slaves could regard themselves as free once they arrived in Britain.

[27] Guillaume-Thomas, Abbé de Raynal (1713–1796): French writer and anti-slavery commentator who challenged both the church and the monarchy. He was most famous for his six-volume history of the colonies of America and India.

[28] Jacques Pierre Brissot de Warville (1754–1793) founded the French abolitionist Société des Amis des Noirs. He was also a French revolutionary who was beheaded in 1793 when the Jacobins defeated the Girondists for control of France.

[29] William Wilberforce (1759–1833): A pioneer of abolitionism in England during the late eighteenth and early nineteenth centuries, and a deeply pious Christian opposed morally to slavery; fought in the House of Commons for the abolition of the slave trade (it was achieved in 1807) and for the abolition of slavery itself, which was achieved just after his death in 1833.

[30] Thomas Clarkson (1760–1846), a close associate of William Wilberforce, wrote several powerful tracts on the horrors of the slave trade. He joined Wilberforce and Sharp, among others, in forming the British Abolition Society in 1787. In 1808, he published a two-volume history of the abolition movement.

[31] Sansom probably is referring to Jacques Necker (1732–1804), a Swiss banker who was director general of finance under Louis XVI and apparently a supporter of the Société des Amis des Noirs.

[32] William Pinkney (1764–1822): Lawyer and politician, and at different times a congressman, senator, attorney general, and ambassador to Great Britain. Early in his career, he had served in the Maryland Legislature where, in 1789, he made speeches against slavery in which he declared that blacks and whites were equal in all capacities, although in later years his anti-slavery fervor seems to have declined.

[33] Sansom refers either to Thomas Mifflin (1740–1800), a Pennsylvania Quaker, American Revolutionary War veteran, and anti-slavery state legislator and activist in the 1780s and 1790s; or to Warner Mifflin (1745–1798), another prominent Quaker abolitionist and cousin of Thomas Mifflin, who took a leading role in the anti-slavery campaign both in Pennsylvania and across the United States.

[34] Beilby Porteus (1731–1808): Bishop of London and an outspoken supporter of the Society for the Propagation of the Gospel, who published numerous tracts against slavery and the slave trade.

[35] James Madison (1751–1836): Fourth president of the United States, author of many of the Federalist Papers, and architect of the three-fifths compromise at the Constitutional Convention of 1787. His position on slavery was vague as he felt that national considerations of unity should come first.

[36] Unidentified.

[37] Benjamin Franklin (1706–1790): The famous American statesman, publisher, author, and inventor, and a leading member of the Pennsylvania Society for the Abolition of Slavery (PAS).

[38] Thomas Scott (1739–1796): U.S. congressman from Pennsylvania and an anti-slavery activist.

[39] Marie-Joseph-Paul-Yves-Roch-Gilbert du Motier, Marquis de Lafayette (1757–1834): Most famous for his military role during the American Revolution. During and after the Revolutionary War, he was an energetic advocate of the abolition of slavery.

[40] Unidentified, although apparently a member of the Société des Amis des Noirs in France.

[41] Elias Boudinot (1740–1821): American lawyer and Revolutionary War veteran who served as a New Jersey Representative to both the Continental Congress and House of Representatives. He opposed slavery and used his legal training to protect free blacks from being enslaved.

THE
INJUSTICE AND IMPOLICY
OF THE
SLAVE TRADE,
AND OF THE
Slavery of the Africans:
ILLUSTRATED IN
A SERMON

PREACHED BEFORE THE CONNECTICUT SOCIETY
FOR THE PROMOTION OF FREEDOM, AND FOR
THE RELIEF OF PERSONS UNLAWFULLY HOL-
DEN IN BONDAGE,

AT THEIR ANNUAL MEETING IN NEW-HAVEN,
SEPTEMBER 15, 1791.

BY JONATHAN EDWARDS, D. D.
PASTOR OF A CHURCH IN NEW-HAVEN.

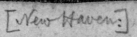

[New Haven.]

Printed by THOMAS and SAMUEL GREEN.

M,DCC,XCI.

[6]
THE INJUSTICE AND IMPOLICY
OF THE SLAVE TRADE
by Jonathan Edwards

Introduction by Sarah Gamertsfelder, University of Maine

Jonathan Edwards the younger (1745–1801) clearly distinguished himself from his famous minister father, Jonathan Edwards the elder (mainstay of the Great Awakening), when he wrote the sermon entitled *The Injustice and Impolicy of the Slave Trade and of the Slavery of the Africans.* Edwards delivered his anti-slavery sermon on September 15, 1791, before the Connecticut Society for the Promotion of Freedom, and for the Relief of Persons Unlawfully Holden in Bondage. The younger Edwards is an important figure in the American anti-slavery movement because he bridges two eras, one in which slave owning was generally acceptable, as it had been for his father, and one that would follow in which increasing numbers of abolitionists would call for an end to slavery. Edwards' position in straddling these two eras is evident in his sermon. While he opposes slavery and denounces it as sinful, he does not go so far as to demand the immediate and universal manumission of slaves. His stance instead is one of gradualism.

Edwards the younger was an eminent New England Congregationalist minister and was best known for his belief in New Divinity, a theological movement characterized by a break from orthodox Calvinism and a desire to instill traditional doctrines with "freshness, immediacy, and contemporaneity."[1] He had inherited most of his theology from his father, but, unlike the elder Edwards, who had been a slave owner, the younger Edwards spoke out against both slavery and the slave trade in this energetic sermon, in which he argues that slavery is neither condoned nor endorsed in the Bible.

Edwards' formative years led to his concern for the plight of blacks and helped shape the reasoning behind his anti-slavery arguments. During his childhood, Edwards had interactions with Native Americans that would prove influential later in life. Born on May 26, 1745, in Northampton, Massachusetts, Edwards was the ninth of eleven children and the second of three sons born to Sarah Pierpont and Jonathan Edwards.[2] When only ten years old, Edwards was sent by his father to stay with the Iroquois to further his education. The elder Edwards hoped to turn his son into a missionary and believed that having experiences with Native Americans would prepare his son for this occupation.[3] Edwards Sr. wrote to his son while he was with the Iroquois, reminding him to "alwaies set God before your Eyes, and live in his Fear, and seek him every Day with all Diligence . . . the eternal salvation of your soul and your all in this life and that which is to come depends on his will & Pleasure."[4] These words would make a deep impression on young Edwards, who devoted himself to the diligent study of the Bible. While his stay with the Iroquois was cut short by the outbreak of the Seven Years' War, his time there gave Edwards a respect for and camaraderie with Native Americans.[5] Edwards also grew fluent in the Mohegan language and spoke it, for a time, with greater comfort than English.[6] Given that Native Americans, as well as blacks, were used as slaves at the time (some of Edwards' own relatives held slaves), these childhood experiences no doubt contributed to the eventual development of Edwards' anti-slavery stance.[7]

Edwards' anti-slavery position was also the result of post-collegiate tutelage from Samuel Hopkins and Joseph Bellamy. Both men had been close associates of the elder Edwards before his death in 1758, and instilled in Edwards the staunch Calvinist doctrines of his father.[8] Hopkins shared more than just religious doctrines with the younger Edwards. As one of the first anti-slavery clergymen in New England and a very active participant in the region's abolition movement, Hopkins worked to aid and improve the position of blacks, and, in doing so, left his stamp upon Edwards.[9] Edwards joined the Rhode Island Missionary Society, where he worked closely with Hopkins, and served as a leader in the Connecticut Society for the Promotion of Freedom, and for the Relief of Persons Unlawfully Holden in Bondage.[10] Edwards was to have a long career in missionary work, ultimately focusing his attention on providing ministers for new churches on the American frontier in the 1780s.[11]

The years leading up to the American Revolution provided an environment conducive to the development and expression of anti-slavery thought. Indeed, Edwards' own anti-slavery views first appeared in print in 1773, in a series of newspaper articles entitled "Some Observations upon the Slavery of Negroes."[12] In this series, printed in October, November, and December of 1773 in the *Connecticut Journal and the New-Haven Post-Boy,* Edwards uses the Revolutionary rhetoric of tyrannical enslavement to highlight the injustice of slavery and the slave trade. Although penned anonymously, the articles have been attributed to Edwards based on their strong phraseological similarities to his 1791 *Injustice and Impolicy* sermon.[13] In the latter, Edwards similarly expounds in the language of liberty, so characteristic of the 1770s, and derides the hypocrisy of the Declaration of Independence's clause that "all men are created equal."

For Edwards, slavery was more than just contradictory to Revolutionary rhetoric. It was also contrary to biblical law. His *Injustice and Impolicy* was a response to the many arguments made by slaveholders, in which they claimed the Bible justified and endorsed slavery. Edwards carefully assesses the arguments presented in favor of slavery, identifying their weaknesses and using biblical support to explain their errors. Edwards' sermon was printed in pamphlet form by Samuel and Thomas Green, two brothers who primarily published religious works.[14]

Among the many arguments Edwards marshals against slavery, biblical precedents and Revolutionary ideals loom large. At various points, he cites biblical injunctions against lording over others. More pointedly, from a Christian perspective, Edwards argues that slavery is a terrible sin and that God-fearing Christians involved in slaveholding must recognize the error of their ways and repent before it is too late. Elsewhere, he complains that slavery is highly inconsistent with Revolutionary rhetoric and ideology, and Americans are hypocritical to bemoan Great Britain's "enslavement" of the colonies while holding others in a state of absolute bondage.

While the *Injustice and Impolicy* sermon seems to have been the only sermon Edwards gave that was centrally concerned with the plight of blacks in society, he continued to be active in the anti-slavery movement in a number of other ways. He had helped to form the Connecticut anti-slavery society and remained active in it while also attending the annual meetings of other anti-slavery societies, and he continued to exchange anti-slavery ideas with Hopkins and other contemporaries.

Despite his insistence that slavery and the slave trade were evil, Edwards did not call for immediate emancipation as Garrisonian abolitionists would do later on in the mid-nineteenth century. Well aware of the widespread fear that anti-slavery radicalism would lead to slave insurrections, Edwards endorsed gradual emancipation. In fact, he did not advocate complete equality. Indeed, his own sermon takes on a racist tone at the end when he discusses the general fear of miscegenation. To temper those fears, he does observe that "[blacks] are so small a proportion of the inhabitants, when mixed with the rest, they will not produce any very sensible diversity of colour."

Despite his occasionally racist tone and gradualist stance, Edwards was advanced for his time, and his position was typical of a transitional period in America's view of slavery. More advanced than his father, who had owned slaves and defended his participation in the institution, the younger Edwards was still far from the radical stance of later abolitionists, who would call for immediate emancipation.

Although Edwards himself did not advocate immediate abolition, his practice of using scripture to undermine pro-slavery arguments would later be utilized by those who did. The anti-slavery views Edwards expressed in 1791 were espoused by abolitionists in the 1830s during a series of religious revivals, which served as the impetus for many reform movements, including abolition. These nineteenth-century abolitionists followed in Edwards' mode of using Christian arguments against slavery, particularly his idea that the horrible treatment of slaves demonstrated slavery's evil and that slavery injured the master as well as the slave. Although not the most charismatic of men, Edwards was remembered and admired for his words in *Injustice and Impolicy*. Speaking of him in a funeral oration delivered August 3, 1801, Robert Smith, pastor of the Presbyterian church in Savannah, recalled Edwards this way: "That all men are born equally free, was his belief; and by this maxim of eternal justice, he regulated his practice."[15]

Notes

[1] Douglas A. Sweeny, *Nathaniel Taylor, New Haven Theology, and the Legacy of Jonathan Edwards* (Oxford: Oxford University Press, 2003), 30.

138

[2] Robert L. Ferm, *A Colonial Pastor, Jonathan Edwards the Younger: 1745–1801* (Grand Rapids: William B. Eerdmans Publishing, 1976), 13–14.

[3] Ferm, 15–16.

[4] Jonathan Edwards Sr. to Jonathan Edwards Jr., May 27, 1755. Yale University Library. Quoted in Ferm, 16.

[5] Ferm, 16.

[6] *The Works of Jonathan Edwards, D.D., Late President of Union College. With a Memoir of his Life and Character,* by Tryon Edwards, 2 vols. American Religious Thought of the 18th and 19th Centuries (New York, Garland Publishing, 1987), xiii.

[7] Kenneth P. Minkema, "Jonathan Edwards on Slavery and the Slave Trade," *The William and Mary Quarterly*, Third Series, vol. 54, Issue 4 (Oct., 1997): 826.

[8] Ferm, 21–22.

[9] Ferm, 93.

[10] Ferm, 92–93.

[11] Ferm, 92.

[12] Ferm, 94.

[13] Ferm, 94.

[14] Isaiah Thomas, *The History of Printing in America with a Biography of Printers, and an Account of Newspapers* (Worcester: The Press of Isaiah Thomas, 1810), 412–414.

[15] Robert Smith, *The Perfect and Upright Man: A Funeral Sermon for Jonathan Edwards the Younger, delivered August 3, 1801*. Quoted in Ferm, 512.

THE

INJUSTICE AND IMPOLICY

OF THE

SLAVE TRADE,

AND OF THE

Slavery of the Africans:

ILLUSTRATED IN

A SERMON

PREACHED BEFORE THE CONNECTICUT SOCIETY
FOR THE PROMOTION OF FREEDOM, AND FOR THE
RELIEF OF PERSONS UNLAWFULLY HOLDEN IN
BONDAGE,

AT THEIR ANNUAL MEETING IN NEW-HAVEN,
SEPTEMBER 15, 1791.

BY JONATHAN EDWARDS, D.D.
PASTOR OF A CHURCH IN NEW-HAVEN.

Printed by THOMAS and SAMUEL GREEN;
M,DCC,XCI.

At a meeting of the Connecticut Society for the Promotion of Freedom, and for the Relief of Persons unlawfully holden in Bondage, at New-Haven, September 15, 1791,

VOTED, That the President return the Thanks of this Society to the Rev. Doctor EDWARDS, for his Sermon this Day delivered before the Society, and that he request a Copy thereof, that it may be printed.–

Test. SIMEON BALDWIN, Sec'y.[1]

The injustice and impolicy of the slave-trade, and of the slavery of the Africans.

MATTHEW VII. 12.

THEREFORE ALL THINGS WHATSOEVER YOU WOULD, THAT MEN SHOULD DO TO YOU, DO YE EVEN SO TO THEM; FOR THIS IS THE LAW AND THE PROPHETS.

THIS precept of our divine Lord hath always been admired as most excellent; and doubtless with the greatest reason. Yet it needs some explanation. It is not surely to be understood in the most unlimited sense, implying that because a prince expects and wishes for obedience from his subjects, he is obliged to obey them: that because parents wish their children to submit to their government, therefore they are to submit to the government of their children: or that because some men wish that others would concur and assist them to the gratification of their unlawful desires, therefore they also are to gratify the unlawful desires of others. But whatever we are conscious, that we should, in an exchange of circumstances, wish, and are persuaded that we might reasonably wish, that others would do to us; that we are bound to do to them. This is the general rule given us in the text; and a very extensive rule it is, reaching to the whole of our conduct: and is particularly useful to direct our conduct toward inferiours, and those whom we have in our power. I have therefore thought it a proper foundation for the discourse which by *the Society for the Promotion of Freedom, and for the Relief of Persons unlawfully holden in Bondage,*[2] I have the honour to be appointed to deliver, on the present occasion.

This divine maxim is most properly applicable to the slave-trade, and to the slavery of the Africans. Let us then make the application.

Should we be willing, that the Africans or any other nation should purchase us, our wives and children, transport us into Africa and there sell us into perpetual and absolute slavery? Should we be willing, that they by large bribes and offers of a gainful traffic should entice our neighbours to kidnap and sell us to them, and that they should hold in perpetual and cruel bondage, not only ourselves, but our posterity through all generations? Yet why is it not as right for them to treat us in this manner, as it is for us to treat them in the same manner? Their colour indeed is different from our's. But does this give us a right to enslave them? The nations from Germany to Guinea[3] have complexions of every shade from the fairest white, to a jetty black: and if a black complexion subject a nation or an individual to slavery; where shall slavery begin? Or where shall it end?

I propose to mention a few reasons against the right of the slave-trade—and then to consider the principal arguments, which I have ever heard urged in favour of it.—What will be said against the slave-trade will generally be equally applicable to slavery itself; and if conclusive against the former, will be equally conclusive against the latter.

As to the slave-trade, I conceive it to be unjust in itself—abominable on account of the cruel manner in which it is conducted—and totally wrong on account of the impolicy of it, or its destructive tendency to the moral and political interests of any country.

I. It is unjust in itself.—It is unjust in the same sense, and for the same reason, as it is, to steal, to rob, or to murder. It is a principle, the truth of which hath in this country been generally, if not universally acknowledged, ever since the commencement of the late war, *that all men are born equally free.*[4] If this be true, the Africans are by nature equally entitled to freedom as we are; and therefore we have no more right to enslave, or to afford aid to enslave them, than they have to do the same to us. They have the same right to their freedom, which they have to their property or to their lives. Therefore to enslave them is as really and in the same sense wrong, as to steal from them, to rob or to murder them.

There are indeed cases in which men may justly be deprived of their liberty and reduced to slavery; as there are cases in which they may be justly deprived of their lives. But they can justly be deprived of neither, unless they have by their own voluntary conduct forfeited it. Therefore still the right to liberty stands on the same basis with the right to life. And that the Africans have done something whereby they have forfeited their liberty must appear, before we can justly deprive them of it; as it must appear, that they have done something whereby they have forfeited their lives, before we may justly deprive them of these.

II. The slave-trade is wicked and abominable on account of the cruel manner in which it is carried on.

Beside the stealing or kidnapping of men, women and children, in the first instance, and the instigation of others to this abominable practice; the inhuman manner in which they are transported to America, and in which they are treated on their passage and in their subsequent slavery, is such as ought forever to deter every man from acting any part in this business, who has any regard to justice or humanity. They are crowded so closely into the holds and between the decks of vessels, that they have scarcely room to lie down, and sometimes not room to sit up in an erect posture; the men at the same time fastened together with irons by two and two; and all this in the most sultry climate. The consequence of the whole is, that the most dangerous and fatal diseases are soon bred among them,[5] whereby vast numbers of those exported from Africa perish in the voyage: others in dread of that slavery which is before them, and in distress and despair from the loss of their parents, their children, their husbands, their wives, all their dear connections, and their dear native country itself, starve themselves to death or plunge themselves into the ocean. Those who attempt in the former of those ways to escape from their persecutors, are tortured by live coals applied to their mouths. Those who attempt an escape in the latter and fail, are equally tortured by the most cruel beating, or otherwise as their persecutors please. If any of them make an attempt, as they sometimes do, to recover their liberty, some, and as the circumstances may be, many, are put to immediate death. Others beaten, bruised, cut and mangled in a most inhuman and shocking manner, are in this situation exhibited to the rest, to terrify them from the like attempt in future: and some are delivered up to every species of torment, whether by the application of the whip, or of any other instrument, even of fire itself, as the ingenuity of the ship-master and of his crew is able to suggest or their situation will admit; and these torments are purposely continued for several days, before death is permitted to afford relief to these objects of vengeance.

By these means, according to the common computation, twenty-five thousand, which is a fourth part of those who are exported from Africa, and by the concession of all, twenty thousand, annually perish before they arrive at the places of their destination in America.[6]

But this is by no means the end of the sufferings of this unhappy people. Bred up in a country spontaneously yielding the necessaries and conveniences of savage life, they have never been accustomed to labour: of course they are but ill prepared to go through the fatigue and drudgery to which they are doomed in their state of slavery. Therefore partly by this cause, partly by the scantiness and badness of their food, and partly from dejection of spirits, mortification and despair, another twenty-five thousand die in the seasoning, as it is called, i.e. within two years of their arrival in America. This I say is the common computation. Or if we will in this particular be as favourable to the trade as in the estimate of the number which perishes on the passage, we may reckon the number which dies in the seasoning to be twenty thousand. So that of the hundred thousand annually exported from Africa to America, fifty thousand, as it is commonly computed, or on the most favourable estimate, forty thousand, die before they are seasoned to the country.

Nor is this all. The cruel sufferings of these pitiable beings are not yet at an end. Thenceforward they have to drag out a miserable life in absolute slavery, entirely at the disposal of their masters, by whom not only every venial fault, every mere inadvertence or mistake, but even real virtues, are liable to be construed into the most atrocious crimes, and punished as such, according to their caprice or rage, while they are intoxicated sometimes with liquor, sometimes with passion.

By these masters they are supplied with barely enough to keep them from starving, as the whole expence laid out on a slave for food, clothing and medicine is commonly computed on an average at thirty shillings sterling annually.[7] At the same time they are kept at hard labour from five o'clock in the morning, till nine at night, excepting time to eat twice during the day. And they are constantly under the watchful eye of overseers and Negro-drivers more tyrannical and cruel than even their masters themselves. From these drivers for every imagined, as well as real neglect or want of exertion, they receive the lash, the smack of which is all day long in the ears of those who are on the plantation or in the vicinity; and it is used with such dexterity and severity, as not only to lacerate the skin, but to tear out small portions of the flesh at almost every stroke.

This is the general treatment of the slaves. But many individuals suffer still more severely. Many, many are knocked down; some have their eyes beaten out; some have an arm or leg broken, or chopt off; and many for a very small or for no crime at all, have been beaten to death merely to gratify the fury of an enraged master or overseer.

Nor ought we on this occasion to overlook the wars among the nations of Africa excited by the trade, or the destruction attendant on those wars. Not to mention the destruction of property, the burning of towns and villages, &c. it hath been determined by reasonable computation, that there are annually exported from Africa to the various parts of America, one hundred thousand slaves, as was before observed; that of these six thousand are captives of war; that in the wars in which these are taken, ten persons of the victors and vanquished are killed, to one taken; that therefore the taking of the six thousand captives is attended with the slaughter of sixty thousand of their countrymen. Now does not justice? does not humanity shrink from the idea, that in order to procure one slave to gratify our avarice, we should put to death ten human beings? Or that in order to increase our property, and that only in some small degree, we should carry on a trade, or even connive at it, to support which sixty thousand of our own species are slain in war?

These sixty thousand, added to the forty thousand who perish on the passage and in the seasoning, give us an hundred thousand who are annually destroyed by the trade; and the whole advantage gained by this amazing destruction of human lives is sixty thousand slaves. For you will recollect, that the whole number exported from Africa is an hundred thousand; that of these forty thousand die on the passage and in the seasoning, and sixty thousand are destroyed in the wars. Therefore while one hundred and sixty thousand are killed in the wars and are exported from Africa, but sixty thousand are added to the stock of slaves.

Now when we consider all this; when we consider the miseries which this unhappy people suffer in their wars, in their captivity, in their voyage to America, and during a wretched life of cruel slavery: and especially when we consider the annual destruction of an hundred thousand lives in the manner before mentioned; who can hesitate to declare this trade and the consequent slavery to be contrary to every principle of justice and humanity, of the law of nature and of the law of God?

III. This trade and this slavery are utterly wrong on the ground of impolicy. In a variety of respects they are exceedingly hurtful to the state which tolerates them.

1. They are hurtful, as they deprave the morals of the people.—The incessant and inhuman cruelties practised in the trade and in the subsequent slavery necessarily tend to harden the human heart against the tender feelings of humanity in the masters of vessels, in the sailors, in the factors, in the proprietors of the slaves, in their children, in the overseers, in the slaves themselves, and in all who habitually see those cruelties. Now the eradication or even the diminution of compassion, tenderness and humanity, is certainly a great depravation of heart, and must be followed with correspondent depravity of manners. And measures which lead to such depravity of heart and manners, cannot but be extremely hurtful to the state, and consequently are extremely impolitic.

2. The trade is impolitic as it is so destructive of the lives of seamen. The ingenious Mr. Clarkson[8] hath in a very satisfactory manner made it appear, that in the slave-trade alone Great-Britain loses annually about nineteen hundred seamen; and that this loss is more than double to the loss annually sustained by Great-Britain in all her other trade taken together. And doubtless we lose as many as Great-Britain in proportion to the number of seamen whom we employ in this trade.—Now can it be politic to carry on a trade which is so destructive of that useful part of our citizens, our seamen?

3. African slavery is extremely impolitic, as it discourages industry. Nothing is more essential to the political prosperity of any state, than industry in the citizens. But in proportion as slaves are multiplied, every kind of labour becomes ignominious: and in fact in those of the United States, in which slaves are the most numerous, gentlemen and ladies of any fashion disdain to employ themselves in business, which in other states is consistent with the dignity of the first families and first offices. In a country filled with Negro slaves, labour belongs to them only, and a white man is despised in proportion as he applies to it.—Now how destructive to industry in all of the lowest and middle class of citizens, such

a situation and the prevalence of such ideas will be, you can easily conceive. The consequence is, that some will nearly starve, others will betake themselves to the most dishonest practices, to obtain the means of living.

As slavery produces indolence in the white people, so it produces all those vices which are naturally connected with it; such as intemperance, lewdness and prodigality. These vices enfeeble both the body and the mind, and unfit men for any vigorous exertions and employments either external or mental. And those who are unfit for such exertions, are already a very degenerate race; degenerate, not only in a moral, but a natural sense. They are contemptible too, and will soon be despised even by their Negroes themselves.

Slavery tends to lewdness not only as it produces indolence, but as it affords abundant opportunity for that wickedness without either the danger and difficulty of an attack on the virtue of a woman of chastity, or the danger of a connection with one of ill fame. A planter with his hundred wenches about him is in some respects at least like the Sultan in his seraglio, and we learn the too frequent influence and effect of such a situation, not only from common fame, but from the multitude of mulattoes in countries where slaves are very numerous.

Slavery has a most direct tendency to haughtiness also, and a domineering spirit and conduct in the proprietors of the slaves, in their children, and in all who have the control of them. A man who has been bred up in domineering over Negroes, can scarcely avoid contracting such a habit of haughtiness and domination, as will express itself in his general treatment of mankind, whether in his private capacity, or in any office civil or military with which he may be vested. Despotism in economics naturally leads to despotism in politics, and domestic slavery in a free government is a perfect solecism in human affairs.

How baneful all these tendencies and effects of slavery must be to the public good, and especially to the public good of such a free country as our's, I need not inform you.

4. In the same proportion as industry and labour are discouraged, is population discouraged and prevented. This is another respect in which slavery is exceedingly impolitic. That population is prevented in proportion as industry is discouraged, is, I conceive, so plain that nothing needs

to be said to illustrate it. Mankind in general will enter into matrimony as soon as they possess the means of supporting a family. But the great body of any people have no other way of supporting themselves or a family, than by their own labour. Of course as labour is discouraged, matrimony is discouraged and population is prevented.—But the impolicy of whatever produces these effects will be acknowledged by all. The wealth, strength and glory of a state depend on the number of its virtuous citizens: and a state without citizens is at least as great an absurdity, as a king without subjects.

5. The impolicy of slavery still further appears from this, that it weakens the state, and in proportion to the degree in which it exists, exposes it to become an easy conquest.—The increase of free citizens is an increase of the strength of the state. But not so with regard to the increase of slaves. They not only add nothing to the strength of the state, but actually diminish it in proportion to their number. Every slave is naturally an enemy to the state in which he is holden in slavery, and wants nothing but an opportunity to assist in its overthrow. And an enemy within a state, is much more dangerous than one without it.

These observations concerning the prevention of population and weakening the state, are supported by facts which have fallen within our own observation. That the southern states, in which slaves are so numerous, are in no measure so populous, according to the extent of territory, as the northern, is a fact of universal notoriety: and that during the late war, the southern states found themselves greatly weakened by their slaves, and therefore were so easily overrun by the British army, is equally notorious.

From the view we have now taken of this subject we scruple not to infer, that to carry on the slave-trade and to introduce slaves into our country, is not only to be guilty of injustice, robbery and cruelty toward our fellow-men; but it is to injure ourselves and our country; and therefore it is altogether unjustifiable, wicked and abominable.

Having thus considered the injustice and ruinous tendency of the slave-trade, I proceed to attend to the principal arguments urged in favour of it.

1. It is said, that the Africans are the posterity of Ham, the son of

Noah; that Canaan one of Ham's sons, was cursed by Noah to be a servant of servants; that by Canaan we are to understand Ham's posterity in general; that as his posterity are devoted by God to slavery, we have a right to enslave them.[9]—This is the argument: to which I answer:

It is indeed generally thought that Ham peopled Africa; but that the curse on Canaan extended to all the posterity of Ham is a mere imagination. The only reason given for it is, that Canaan was only one of Ham's sons; and that it seems reasonable, that the curse of Ham's conduct should fall on all his posterity, if on any. But this argument is insufficient. We might as clearly argue, that the judgments denounced on the house of David, on account of his sin in the matter of Uriah,[10] must equally fall on all his posterity. Yet we know, that many of them lived and died in great prosperity. So in every case in which judgments are predicted concerning any nation or family.

It is allowed in this argument, that the curse was to fall on the *posterity* of Ham, and not immediately on Ham himself; If otherwise, it is nothing to the purpose of the slave-trade, or of any slaves now in existence. It being allowed then, that this curse was to fall on Ham's posterity, he who had a right to curse the whole of that posterity, had the same right to curse a part of it only, and the posterity of Canaan equally as any other part; and a curse on Ham's posterity in the line of Canaan was as real as a curse on Ham himself, as a curse on all his posterity would have been.

Therefore we have no ground to believe, that this curse respected any others, that the posterity of Canaan, who lived in the land of Canaan,[11] which is well known to be remote from Africa. We have a particular account, that all the sons of Canaan settled in the land of Canaan; as may be seen in Gen. X. 15–20. "And Canaan begat Sidon his first born, and Heth, and the Jebusite, and the Emorite, and the Girgasite, and the Hivite, and the Arkite, and the Sinite, and the Arvadite, and the Zemorite, and the Hamathite; and afterward were the families of the Canaanites spread abroad. And the border of the Canaanites was from Sidon, as thou goest to Gerar, unto Gaza; as thou goest unto Sodom and Gomorrah, Admah, and Zeboim, even unto Lashah." —Nor have we account that any of their posterity except the Carthaginians afterward removed to any part of Africa: and none will pretend that these peopled

Africa in general; especially considering, that they were subdued, destroyed and so far extirpated by the Romans.

This curse then of the posterity of Canaan, had no reference to the inhabitants of Guinea, or of Africa in general; but was fulfilled partly in Joshua's time, in the reduction and servitude of the Canaanites, and especially of the Gibeonites; partly by what the Phoenicians[12] suffered from the Chaldeans, Persians and Greeks; and finally by what the Carthaginians suffered from the Romans.[13]

Therefore this curse gives us no right to enslave the Africans, as we do by the slave-trade, because it has no respect to the Africans whom we enslave. Nor if it had respected them, would it have given any such right; because it was not an institution of slavery, but a mere prophecy of it. And from this prophecy we have no more ground to infer the right of slavery, than we have from the prophecy of the destruction of Jerusalem by Nebuchadnezzar,[14] or by the Romans, to infer their right respectively to destroy it in the manner they did; or from other prophecies to infer the right of Judas[15] to betray his master, or of the Jews to crucify him.

2. The right of slavery is inferred from the instance of Abraham,[16] who had servants born in his house and bought with his money.—But it is by no means certain, that these were slaves, as our Negroes are. If they were, it is unaccountable, that he went out at the head of an army of them to fight his enemies.[17] No West-India planter would easily be induced to venture himself in such a situation. It is far more probable, that similar to some of the vassals under the feudal constitution, the servants of Abraham were only in a good measure dependant on him, and protected by him. But if they were to all intents and purposes slaves, Abraham's holding of them will no more prove the right of slavery, than his going in to Hagar,[18] will prove it right for any man to cohabit with his wench.

3. From the divine permission given the Israelites to buy servants of the nations round about them, it is argued, that we have a right to buy the Africans and hold them in slavery. See Lev. xxv. 44–47. "Both thy bondmen and thy bondmaids, which thou shalt have, shall be of the heathen that are round about you; of them shall ye buy bondmen and bondmaids. Moreover, of the children of the strangers that do sojourn among you, of them shall ye buy, and of their families, that are with you, which they

begat in your land; and they shall be your possession. And ye shall take them as an inheritance for your children after you, to inherit them for a possession; they shall be your bondmen for ever: but over your brethren the children of Israel ye shall not rule one over another with rigour." But if this be at all to the purpose, it is a permission to every nation under heaven to buy slaves of the nations round about them; to us, to buy of our Indian neighbours; to them, to buy of us, to the French, to buy of the English, and to the English to buy of the French; and so through the world. If then this argument be valid, every man has an entire right to engage in this trade, and to buy and sell any other man of another nation, and any other man of another nation has an entire right to buy and sell him. Thus according to this construction, we have in Lev. xxv. 43, &c. an institution of an universal slave-trade, by which every man may not only become a merchant, but may rightfully become the merchandize itself of this trade, and may be bought and sold like a beast.—Now this consequence will be given up as absurd, and therefore also the construction of scripture from which it follows, must be given up. Yet it is presumed, that there is no avoiding that construction or the absurdity flowing from it, but by admitting, that this permission to the Israelites to buy slaves has no respect to us, but was in the same manner peculiar to them, as the permission and command to subdue, destroy and extirpate the whole Canaanitish nation; and therefore no more gives countenance to African slavery, than the command to extirpate the Canaanites, gives countenance to the extirpation of any nation in these days, by an universal slaughter of men and women, young men and maidens, infants and sucklings.

4. It is further pleaded, that there were slaves in the time of the apostles; that they did not forbid the holding of those slaves, but gave directions to servants, doubtless referring to the servants of that day, to obey *their masters*, and *count them worthy of all honour.*[19]

To this the answer is, that the apostles teach the general duties of servants who are righteously in the state of servitude, as many are or may be, by hire, by indenture, and by judgment of a civil court. But they do not say, whether the servants in general of that day were justly holden in slavery or not. In like manner they lay down the general rules of obedience to civil magistrates, without deciding concerning the characters of the magistrates of the Roman empire in the reign of Nero.[20] And as the apostle Paul requires masters *to give their servants that which is just and equal,* (Col. iv. I.) so if any were enslaved unjustly, of course he in this text requires of the masters of such, to give them their freedom.—Thus the apostles treat the slavery of that day in the same manner that they treat the civil government; and say nothing more in favour of the former, than they say in favour of the latter.

Besides, this argument from the slavery prevailing in the days of the apostles, if it prove any thing, proves too much, and so confutes itself. It proves, that we may enslave all captives taken in war, of any nation, and in any the most unjust war, such as the wars of the Romans, which were generally undertaken from the motives of ambition or avarice. On the ground of this argument we had a right to enslave the prisoners, whom we, during the late war, took from the British army; and they had the same right to enslave those whom they took from us; and so with respect to all other nations.

5. It is strongly urged, that the Negroes brought from Africa are all captives of war, and therefore are justly bought and holden in slavery.— This is a principal argument always urged by the advocates for slavery; and in a solemn debate on this subject, it hath been strongly insisted on, very lately in the British parliament. Therefore it requires our particular attention.

Captives in a war just on their part, cannot be justly enslaved; nor is this pretended. Therefore the captives who may be justly enslaved, must be taken in a war unjust on their part. But even on the supposition, that captives in such a war may be justly enslaved, it will not follow, that we can justly carry on the slave-trade, as it is commonly carried on from the African coast. In this trade any slaves are purchased, who are offered for sale, whether justly or unjustly enslaved. No enquiry is made whether they were captives in any war; much less, whether they were captivated in a war unjust on their part.

By the most authentic accounts, it appears, that the wars in general in Africa are excited by the prospect of gain from the sale of the captives of the war. Therefore those taken by the assailants in such wars, cannot be justly enslaved. Beside these, many are kidnapped by those of neighbouring nations; some by their own neighbours; and some by their kings or his agents; others for debt or some trifling crime are condemned to perpetual slavery—But none of these are justly enslaved. And the traders make no enquiry concerning the mode or occasion of their first enslavement. They buy all that are offered, provided they like them and the price.—So that the plea, that the African slaves are captives in war, is entirely insufficient to justify the slave-trade as now carried on.

But this is not all; if it were ever so true, that all the Negroes exported from Africa were captives in war, and that they were taken in a war unjust on their part; still they could not be justly enslaved.—We have no right to enslave a private foe in a state of nature, after he is conquered. Suppose in a state of nature one man rises against another and endeavours to kill him; in this case the person assaulted has no right to kill the assailant, unless it be necessary to preserve his own life. But in wars between nations, one nation may no doubt secure itself against another, by other means than the slavery of its captives. If a nation be victorious in the war, it may exact some towns or a district of country, by way of caution; or it may impose a fine to deter from future injuries. If the nation be not victorious, it will do no good to enslave the captives whom it has taken. It will provoke the victors, and foolishly excite vengeance which cannot be repelled.

Or if neither nation be decidedly victorious, to enslave the captives on either side can answer no good purpose, but must at least occasion the enslaving of the citizens of the other nation, who are now, or in future may be in a state of captivity. Such a practice therefore necessarily tends to evil and not good.

Besides; captives in war are generally common soldiers or common citizens; and they are generally ignorant of the true cause or causes of the war, and are by their superiours made to believe, that the war is entirely just on their part. Or if this be not the case, they may by force be compelled to serve in a war which they know to be unjust. In either of these cases they do not deserve to be condemned to perpetual slavery. To inflict perpetual slavery on these private soldiers and citizens is manifestly not to do, as we would wish that men should do to us. If we were taken in a war unjust on our part, we should not think it right to be condemned to perpetual slavery. No more right is it for us to condemn and hold in perpetual slavery others, who are in the same situation.

6. It is argued, that as the Africans in their own country, previously to the purchase of them by the African traders, are captives in war; if they were not bought up by those traders, they would be put to death: that therefore to purchase them and to subject them to slavery instead of death, is an act of mercy not only lawful, but meritorious.

If the case were indeed so as is now represented, the purchase of the Negroes would be no more meritorious, than the act of a man, who, if we were taken by the Algerines,[21] should purchase us out of that slavery. This would indeed be an act of benevolence, if the purchaser should set us at liberty. But it is no act of benevolence to buy a man out of one state into another no better. Nay, the act of ransoming a man from death gives no right to the ransomer to commit a crime or an act of injustice to the person ransomed. The person ransomed is doubtless obligated according to his ability to satisfy the ransomer for his expense and trouble. Yet the ransomer has no more right to enslave the other, than the man who saves the life of another who was about to be killed by a robber or an assassin, has a right to enslave him.—The liberty of a man for life is a far greater good, than the property paid for a Negro on the African coast. And to deprive a man of an immensely greater good, in order to recover one immensely less, is an immense injury and crime.

7. As to the pretence, that to prohibit or lay aside this trade, would be hurtful to our commerce; it is sufficient to ask, whether of the supposition, that it were advantageous to the commerce of Great-Britain to send her ships to these states, and transport us into perpetual slavery in the West-Indies, it would be right that she should go into that trade.

8. That to prohibit the slave trade would infringe on the property of those, who have expended large sums to carry on that trade, or of those who wish to purchase the slaves for their plantations, hath also been urged as an argument in favour of the trade.—But the same argument would prove, that if the skins and teeth of the Negroes were as valuable articles of commerce as furs and elephant's teeth, and a merchant were to lay out his property in this commerce, he ought by no means to be obstructed therein.

9. But others will carry on the trade, if we do not.—So others will rob, steal and murder, if we do not.

10. It is said, that some men are intended by nature to be slaves.—If this mean, that the author of nature has given some men a licence, to enslave others; this is denied and proof is demanded. If it mean, that God hath made some of capacities inferior to others, and that the last have a right to enslave the first; this argument will prove, that some of the citizens of every country, have a right to enslave other citizens of the same country; nay, that some have a right to enslave their own brothers and sisters.—But if this argument mean, that God in his providence suffers some men to be enslaved, and that this proves, that from the beginning he intended they should be enslaved, and made them with this intention; the answer is, that in like manner he suffers some men to be murdered, and in this sense, he intended and made them to be murdered. Yet no man in his senses will hence argue the lawfulness of murder.

11. It is further pretended, that no other men, than Negroes, can endure labour in the hot climates of the West-Indies and the southern states.—But does this appear to be fact? In all other climates, the labouring people are the most healthy. And I confess I have not yet seen evidence, but that those who have been accustomed to labour and are inured to those climates, can bear labour there also.—However, taking for granted the fact asserted in this objection, does it follow, that the inhabitants of those countries have a right to enslave the Africans to labour for them? No more surely than from the circumstance, that you are feeble and cannot labour, it follows, that you have a right to enslave your robust neighbour. As in all other cases, the feeble and those who choose not to labour, and yet wish to have their lands cultivated, are necessitated to hire the robust to labour for them; so no reason can be given, why the inhabitants of hot climates should not either perform their own labour, or hire those who can perform it, whether Negroes or others.

If our traders went to the coast of Africa to murder the inhabitants, or to rob them of their property, all would own that such murderous or piratical practices are wicked and abominable. Now it is as really wicked to rob a man of his liberty, as to rob him of his life; and it is much more wicked, than to rob him of his property. All men agree to condemn highway robbery. And the slave-trade is as much a greater wickedness than highway robbery, as liberty is more valuable than property. How strange is it then, that in the same nation highway robbery should be punished with death, and the slave-trade be encouraged by national authority.

We all dread political slavery, or subjection to the arbitrary power of a king or of any man or men not deriving their authority from the people. Yet such a state is inconceivably preferable to the slavery of the Negroes. Suppose that in the late war we had been subdued by Great-Britain; we should have been taxed without our consent. But these taxes would have amounted to but a small part of our property. Whereas the Negroes are deprived of all their property; no part of their earnings is their own; the whole is their masters.—In a conquered state we should have been at liberty to dispose of ourselves and of our property in most cases, as we should choose. We should have been free to live in this or that town or place; in any part of the country, or to remove out of the country; to apply to this or that business; to labour or not; and expecting a sufficiency for the taxes, to dispose of the fruit of our labour to our own benefit, or that of our children, or of any other person. But the unhappy Negroes in slavery can do none of these things. They must do what they are commanded and as much as they are commanded, on pain of the lash. They must live where they are placed, and must confine themselves to that spot, on pain of death.

So that Great-Britain in her late attempt to enslave America, committed a very small crime indeed in comparison with the crime of those who enslave the Africans.

The arguments which have been urged against the slave-trade, are with little variation applicable to the holding of slaves. He who holds a slave, continues to deprive him of that liberty, which was taken from him on the coast of Africa. And if it were wrong to deprive him of it in the first instance, why not in the second? If this be true, no man hath a better right to retain his Negro in slavery, than he had to take him from his native African shores. And every man who cannot show, that his Negro hath by his voluntary conduct forfeited his liberty, is obligated immediately to manumit him. Undoubtedly we should think so were we holden in the same slavery in which the Negroes are: And our text requires us to do to others, as we would that they should do to us.

To hold a slave, who has a right to his liberty, is not only a real crime, but a very great one. Many good Christians have wondered how Abraham, the father of the faithful, could take Hagar to his bed; and how Sarah, celebrated as an holy woman, could consent to this transaction: Also, how David and Solomon could have so many wives and concubines, and yet be real saints. Let such inquire how it is possible, that our fathers and men now alive, universally reputed pious, should hold Negro slaves, and yet be the subjects of real piety? And whether to reduce a man, who hath the same right to liberty as any other man, to a state of absolute slavery, or to hold him in that state, be not as great a crime as concubinage or fornication. I presume it will not be denied, that to commit theft or robbery every day of a man's life, is as great a sin as to commit fornication in one instance. But to steal a man or to rob him of his liberty is a greater sin, than to steal his property, or to take it by violence. And to hold a man in a state of slavery, who has a right to his liberty, is to be every day guilty of robbing him of his liberty, or of man stealing. The consequence is inevitable, that other things being the same, to hold a Negro slave, unless he have forfeited his liberty, is a greater sin in the sight of God, than concubinage or fornication.

Does this conclusion seem strange to any of you? Let me entreat you to weigh it candidly before you reject it. You will not deny, that liberty is more valuable than property; and that it is a greater sin to deprive a man of his whole liberty during life, than to deprive him of his whole property; or that man-stealing is a greater crime than robbery. Nor will you deny, that to hold in slavery a man who was stolen, is substantially the same crime as to steal him. These principles being undeniable, I leave it to yourselves to draw the plain and necessary consequence. And if your consciences shall, in spite of all opposition, tell you, that while you hold your Negroes in slavery, you do wrong, exceedingly wrong; that you do not, as you would that men should do to you; that you commit sin in the sight of God; that you daily violate the plain rights of mankind, and that in a higher degree, than if you committed theft or robbery; let me beseech you not to stifle this conviction, but to attend to it and act accordingly; lest you add to your former guilt, that of sinning against the light of truth, and of your own consciences.

To convince yourselves, that your information being the same, to hold a Negro slave is a greater sin than fornication, theft or robbery, you need only bring the matter home to yourselves. I am willing to appeal to your own consciences, whether you would not judge it to be a greater sin for a man to hold you or your child during life in such slavery, as that of the Negroes, than for him to spend one night in a brothel, or in one instance to steal or rob. Let conscience speak, and I will submit to its decision.

This question seems to be clearly decided by revelation. Exod. xxi. 16. "He that stealeth a man and selleth him, or if he be found in his hand, he shall surely be put to death." Thus death is, by the divine express declaration, the punishment due to the crime of man-stealing. But death is not the punishment declared by God to be due to fornication, theft or robbery in common cases. Therefore we have the divine authority to assert, than man-stealing is a greater crime than fornication, theft or robbery. Now to hold in slavery a man who has a right to liberty, is substantially the same crime as to deprive him of his liberty. And to deprive of liberty and reduce to slavery, a man who has a right to liberty, is man-stealing. For it is immaterial whether he be taken and reduced to slavery clandestinely or by open violence. Therefore if the Negroes have a right to liberty, to hold them in slavery is man-stealing, which we have seen is, by God himself, declared to be a greater crime than fornication, theft or robbery.

Perhaps, though this truth be clearly demonstrable both from reason and revelation, you scarcely dare receive it, because it seems to bear hardly on the characters of our pious fathers, who held slaves. But they did it ignorantly and in unbelief of the truth; as Abraham, Jacob, David and Solomon were ignorant, that polygamy or concubinage was wrong. As to domestic slavery our fathers lived in a "time of ignorance which God winked at; but now he commandeth all men every where to repent[22] of this wickedness, and to break off this sin by righteousness, and this iniquity by shewing mercy to the poor, if it may be a lengthening out of their tranquility." You therefore to whom the present blaze of light as to this subject has reached, cannot sin at so cheap a rate as our fathers.

But methinks I hear some say, I have bought my Negro; I have paid a large sum for him; I cannot lose this sum, and therefore I cannot manumit him.—Alas! This is "hitting the nail on the head." This brings into view the true cause which makes it so difficult to convince men of what is right in this case.—You recollect the story of Amaziah's hiring an hundred thousand men of Israel, for an hundred talents, to assist him against the Edomites;[23] and that when by the word of the Lord, he was forbidden to take those hired men with him to the war, he cried out, "But what shall we do for the hundred talents, which I have given to the army of Israel?" In this case, the answer of God was, "The Lord is able to give thee much more than this."[24]—To apply this to the subject before us, God is able to give thee much more than thou shalt lose by manumitting thy slave.

You may plead, that you use your slave well; you are not cruel to him, but feed and clothe him comfortably, &c. Still every day you rob him of a most valuable and important right. And a highway man, who robs a man of his money in the most easy and complaisant manner, is still a robber; and murder may be effected in a manner the least cruel and tormenting; still it is murder.

Having now taken that view of our subject, which was proposed, we may in reflection see abundant reason to acquiesce in the institution of this society. If the slave-trade be unjust, and as gross a violation of the rights of mankind, as would be, if the Africans should transport us into perpetual slavery in Africa; to unite our influence against it, is a duty which we owe to mankind, to ourselves and to God too. It is but doing as we would that men should do to us.—Nor is it enough that we have formed the society; we must do the duties of it. The first of these is to put an end to the slave-trade. The second is to relieve those who, contrary to the laws of the country, are holden in bondage. Another is to defend those in their remaining legal and natural rights, who are by law holden in bondage. Another and not the least important object of this society, I conceive to be, to increase and disperse the light of truth with respect to the subject of African slavery, and so prepare the way for its total abolition. For until men in general are convinced of the injustice of the trade and of the slavery itself, comparatively little can be done to effect the most important purposes of the institution.

It is not to be doubted, that the trade is even now carried on from this state. Vessels are from time to time fitted out for the coast of Africa, to transport the Negroes to the West-Indies and other parts. Nor will an end be put to this trade, without vigilance and strenuous exertion on the part of this society, or other friends of humanity, nor without a patient enduring of the opposition and odium of all who are concerned in it, of their friends and of all who are the opinion that it is justifiable. Among these we are doubtless to reckon some of large property and considerable influence. And if the laws and customs of the country equally allowed of it, many, and perhaps as many as now plead for the right of the African slave-trade, would plead for the right of kidnapping us, the citizens of the United States, and of selling us into perpetual slavery.—If then we dare not incur the displeasure of such men, we may as well dissolve the society, and leave the slave-trade to be carried on, and the Negroes to be kidnapped, and though free in this state, to be sold into perpetual slavery in distant parts, at the pleasure of any man, who wishes to make gain by such abominable practices.

Though we must expect opposition, yet if we be steady and persevering, we need not fear, that we shall fail of success. The advantages, which the cause has already gained, are many and great. Thirty years ago scarcely a man in this country thought either the slave-trade or the slavery of Negroes to be wrong. But now how many and able advocates in private life, in our legislatures, in Congress, have appeared and have openly and irrefragably pleaded the rights of humanity in this as well as other instances? Nay, the great body of the people from New-Hampshire to Virginia inclusively, have obtained such light, that in all those states the further importation of slaves is prohibited by law. And in Massachusetts and New-Hampshire, slavery is totally abolished.[25]

Nor is the light concerning this subject confined to America. It hath appeared with great clearness in France, and produced remarkable effects in the National Assembly. It hath also shone in bright beams in Great-Britain. It flashes with splendor in the writings of Clarkson and in the proceedings of several societies formed to abolish the slave-trade.[26] Nor hath it been possible to shut it out of the British parliament. This light is still increasing, and in times will effect a total revolution. And if we judge of the future by the past, within fifty years from this time, it will be as shameful for a man to hold a Negro slave, as to be guilty of common robbery or theft. But it is our duty to remove the obstacles which intercept the rays of this light, that it may reach not only public bodies, but every individual. And when it shall have obtained a general spread, shall have dispelled all darkness, and slavery shall be no more; it will be an honour to be recorded in history, as a society which was formed, and which exerted itself with vigour and fidelity, to bring about an event so necessary and conducive to the interests of humanity and virtue, to the support of the rights and to the advancement of the happiness of mankind.

APPENDIX.

S O M E objections to the doctrine of the preceding sermon, have been mentioned to the author, since the delivery of it. Of these it may be proper to take some notice.

1. The slaves are in a better situation than that in which they were in their own country; especially as they have opportunity to know the Christian religion and to secure the saving blessings of it. Therefore it is not an injury, but a benefit to bring them into this country, even though their importation be accompanied and followed with slavery. It is also said, that the situation of many Negroes under their masters is much better, than it would be, were they free in this country; that they are much better fed and clothed, and are much more happy; that therefore to hold them in slavery is so far from a crime, that it is a meritorious act.

With regard to these pleas, it is to be observed, that every man hath a right to judge concerning his own happiness, and to chose the means of obtaining or promoting it; and to deprive him of this right is the very injury of which we complain; it is to enslave him. Because we judge, that the Negroes are more happy in this country, in a state of slavery, than in the enjoyment of liberty in Africa, we have no more right to enslave them and bring them into this country, than we have to enslave any of our neighbours, who we judge would be more happy under our control, than they are at present under their own. Let us make the case our own. Should we believe, that we were justly treated, if the Africans should carry us into perpetual slavery in Africa, on the ground that they judged, that we should be more happy in that state, than in our present situation?

As to the opportunity which the Negroes in this country are said to have, to become acquainted with Christianity; this with respect to many is granted: But what follows from it? It would be ridiculous to pretend, that this is the motive on which they act who import them, or they who buy and hold them in slavery. Or if this were the motive, it would not sanctify either the trade or the slavery. We are not at liberty to do evil, that good may come; to commit a crime more aggravated than theft or robbery, that we may make a proselyte to Christianity. Neither our Lord Jesus Christ, nor any one of his apostles has taught us this mode of propagating the faith.

2. It is said, that the doctrine of the preceding sermon imputes that as a crime to individuals, which is owing to the state of society. This is granted; and what follows? It is owing to the state of society, that our neighbours, the Indians roast their captives: and does it hence follow, that such conduct is not to be imputed to the individual agents as a crime? It is owing to the state of society in Popish countries, that thousands worship the beast and his image: and is that worship therefore not to be imputed as a crime to those, who render it? Read the Revelation of St. John.[27] The state of society is such, that drunkenness and adultery are very common in some countries; but will it follow, that those vices are innocent in those countries?

3. If I be ever so willing to manumit my slave, I cannot do it without being holden to maintain him, when he shall be sick or shall be old and decrepit. Therefore I have a right to hold him as a slave.—The same argument will prove, that you have a right to enslave your children or your parents; as you are equally holden to maintain them in sickness and in decrepit old age.—The argument implies, that in order to secure the money, which you are afraid the laws of your country will some time or other oblige you to pay; it is right for you to rob a free man of his liberty or be guilty of man-stealing. On the ground of this argument every town or parish obligated by law, to maintain its helpless poor, has a right to sell into perpetual slavery all the people, who may probably or even possibly occasion a public expence.

4. After all, it is not safe to manumit the Negroes: they would cut our throats; they would endanger the peace and government of the state. Or

at least they would be so idle, that they would not provide themselves with necessaries: of course they must live by thievery and plundering.

This objection requires a different answer, as it respects the northern, and as it respects the southern states. As it respects the northern, in which slaves are so few, there is not the least foundation to imagine, that they would combine or make insurrection against the government; or that they would attempt to murder their masters. They are much more likely to kill their masters, in order to obtain their liberty, or to revenge the abuse they receive, while it is still continued, than to do it after the abuse hath ceased, and they are restored to their liberty. In this case, they would from a sense of gratitude, or at least from a conviction of the justice of their masters, feel a strong attachment, instead of a murderous disposition.

Nor is there the least danger, but that by a proper vigilance of the select-men, and by a strict execution of the laws now existing, the Negroes might in a tolerable degree be kept from idleness and pilfering.

All this hath been verified by experiment. In Massachusetts, all the Negroes in the commonwealth were by their new constitution liberated in a day: and none of the ill consequences objected followed either to the commonwealth or to individuals.

With regard to the southern states, the case is different. The Negroes in some parts of those states are a great majority of the whole, and therefore the evils objected would, in case of a general manumission at once, be more likely to take place. But in the first place there is no prospect, that the conviction of the truth exhibited in the preceding discourse, will at once, take place in the minds of all the holders of slaves. The utmost that can be expected, is that it will take place gradually in one after another, and that of course the slaves will be gradually manumitted. Therefore the evils of a general manumission at once, are dreaded without reason.

If in any state the slaves should be manumitted in considerable numbers at once, or so that the number of free Negroes should become large; various measures might be concerted to prevent the evils feared. One I beg leave to propose: That overseers of the free Negroes be appointed from among themselves, who shall be empowered to inspect the morals and management of the rest, and report to proper authority, those who are vicious, idle or incapable of managing their own affairs, and that such authority dispose of them under proper masters for a year or other term, as is done, perhaps in all the states, with regard to the poor white people in like manner vicious, idle or incapable of management. Such black overseers would naturally be ambitious to discharge the duties of their office; they would in many respects have much more influence than white men with their country men: and other Negroes looking forward to the same honourable distinction, would endeavour to deserve it by their improvement and good conduct.

But after all, this whole objection, if it were ever so entirely founded on truth; if the freed Negroes would probably rise against their masters, or combine against government; rests on the same ground, as the apology of the robber, who murders the man whom he has robbed. Says the robber to himself, I have robbed this man, and now if I let him go he will kill me, or he will complain to authority and I shall be apprehended and hung. I must therefore kill him. There is no other way of safety for me.— The coincidence between this reasoning and that of the objection under consideration, must be manifest to all. And if this reasoning of the robber be inconclusive; if the robber have no right on that ground to kill the man whom he hath robbed; neither have the slave-holders any more right to continue to hold their slaves. If the robber ought to spare the life of the man robbed, take his own chance and esteem himself happy, if he can escape justice; so the slave-holders ought immediately to let their slaves go free, treat them with the utmost kindness, by such treatment endeavour to pacify them with respect to past injuries, and esteem themselves happy, if they can compromise the matter in this manner.

In all countries in which slaves are a majority of the inhabitants, the masters lie in a great measure at the mercy of the slaves, and may most rationally expect sooner or later, to be cut off, or driven out by the slaves, or to be reduced to the same level and to be mingled with them into one common mass. This I think is by ancient and modern events demonstrated to be the natural and necessary course of human affairs. The hewers of wood and drawers of water among the Israelites, the Helots among the Lacedemonians, the slaves among the Romans, the villains and vassals in most of the kingdoms of Europe under the feudal system, have long since mixed with the common mass of the people, and shared the common privileges and honours of their respective countries. And in the French West-Indies the Mulattoes and free Negroes are already become so numerous and powerful a body, as to be allowed by the National Assembly to enjoy the common rights and honours of free men.[28] These facts plainly show, what the whites in the West-Indies and the Southern States are to expect concerning their posterity, that it will infallibly be a mongrel breed, or else they must quit the country to the Negroes whom they have hitherto holden in bondage.

Thus it seems, that they will be necessitated by Providence to make in one way or another compensation to the Negroes for the injury which they have done them. In the first case, by taking them into affinity with themselves, giving them their own sons and daughters in marriage, and making them and their posterity the heirs of all their property and all their honours, and by raising their colour to a partial whiteness, whereby a part at least of that mark which brings on them so much contempt, will be wiped off. In the other case, by leaving to them all their real estates. It is manifest by the bare stating of the two cases, that the compensation in the latter case is by much the least. In the former case, the compensation will include all that is included in the latter and much more. If therefore our southern brethren and the inhabitants of the West-Indies would balance their accounts with their Negro slaves, at the cheapest possible rate, they will doubtless judge it prudent, to leave the country with all their houses, lands and improvements to their quiet possession and dominion; as otherwise Providence will compel them to much dearer settlement, and one attended with a circumstance inconceivably more mortifying, than the loss of all their real estates, I mean the mixture of their blood with that of the Negroes into one common posterity.

At least it is to be hoped, that these considerations will induce them to forbear any further importation of slaves, as the more numerous the slaves are, the more dangerous they will be, and the more deeply tinged will be the colour of their mulatto posterity.

It is not to be doubted, but that the Negroes in these northern states also will, in time, mix with the common mass of the people. But we have this consolation, that as they are so small a proportion of the inhabitants, when mixed with the rest, they will not produce any very sensible diversity of colour.

———

THE END.

Notes

[1] Simeon Baldwin (1761–1851): Connecticut-born lawyer and jurist, and from 1789 to 1800, New Haven city clerk.

[2] The Connecticut Society for the Promotion of Freedom, and for the Relief of Persons Unlawfully Holden in Bondage, established circa 1790.

[3] "Guinea" was widely used in Europe, beginning in the fifteenth century, to refer to the coastal regions of West Africa between River Senegal (modern Senegal) and Cape Lopez (modern Gabon).

[4] Edwards refers to the language of The Declaration of Independence: "We hold these truths to be self-evident, that all men are created equal, that they are endowed by their Creator with certain inalienable Rights, that among these are Life, Liberty, and the pursuit of Happiness."

[5] Small pox and dysentery were among the most common diseases found aboard slave vessels, and given the cramped quarters, these diseases spread rapidly.

[6] Mortality rates aboard ships ranged from 13 to 33 percent, depending upon the ship's conditions and route.

[7] Roughly equivalent to 106 pounds, or about 190 dollars, in 2002. See Economic History Services, http://www.eh.net/.

[8] Thomas Clarkson (1760–1846): British abolitionist who wrote about the slave trade and slavery. Edwards refers to Clarkson's major works, which included *An Essay on the Slavery and Commerce of the Human Species* (1786) and *The Substance of the Evidence of Sundry Persons on the Slave-Trade, Collected in the Course of a Tour Made in the Autumn of the Year 1788* (1789).

[9] Genesis 9:20–27 relates the story of Noah's curse upon Ham's son Canaan and his descendents, which was often cited by defenders of slavery to justify the institution. According to this passage, Ham, Noah's son, found his father drunk and naked in his tent and failed to cover him. This disrespectful behavior led to Noah declaring a curse upon Ham's son, Canaan. This and all subsequent Biblical references are from the Authorized (King James) Version of the Bible.

[10] 2 Samuel 11 tells of how David arranged to have Uriah, an officer in his army, killed in battle so that he would be free to marry Uriah's wife, Bathsheba.

[11] Present-day Lebanon and Israel.

[12] A people culturally descended from the Canaanites.

[13] Possibly a reference to the Punic Wars, the first of which occurred from 264 to 241 BCE, the second from 218 to 201 BCE, and the third from 149 to 146 BCE. These wars culminated with the destruction of the city of Carthage and the end of Carthaginian power.

[14] Nebuchadnezzar: Conquered Jerusalem 627 BCE; King of Babylonia, 605–562 BCE.

[15] Judas Iscariot, one of the apostles of Jesus Christ, betrayed Christ's identity to Jewish authorities who sentenced him to death.

[16] Genesis 17. Often credited as the progenitor of the Hebrews and the founder of Judaism.

[17] Edwards possibly refers to Genesis 14:14.

[18] Genesis 16. Haggar was the Egyptian servant of Sarah, Abraham's wife, who was offered to Abraham to bear him a child due to Sarah's sterility. Hagar bore Abraham a son, Ishmael, and was turned out of the house by Sarah.

[19] I Timothy 6:1.

[20] Nero: Roman Emperor from 54 to 68 CE, notorious for his murderous cruelty and long-rumored to have instigated the fire that burned Rome in the year 64 CE.

[21] Algerians: A reference to the Barbary pirates who abducted European and American merchants from their ships and either ransomed or enslaved them.

[22] Here Edwards splices together quotations from Acts of the Apostles 17:30 and Daniel 4:27.

[23] 2 Kings 14:7. Amaziah, king of Judah from 800 to 783 BCE, killed 10,000 Edomites, a people who lived adjacent to the Israelites at the southeast end of the Dead Sea.

[24] 2 Chronicles 25:9.

[25] Slavery was abolished in Massachusetts in 1780 and in New Hampshire in 1784, in both cases as inscribed in new state constitutions.

[26] In 1787, a national anti-slavery committee was established in Great Britain. Headed by Granville Sharp and Thomas Clarkson, the committee first sought to suppress the slave trade. Shortly thereafter, William Wilberforce joined the cause, giving them parliamentary backing. Wilberforce's 1789 parliamentary motion to end the slave trade received more than 100 petitions in support, but ultimately failed. Another attempt, in 1791, to abolish the slave trade proved equally unsuccessful. But finally in 1807, Lord Grenville steered a bill through the House of Lords that abolished the transatlantic slave trade. In 1823, the anti-slavery movement gained momentum with the formation of the Anti-Slavery Society by Evangelicals, Quakers, and Methodists. In 1833 slavery was abolished throughout the British colonies, and replaced by apprenticeship terms of seven years, which were eliminated in 1838.

[27] More commonly known as the book of Revelation in the Bible.

[28] In 1791, the French National Assembly extended suffrage to all colonists, regardless of their color, providing they met the property requirements and were born of free parents.

BEACON HILL.

A Local Poem,

HISTORIC and DESCRIPTIVE.

BOOK I.

Publifhed according to Act of Congrefs.

(Morton, Sarah Wentworth Apthorp)

Printed by MANNING & LORING for the *AUTHOR.*

1797.

Reproduced courtesy of the American Antiquarian Society

POEMS,

ON

VARIOUS SUBJECTS.

By ISABELLA OLIVER,
Of Cumberland County, Pennsylvania.

ALL hail, ye mighty masters of the lay,
Nature's true sons, the friends of men and truth!
Whose song, sublimely sweet, serenely gay,
Amus'd my childhood, and inform'd my youth.

BEATTIE'S MINSTREL.

Carlisle:

FROM THE PRESS OF A. LOUDON,
(WHITEHALL.)

1805.

TO THE

INHABITANTS

OF

CHARLESTON,

SOUTH CAROLINA.

——————

PHILADELPHIA:

PRINTED BY KIMBER, CONRAD, & CO.

——◄◆►——

1805.

[7]
THREE ANTI-SLAVERY WOMAN WRITERS

Introduction by Kathryn Gin, Stanford University

The short works reprinted here share two defining characteristics: they were all written by women and they all reflect, in different ways, the anti-slavery movement between 1790 and 1810. The first of these, *The African Chief,* about the capture and enslavement of a fictional Gambian, was written in 1792 by Sarah Wentworth Apthorp Morton, a member of Boston society. Morton went on to publish, in 1797, her epic poem *Beacon Hill,* which celebrates the new republic, but, at the same time, lambasts Southern slavery. Eight years later and roughly 400 miles away, Isabella Oliver Sharp, a Presbyterian from South Central Pennsylvania, included the searing verse essay "On Slavery" in her new book of poetry. Also in 1805, Ann Tuke Alexander, a British Quaker visiting Philadelphia, attacked the African slave trade in *An Address to the Inhabitants of Charleston, South Carolina.* Together, these documents are significant not only because they pre-date the more well known abolition movement that was to begin in the 1820s, but, because they were written by women, they address a gap in our understanding of early anti-slavery sentiments from a group that was itself marginalized in society.

The marginalization of women in the early republic made the publication of their texts particularly significant. During the Revolution, many women found themselves immersed in public events, making sacrifices for the republic and acquiring political identities as patriots or loyalists. Women were encouraged, as "Republican Mothers," to be acquainted with the political world so they could teach their sons to become informed and virtuous citizens.[1] Many women hoped their status would improve with American independence; however, the ideal of "Republican Motherhood" instead developed into what many scholars have termed the "Cult of True Womanhood," an antebellum ideal of femininity that defined a woman's proper sphere more sharply than it had been previously. Americans of both sexes began to view women as morally and spiritually superior to men, but believed the public sphere was too competitive and corrupt for them. Women were increasingly shut out of the political arena and encouraged instead to perfect the arts of domesticity, making the home a haven from the outside world. Because women were supposed to focus on the home, female authors had to assure their audience that they did not, as Morton wrote, "neglect . . . appropriate duties" when they took time to write.[2] Women who publicly opposed slavery faced an even greater challenge. While the ideal of "True Womanhood" made it acceptable for the morally superior woman to privately feel that slavery was wrong, it discouraged her from publicly airing her views.[3]

Morton, Oliver,[4] and Alexander published their views despite these gender constraints. Though none of the works reprinted here could be called great literature, they deserve attention because they belie the conventional notion that women did not publicly oppose slavery until the 1830s. Much has been written about the women abolitionists of the 1830s and later, who used the ideal of women as moral guardians to justify their public criticisms, attacking slavery on the grounds, for example, that it broke up slaves' families and made impossible a stable home.[5] The writings here show that women in this earlier period similarly used their position as women and the prevailing ideal of womanhood to offer criticisms of the new republic.

To be sure, earlier writers like Morton, Oliver, and Alexander were not as vocal and persistent in expressing their views as later women like the Grimké sisters and Lucretia Mott, radical abolitionists in favor of immediate emancipation. The different approaches taken by earlier and later anti-slavery women reflect the differences in the institution of slavery at the end of the Revolutionary War and in the 1830s. Although all Northern states had passed emancipation acts by 1804, and Congress had abolished the African slave trade in 1807, the introduction of Eli Whitney's cotton gin gave new life to slavery and made it economically viable in vast new areas of the South.[6] The rise of "King Cotton" and the associated increase in the slave population paralleled the rise of radical women abolitionists in the first decades of the 1800s.

The publications of earlier anti-slavery writers like Morton, Oliver, and Alexander reflected a different situation. Though their writings dramatized the evils of slavery and the slave trade from Africa to the Americas, they were less urgent than the public orations of later women abolitionists. Whereas the later radical abolitionists united in favor of immediate emancipation, early anti-slavery advocates shared no such unanimity. Some favored the removal of slaves to colonies, others favored gradual emancipation, and still others thought that the end of the transatlantic slave trade would spell the end of an already weak institution. Yet most agreed that slavery was evil.

SARAH WENTWORTH APTHORP MORTON (1759–1846)

Sarah Wentworth Apthorp Morton received a thorough education as part of her privileged Boston upbringing. In 1781 she married Perez Morton, a well-connected lawyer and orator. After giving birth to six children in the 1780s (one of whom died) and enduring a scandalous affair between her husband and sister, Morton began, in the 1790s, to publish poetry, often under the penname Philenia, and she quickly became one of the most famous woman poets of her day.[7]

While it is unclear how involved Morton became in the fledgling abolition societies of the late eighteenth century,[8] her interest in slavery and the slave trade is apparent in several of her poems. Her first known anti-slavery poem, the 1791 *Tears of Humanity,* was a response to the failure of the British House of Commons to abolish the slave trade.[9] A year later, she wrote *The African Chief,* which became her most successful short work. First published in the *Columbian Centinel* in 1792, it was reprinted in a number of newspapers from Massachusetts to New York, and republished in Morton's 1823 *My Mind and Its Thoughts, In Sketches, Fragments, and Essays.*

Though the latter version has become the standard text in reprints of *The African Chief* (including the one here), in the original printing in the *Columbian Centinel,* a short *History of the West-India Islands* preceded the poem to help the reader understand its context. This history explained that "imported Africans" were brought to the islands "with dissatisfied and exasperated minds" made worse by the inhumane treatment they received and implied that the slave trade was a cause of slave insurrections. The poem, which describes the valiant struggle of a Gambian chief resentful of his capture, was written while insurrections were occurring in St. Domingue (modern Haiti). *The African Chief* also had roots in a vein of anti-slavery writing stretching back to Aphra Behn's 1688 *Oroonoko, or the Royal Slave,* which tells the story of an enslaved African prince who led a slave rebellion in Surinam.[10]

Probably much of Morton's initial audience of newspaper readers agreed with her criticisms of the slave trade. That a publication like the *Columbian Centinel* included a description of the West Indies before her poem and printed other works related to slavery suggests similar anti-slavery views among its editors and contributors. *The African Chief* was also popular long after its original publication in 1792. John Greenleaf Whittier, a prominent abolitionist of the later movement, called it one of his favorite poems,[11] and an 1849 article in the *North American Review* called the poem "as familiar as our nursery rhymes."[12]

In contrast, Morton's *Beacon Hill* was not as successful or as well received. Printed in 1797 by Manning & Loring, a press that served clients ranging from Harvard University to the United States government, the poem did not sell as expected, and reviews were not as effusive as Morton had hoped.[13] Its ill success was probably due more to Morton's overwrought style than to her subject. One scholar suggests that "epic poetry proved to be beyond Philenia's slender talents."[14]

The poetic merits of *Beacon Hill* aside, what is most useful for students of early anti-slavery writings is the section reprinted here. The poem belongs to a period in the early republic in which many authors strived to create a distinctly American literature,[15] and though the poem as a whole is ardently pro-American, Morton tempers her descriptions of beautiful landscapes and heroic patriots with criticisms of southern slavery. The 52-page *Beacon Hill* is not an anti-slavery poem in the typical sense, but its passages on slavery expose the contradiction between espousing freedom and enslaving blacks.

ISABELLA OLIVER SHARP (1771 OR 1777[16]–1843)

Whereas Sarah Morton's fame guaranteed her presence in the historical record, not much information survives about Isabella Oliver Sharp, a lifelong resident of Cumberland County, Pennsylvania. Most of what we know about her comes from her 1805 book, *Poems, on Various Subjects,* in which "On Slavery" was printed. She did not receive a formal education and may not even have been very fluent with the pen, instead dictating her poems for someone else to copy.[17] She published her book of poems in 1805, seven years before her marriage to Captain Alexander Sharp. Whether domestic or other concerns kept her from publishing thereafter, she seems not to have written anything else for publication.

Published by Archibald Loudon, a local printer and bookseller whose business was not as grand, perhaps, as Morton's Boston publishers,[18] *Poems, on Various Subjects* was similar to other women's poetry of the early nineteenth century. Its title was a common one used by a number of poets, and its subjects—including religion and the commemoration of the dead—were typical of women's poetry of the period. "On Slavery" is Oliver's only poem that focuses specifically on slavery, though several other poems mention her sympathy for "all who wear the human form"[19] and her belief that having anti-slavery sentiments was a virtue befitting women.[20]

"On Slavery" depicts the horrors of slavery, calls on lawmakers to "stop this most unnat'ral trade in man," and attacks popular arguments used to defend slavery. For example, Oliver debunks the "curse of Canaan," a common defense of slavery from the book of Genesis, in which Canaan is cursed as "a servant of servants," and Africans' black skin was taken to be the mark of this curse.[21] Unfortunately, we do not know much about how "On Slavery" or Oliver's other poems were received. Pennsylvania had enacted a gradual emancipation law in 1780, which meant that, in 1805, there were still slaves in the state and notices for runaways in Cumberland County papers. Because slavery persisted in Pennsylvania, Oliver's audience may not have been as uniformly anti-slavery as Morton's (in Massachusetts, the abolition of slavery by a 1783 court case resulted in the freeing of the last slaves by 1790). Judging from the long list of subscribers to the book, though, we can speculate that it was at least fairly well received.

ANN TUKE ALEXANDER (1767–1849)

While Morton and Oliver were both American and mainstream Protestants, Ann Alexander was a British Quaker from York, raised with very different ideals of womanhood. Although in Britain, as in America, industrialization was dividing the male and female spheres into the public and the private, Quaker families were notable for their relative egalitarianism. Many women in Alexander's family became Quaker ministers, including Alexander herself at the young age of eighteen.[22] Her ministries led her to travel extensively, visiting families and holding Meetings.[23] Concerned with the "misery and oppression" she saw around her, Alexander's writings included not only the anti-slavery text reprinted here, but also a hymnal for prisoners and works related to child labor. Her personal life rarely interfered with her ministries and her writing, and her family supported her in many ways. When she traveled to America between 1803 and 1805, for example, she left her young sons with her husband, William Alexander, a fellow Quaker who published a number of his wife's works and shared her interest in the anti-slavery movement.[24]

Ann Alexander's travels in America brought her face to face with the institution of slavery, "call[ing] forth the tender feelings of [her] heart."[25] Written during her stay in America, Alexander's *Address to the Inhabitants of Charleston, South Carolina* relies heavily on the Bible for its arguments, and focuses on the "barbarous" and "repugnant" African slave trade. Alexander's focus reflects the anti-slavery strategy of many Quakers, leaders in the fight against the slave trade before 1807, when bills to abolish the trade were passed in Great Britain and America.[26] Alexander's short pamphlet was printed in Philadelphia by Kimber, Conrad & Co., a prominent Bible publisher that also printed other texts, including anti-slavery documents.[27] Alexander's decision, in 1805, to address her pamphlet to "the inhabitants of Charleston" was prompted by South Carolina's reopening of the African slave trade in 1803, sixteen years after the state legislature had banned it. The phenomenal rise in cotton production, beginning in the 1790s, had greatly increased the demand for slaves in the deep South,[28] and the reopening of the trade in South Carolina led to a massive importation of slaves from 1803 until 1808, when the national prohibition of the slave trade went into effect.

Unfortunately, information about the distribution and reception of Alexander's pamphlet is lacking. We do not even know if Alexander actually succeeded in reaching "the inhabitants of Charleston," as it was printed in Philadelphia. Regardless of how far her readership actually extended, the fact that a Quaker woman from Britain could travel to America and publish an anti-slavery tract there is a significant reminder that as the slave trade was transatlantic, so too was the anti-slavery movement.

How Morton, Oliver, and Alexander came to their anti-slavery views is subject to speculation. Though none of the women lived in an area where slavery was an inescapable part of daily life, Alexander saw slaves when she visited the American South, and Morton and Oliver were both born when slavery was still legal in their respective states. But firsthand experience was not a prerequisite to forming anti-slavery sentiments. The women may have formed their views by reading other anti-slavery works. For instance, Morton, in *Beacon Hill,* cites John Lendrum's 1795 *A Concise and Impartial History of the American Revolution,* a text that is critical of slavery and the "infamous commerce of human flesh."[29] Another contributing factor may have been the influence of the fledgling anti-slavery movements around them, such as the Pennsylvanian Quakers' initiatives to end slavery beginning in the mid-eighteenth century and the York Anti-Slavery Society's agitation for the end of the slave trade.[30] Still another possibility is the general climate of ideas by which these women, in an age of democratic revolutions, keenly felt the hypocrisy of the rhetoric used to decry America's "enslavement" to Britain, while America itself enslaved blacks.

Regardless of how they came to their views, Morton, Oliver, and Alexander were compelled to write about their anti-slavery sentiments well before what is traditionally viewed as the start of the abolitionist movement in the 1830s. Even allowing for the apparent artificiality of grouping these four works by the gender of their authors, it is significant that these three women of different nationalities and religious persuasions should all be moved to focus on African slavery as the defining moral issue of their time.

Notes

[1] Linda Kerber, *Women of the Republic: Intellect and Ideology in Revolutionary America* (Chapel Hill: University of North Carolina Press, 1980), 235.

[2] Sarah Wentworth Apthorp Morton, "Apology for the Poem," *Beacon Hill* (Boston: Manning and Loring, 1797), ix.

[3] Jacqueline Bacon, *The Humblest May Stand Forth: Rhetoric, Empowerment, and Abolition* (Columbia: The University of South Carolina Press, 2002), 36–37.

[4] Isabella Oliver Sharp published *Poems, on Various Subjects* under the last name "Oliver." The few references to her that exist generally refer to her as Isabella Oliver, and she will be referred to as such here.

[5] Bacon, 30, 112.

[6] Steven Mintz, *Moralists and Modernizers: America's Pre-Civil War Reformers* (Baltimore: Johns Hopkins University Press, 1995), 23–24, 119–120.

[7] Emily Pendleton and Milton Ellis, *Philenia: The Life and Works of Sarah Wentworth Morton, 1759–1846* (Orono: University Press of Maine, 1931); Janet Wilson James, *Changing Ideas About Women in the United States, 1776–1825* (New York: Garland Publishing, 1981), 246. Morton's use of a penname was not an attempt to hide her identity as a writer, but a "stylish convention" practiced by men and women.

[8] Pendleton and Ellis, 56.

[9] Sarah Wentworth Apthorp Morton, "The Tears of Humanity," *Columbian Centinel*, Aug. 6, 1791. The poem was introduced with the lines "Occasioned by the loss of the question for the abolition of the slave trade, in the British Parliament." It was dedicated to "the BENIGNANT minority"—those brave members of parliament who had voted with William Wilberforce, unsuccessfully, to end the slave trade.

[10] James Basker, *Amazing Grace: An Anthology of Poems About Slavery, 1660–1810* (New Haven: Yale University Press, 2002), 18.

[11] Basker, 467.

[12] "The American Female Poets," *The North American Review* 68 (Apr. 1849).

[13] *Columbian Centinel,* Nov. 4, 1797. The reviewer praises the virtues of *Beacon Hill,* but sounds rather doubtful as to its reception: "'Beacon-hill' is certainly a work of great merit. We hope it will be extensively patronized by the citizens of America. But if it meet not the encouragement it deserves, it will nevertheless procure reputation for its author."

[14] James, 259.

[15] Emily Stipes Watts, *The Poetry of American Women from 1632 to 1945* (Austin: University of Texas Press, 1971), 63.

[16] Some sources give Oliver's date of birth as 1771, while other equally credible sources give the date as 1777. The discrepancy might be due to the fading of Oliver's grave marker.

[17] Robert Davidson, "To the Editor," *Poems, on Various Subjects* (Carlisle: A. Loudon, 1805), 3–5.

[18] James Hamilton, "Recollections of Men and Things in Penna, About 1800," *Two Hundred Years in Cumberland County*, ed. D.W. Thompson et al. (Carlisle: The Hamilton Library and Historical Association of Cumberland County, 1951), 94.

[19] Isabella Oliver, "A Morning Piece," *Poems, on Various Subjects* (Carlisle: A. Loudon, 1805), 42.

[20] Isabella Oliver, "Lucinda," *Poems, on Various Subjects* (Carlisle: A. Loudon, 1805), 147.

[21] See Genesis 9:19–29.

[22] "Memoir of Ann Alexander," *Friends' Review: A Religious, Literary and Miscellaneous Journal* 3, no. 22 and 23 (1850).

[23] Sheila Wright, *Friends in York: The Dynamics of Quaker Revival, 1780–1860* (Keele: Keele University Press, 1995), 45.

[24] Wright, 100.

[25] "Memoir of Ann Alexander."

[26] Wright, 103.

[27] Ralph R. Shaw and Richard H. Shoemaker, *American Bibliography: A Preliminary Checklist for 1805, Items 7819–9785* (New York: The Scarecrow Press, 1958); John Tebbel, *vol. 1: The Creation of an Industry, 1630–1865, A History of Book Publishing in the United States* (New York: R.R. Bowker, 1972), 508–509.

[28] Ira Berlin, *Many Thousands Gone: The First Two Centuries of Slavery in North America* (Cambridge: Harvard University Press, 1998), 308–309; Walter J. Fraser Jr., *Charleston! Charleston! The History of a Southern City* (Columbia: University of South Carolina Press, 1989), 177–186.

[29] John Lendrum, *A Concise and Impartial History of the American Revolution: to Which Is Prefixed, a General History of North and South America; Together with an Account of the Discovery and Settlement of North America, and a View of the Progress, Character, and Political State of the Colonies Previous to the Revolution. . . .* (Boston: Thomas and Andrews, 1795; repr. Trenton: James Oram, 1811), 211–212.

[30] Wright, 103.

"The African Chief"[1]

as reprinted in

𝔐𝔶 𝔐𝔦𝔫𝔡

AND

ITS THOUGHTS,

IN

SKETCHES, FRAGMENTS, AND ESSAYS;

——————

BY SARAH WENTWORTH MORTON,

OF DORCHESTER, MASS.

——————

"I stood among them, but not of them—
In a shroud of thoughts, which were not *their* thoughts."[2]

——————

BOSTON:

WELLS AND LILLY—COURT-STREET.

....

1823.

THE AFRICAN CHIEF.*

See how the black ship cleaves the main,
    High bounding o'er the dark blue wave,
Remurmuring with the groans of pain,
    Deep freighted with the princely slave!

Did all the Gods of Afric sleep,
    Forgetful of their guardian love,
When the white tyrants of the deep,
    Betrayed him in the palmy grove.

A Chief of *Gambia's*[3] golden shore,
    Whose arm the band of warriors led,
Or more—the lord of generous power,
    By whom the foodless poor were fed.

Does not the voice of reason cry,
    Claim the first right that nature gave,
From the red scourge of bondage fly,
    Nor deign to live a burdened slave.

Has not his suffering offspring clung,
    Desponding round his fettered knee;
On his worn shoulder, weeping hung,
    And urged one effort to be free!

His wife by nameless wrongs subdued,
    His bosom's friend to death resigned;
The flinty path-way drenched in blood;
    He saw with cold and phrenzied mind.

* Taken in arms, fighting for his freedom, and inhumanly butchered by his conquerors! This affecting event was fully delineated in the various Gazettes of that period. [Here and throughout, Morton's notes, which were originally printed as endnotes, have been transformed into footnotes.]

Strong in despair, then sought the plain,
    To heaven was raised his stedfast eye,
Resolved to burst the crushing chain,
    Or mid the battle's blast to die.

First of his race, he led the band,
    Guardless of danger, hurling round,
Till by his red avenging hand,
    Full many a despot stained the ground.

When erst *Messenia's*[*] sons oppressed,[4]
    Flew desperate to the sanguine field,
With iron cloathed each injured breast,
    And saw the cruel Spartan yield.

Did not the soul to heaven allied,
    With the proud heart as greatly swell,
As when the *Roman Decius*[5] died,
    Or when the *Grecian victim* fell.[†6]

Do later deeds quick rapture raise,
    The boon *Batavia's William* won,[7]
Paoli's[8] time-enduring praise,
    Or the yet greater *Washington!*

If these exalt thy sacred zeal,
    To hate oppression's mad controul,
For bleeding *Afric* learn to feel,
    Whose Chieftain claimed a kindred soul.

---

[*] The *Messenians* being conquered by the *Spartans*, and agreeably to the custom of the age, the miserable remnant led into slavery, under these circumstances were so inhumanly oppressed, that rising, and united in arms, they seized upon a Spartan fortress, and after innumerable injuries, inflicted and reciprocated, finally obtained their freedom.

[†] Leonidas.

Ah, mourn the last disastrous hour,
    Lift the full eye of bootless grief,
While victory treads the sultry shore,
    And tears from hope the captive Chief.

While the hard race of *pallid hue,*
    Unpracticed in the power to feel,
Resign him to the murderous crew,
    The horrors of the quivering wheel.[9]

Let sorrow bathe each blushing cheek,
    Bend piteous o'er the tortured slave,
Whose wrongs compassion cannot speak,
    Whose only refuge was the grave.

Notes

[1] Morton's "The African Chief" was first printed in 1792 in the *Columbian Centinel*, and reprinted in 1823 in Morton's *My Mind and Its Thoughts, in Sketches, Fragments, and Essays*. The text reprinted here is the 1823 version. Morton's note in the 1792 version reads: "Captured in arms at St. Domingo, fighting for his Freedom." Morton's notes, the date when the poem was first published, and the phrase "the horrors of the quivering wheel" found in stanza 14 suggest that the title character was loosely based on Vincent Ogé, a free mulatto who led a failed insurrection in St. Domingue in 1790 and was executed.

[2] Byron, George Gordon, Lord, *Childe Harold's Pilgramage. Canto the Third* (London, 1816), stanza 113.

[3] Modern-day Gambia surrounds the River Gambia, which flows into the Atlantic Ocean. Before the abolition of the slave trade by Great Britain and the United States in 1807 (put into effect in 1808), the River Gambia served as an important trade route, used also for exporting slaves.

[4] During the First and Second Messenian Wars in the eighth and seventh centuries BCE, Sparta conquered Messenia, a region in the southwestern Peloponnese, and turned the Messenians into helots, a status between slaves and citizens. Messenia regained its independence in 369 BCE.

[5] Gaius Messius Quintus Traianus Decius (d. 251): Emperor of Rome from 249 CE to his death in 251 CE. According to Christian accounts, he was the first Roman emperor to persecute Christians across the empire. Decius died in a battle against Cniva, king of the Goths.

[6] Leonidas (d. 480 BCE): King of Sparta in the fifth century BCE. He died valiantly, leading a Greek force defending the Thermopylae Pass against the Persian army.

[7] William I of Orange (1533–1584): Known as William the Silent, won independence from Spain for the northern provinces of the Netherlands in the 1570s.

[8] Pasquale di Paoli (1725–1807): Corsican patriot famous for his efforts to win Corsica's independence from Genoa in the eighteenth century.

[9] Morton refers to the wheel as an instrument of torture and/or execution. Vincent Ogé, the mulatto who led an uprising in St. Domingue in 1791, was tortured to death on the wheel.

BEACON HILL.

A Local Poem,

HISTORIC AND DESCRIPTIVE.

BOOK I.

Published according to Act of Congress.

Boston.

Printed by MANNING & LORING for the *AUTHOR*.

—

1797.

[Excerpt from *Beacon Hill*, Book I
by Sarah Wentworth Apthorp Morton]

VIRGINIA! blest beyond each bordering clime,
The noblest plume, that lifts the wing of time!—
Not that luxuriance decks her festive bowers,
While the rich weed[1] its curling fragrance pours;
That fatal weed, with many a blossom fair,
Was nursed by tears, and ripen'd in despair!—
Not that her ample skirts redundant spread,
And towering mountains crown her princely head;
The wasteful wilderness unheeded lies,
And round those heights the fiend of Slavery hies!—[2]
Yet thou, *Virginia*, fairest of the fair,
More bright than all thy radiant sisters are,
Shalt rise supreme, and every wreath of fame
Twine its rich foliage round thy *elder* name;*[3]
Since to those sovereign skies, that ruling earth,
An infant nation owes its brilliant *birth*;
Enlighten'd empires shall thy influence own,
And hail the clime, that bore a WASHINGTON!—
In age, in wisdom, and in glory blest,
Thou first-born daughter of the blooming west,
What happier fate can mark thy golden days!
What other hero win the voice of praise!
And yet thy shores two laurel'd leaders yield,
Brave as the foremost veterans of the field;
GATES,[4] train'd to war in *Britain's* regal band,
Now call'd to freedom bears her loved command,
While MERCER,[5] by the clans of *Scotia* bred,
A chosen corps with equal honor led.—

---

* "VIRGINIA was the first province settled by the English. It was colonized by
the influence of Sir *Walter Raleigh* under the reign of the *Virgin* Queen, *Elizabeth*,
from whom it derived its name.—The first motion for Independence was made
by *Richard Henry Lee*, member from that State, which is the largest in the Union."
LENDRUM.

—And next, neglectful of each pleasing care,
A young Marcellus[*][6] joins the growing war;
Led by his worth, the sons of Fortune roam
Through dreary wilds, and leave their happy home,
Where the bold *Chesapeak*,[7] by tempests borne,
Round many an island winds his moony horn,
Sees the rich land display its cultured green,
And grace the name of *Britain's* exiled Queen,—
Maria, hapless fair! to FORTUNE known
By each extreme, that marks her smile or frown,[†][8]
When, soaring high, she waves her silver plume,
Or points to earth, the scaffold and the tomb!
—Could birth, could beauty no protection claim,
Nor e'en thy glorious father's deathless fame!—
Yet shall the clime, with vernal blushes fair,
That hapless name in proud distinction wear,
And every trophy of her patriot-brave
Recal thy life, and triumph o'er the grave,
Till the bold race, by hardy valor crown'd,
Shall free those fields, and reap that laurel'd ground.—
—CHILD OF THE SUN, proud *Carolina*, rise!
And say what chief thy haughty hand supplies!
Canst thou contend for freedom, while yon vale
Pours its deep sorrows on the sultry gale!
Thus rise with patriot heart supremely brave,
Nor heed the scourge, that breaks thy shackled slave!—
What boots the fleecy field, and ricy mead,
If mid their bloom the culturing captive bleed!
Or what avails, that many a sumptuous dome

---

[*] General SMALLWOOD.

[†] MARYLAND was named in honor of *Henrietta Maria*, wife of Charles I. of England, and daughter of *Henry the Great*, of France. A corps of young men of the first fortune and distinction under General *Smallwood* joined the war from this State, and unhappily were nearly all cut off at the battle of Long-Island. *See* LENDRUM's *Selection*.

To every traveller yields a generous home,
If the rich banquet, and the costly cheer,
Are fan'd by sighs, and moisten'd with a tear!—
Thine is the grace of courts, the polish'd pride,
That bears no equal at its lordly side,*
On the poor artist bends its frowning eye,
And bids discarded commerce shrink and die;
But still the stranger gladdens at the feast,
An ever welcome, ever valued guest,
The *robe*, the *gown*, with PEAN's *healing art*,[9]
Shine at the board, and share the master's heart.—
When tired with toils of indolence and ease,
Sick at the sun, or shuddering at the breeze,
The listless fair, on silken sofas spread,
Hang the white hand, and droop the graceful head,
While thousand menials loiter in their train,
And speak the despot of a new domain.—
What leader, worthy of this lofty band,
What brave patrician claims the high command!
Thou, MOULTRIE![10] famed in camps, to glory known,
By deeds more brilliant, than a regal crown,—
Great in thyself,—most *noble* in thy fame,—
And *rich* in all, that worth and valor claim.—
—While in the south proud *Carolina* towers,
Famed for her palmy plains, and myrtle bowers,
Without her stately mind, and polish'd charms,
Her PALLID SISTER lifts her languid arms;—†[11]

---

* THE original constitution of *Carolina* was framed by the celebrated Mr. *Locke*, of an aristocratical form, establishing orders of Nobility. *Lend.* Vol. I. And although now its principles are those of a democratic Republic, there is no State in the Union, in which the distinction of rank and situation is so tenaciously observed: The planter disdains to associate with the mechanic, and even the merchant; yet their characteristic, though haughty, is hospitable, generous and enlightened.

† THE outlawed inhabitants of the west part of *North Carolina*, who had formerly denominated themselves *Regulators*, and under that character attempted to

When from her woods the *regulating band,*
Discarded children of their native land,
Urged by insidious power, and cherish'd hate,
Aim'd at her bleeding heart the bolts of fate,
She calls her *faithful sons* in bold array
To stem the torrent of their wasteful way;—
Raised at her voice, intrepid MOORE[12] appears,
Restores her hopes, and stills her patriot fears;
He guards the culture of her labor'd fields,
Whose sandy soil a golden vintage yields,
Whose native pine its spiky summit rears,
And pours profusion from its fragrant tears;
While *Health,* auspicious to their balmy stream,
Fills the loose breeze, and fans the sweltering beam,
O'er the wan cheek *her* vernal lily throws,
But bears to colder climes her ruddy rose.—
—An ardent youth the sultry race commands,
Where green *Savannah* folds the level lands,
And *Altimaha's*[13] sounding waters run
With headlong fury to the vertic sun,
Where the mail'd reptile of Egyptian Nile
From shore to shore directs his floating file.*
While, from the cavern of his clashing jaw,
The hands of death an hundred arrows draw,
He crops the verdure of the growing grain,
Or drags the wailing baby from the plain;
E'en while the watchful fisher reads the skies,

---

change the government of the colony, from a principle of revenge against the other citizens, who had opposed them in the field, were easily persuaded to join the royal standard at the beginning of the Revolution, when they were totally defeated by General *Moore,* and their brave commander, *McDonald,* was taken. LENDRUM.

* THE *alligators* or *crocodiles* of Georgia proceed through the lakes or rivers in large companies, like a file of soldiers, ranged under one chief, who is the largest and most ferocious of the party. The clashing jaws of these reptiles may be heard at a great distance. *See Bartram's Travels through the interior Parts of America.*

He feels his leaning bark unconscious rise,
Then whirl impetuous to the plunging wave,
Drink the salt surge, and dash the billowy grave.—
Yet round these shores prolific plenty twines,
Stores the thick field, and swells the clustering vines,
A thousand groves their glossy leaves unfold,
Where the rich orange rolls its ruddy gold,
China's green shrub, divine magnolia's bloom,*
With mingling odors fling their high perfume;—
A depth of forest, and a breadth of plain,
Screens the hot soil, and spreads the opening main,
Whence freighted fleets, with many a streamer gay,
To eastern empires bend their wealthy way,
While the blythe sons of jovial commerce stand
Round the high deck, and bless the parting land;—
Land last of Freedom! youngest child of Fame!
Graced with thy great Defender's glorious name,
Bright *Georgia,* hail!—Though fiery Summer pours
His fierce electric round thy blasted bowers,
While in black streams the turbid clouds descend,
And peals on peals the flashing concave rend,—
Though many a reptile rear its slimy brood
On the moist bosom of thy breezeless wood,—
Though *Afric* feel thee on her ravaged plain,†
And stay thy step, and stop thy hand in vain . . .

---

* THE *Tea-Plant* was introduced into *Georgia* by Mr. *Samuel Bowen,* about the year 1770. LENDRUM.

†GEORGIA for a long time after its first settlement opposed the importation of African slaves; but finally, influenced by the bad example of the neighboring colonies, she fell into the pernicious traffic, and the lands are now generally cultivated by that unhappy people. Georgia is the only colony that derived its entire settlement and support from the crown, and was the last to consent to Union and Independence. LENDRUM.

Notes

[1] Morton is probably referring to tobacco, since one of her main sources of information, John Lendrum's 1795 *A Concise and Impartial History of the American Revolution*, highlights the importance of tobacco as a "staple production" of Virginia.

[2] "Negro slavery was first introduced [in Virginia]; and has had a baneful effect upon the manners and morals of the people," John Lendrum, *A Concise and Impartial History of the American Revolution* (Boston: Thomas and Andrews, 1795; repr. Trenton: James Oran, 1811), 116.

[3] Morton's footnote refers to Sir Walter Raleigh (1552–1618), an English explorer who tried unsuccessfully to settle Virginia from 1584 to 1589, and Richard Henry Lee (1732–1794), a Virginia delegate to the Continental Congress.

[4] Born in Britain, Horatio Gates (1727–1806) fought for the patriots in the American Revolution. He was victorious over the British in the Battle of Saratoga, but was defeated in Camden, South Carolina.

[5] Born in Scotland, Hugh Mercer (1721–1777) served as a physician, colonel, and brigadier general with a Virginia regiment during the Revolutionary War. He was killed in 1777 at the battle of Princeton.

[6] Morton's footnote refers to William Smallwood (1732–1792), who led the First Maryland Regiment during the Revolutionary War, and saved the American army from disaster following the defeat of Horatio Gates in South Carolina. "Marcellus" probably refers to Marcus Claudius Marcellus (d. 208 BCE), a Roman general who showed considerable military prowess during the Second Punic War.

[7] The Chesapeake Bay is located between the eastern shore of Maryland on the east and the western shore of Maryland and then Virginia on the west, and extends from the mouth of the Susquehanna River out to the Atlantic Ocean.

[8] Queen Henrietta Maria, wife of Charles I (1625–1649), who granted the Maryland Charter to Lord Baltimore to found the colony as a settlement for Catholics from England. Henrietta Maria (1609–1669), French by birth and Roman Catholic, was unpopular, and fled to France during the English Civil War. Morton's reference in the footnote to a "corps of young men" probably refers to the battalion from Maryland commanded by William Smallwood, which joined forces with Washington's troops in the Battle of Long Island, a significant defeat for the patriots.

[9] Homer in *The Iliad* refers to Pean, or Paean, as a god of healing, elsewhere referred to as Apollo.

[10] William Moultrie (1730–1805) commanded a South Carolina regiment dur-

ing the Revolutionary War. Moultrie's troops repelled a British attack on Sullivan's Island in Charleston harbor, a success for which Congress gave Moultrie an official commendation.

[11] Donald McDonald (d. 1788), a Scottish officer in the British army who commanded Scots loyalists in North Carolina but was defeated by James Moore and his patriot militia at Moore's Creek Bridge.

[12] James Moore (1737–1777) was born in North Carolina and was regarded as the best military leader from that state. He led the patriots in a defeat of southern loyalists at Moore's Creek Bridge in North Carolina. He died soon after being given command of the Southern Department.

[13] "The whole territory between the rivers Savannah and Altamaha [was set aside for] the accommodation of poor people in Great Britain and Ireland, and for the farther security of Carolina," (Lendrum, 194). The Savannah River still forms the eastern border between Georgia and South Carolina.

"On Slavery"

as printed in

POEMS,

ON

VARIOUS SUBJECTS.

By ISABELLA OLIVER,

Of Cumberland County, Pennsylvania.

ALL hail, ye mighty masters of the lay,
Nature's true sons, the friends of men and truth!
Whose song, sublimely sweet, serenely gay,
Amus'd my childhood, and inform'd my youth.

BEATTIE'S MINSTREL.[1]

Carlisle:

FROM THE PRESS OF A. LOUDON,

(WHITEHALL.)

1805.

ON SLAVERY

AMONG the moral evils which disgrace
The page historic of the human race,
Slavery seems most to blacken the records;
It militates against our blessed Lord's
Divine instructions.² Is it not a shame
For any that assume the christian name,
Who say the influence of his blood extends
From sea to sea, to earth's remotest ends,
To trade in human flesh, to forge a chain
For those who may with them in glory reign?
But, independent of the christian light,³
Humanity is outrag'd, every right
Of human nature trampled to the ground;
By men who deify an empty sound,
And call it liberty, or what they please;
But God will visit for such crimes as these.
Behold the fruitful islands of the main;⁴
Where sweetness is extracted from the cane⁵
Where luscious fruits in rich profusion grow,
And streams of milk and honey us'd to flow;
The cords of slav'ry were so tighten'd there,
Its hapless victims could no longer bear;
But desperation work'd in every brain,
And gave them strength to break the iron chain.
A scene of terror and of blood ensues!
The bare idea petrifies the muse!
Here is a glass: let each oppressing state
Forsake their practice, or expect their fate.
Slavery's a very monster on the earth,
Which strangles every virtue in its birth:
From the first dawning of the human mind,
Children should be instructed to be kind;

To treat no human being with disdain,
Nor give the meanest insect useless pain:
Yet mark how babes and suckling learn to rack,
And trample down, the poor defenceless black;
Their little humours ample scope may have,
When only vented—on a wretched slave.
God's image[6] in his creature they deride,
And daily grow in indolence and pride,
With ignorance and cruelty combin'd;
A Slavery of the most ignoble kind!

    O ye, who make and execute the laws,
Exert your influence in so good a cause;
Pursue with zeal some well-arranged plan,
To stop this most unnat'ral trade in man:
This interesting object keep in view:
Much has been done, but much is still to do.
Forever honour'd be their names, who strive
To keep divine philanthropy alive:
But horror seizes every feeling mind,
To hear of depredation on mankind!
Till this inhuman commerce disappears,
Our country must claim kindred with Algiers.[7]
AMERICA! wipe out this dire disgrace,
Which stains the brightest glories of thy face.
'Twas thine against oppressive power to raise
A noble standard, and attract the gaze
Of the surrounding nations, who approve
Thy arduous struggle, rising from a love
Of liberty. Your rights you understood,
And rose, resolv'd like men to make them good;
Through every rank the gen'rous ardour ran;
The poorest lab'rer feels himself a man.
COLUMBIA'S[8] sons put forth their talents now;
Intrepid soldiers, starting from the plough,

A virtuous independence to secure,
Hunger and thirst and nakedness endure.
Such great occasions noble minds invite,
And bring conceal'd abilities to light;
Consummate statesmen in our councils rise,
Fit for their station, honest, brave, and wise;
Our gallant leaders in the martial field
To neither Greece nor Rome the laurels yield;
Nor were it just to pass Columbia's fair;
Who share the burden should the garland share.
Thy charms, O Liberty! their souls impress,
Behold them patriots even in their dress;
The graceful vestments of the most refin'd,
By their own hands have been with pleasure twin'd;
They throw the shuttle, and they mix the dye,
And ev'n the famed Spartan dames[9] outvie;
Their tenderness and modesty retain;
Gentle, not weak, they vigorously sustain,
Without a murmur, the severest toil;
With their fair hands they cultivate the soil;
Expos'd to summer's heat and winter's cold;
Prepare the fuel, and attend the fold;
To give the husband, brother, or the sire
To the hard duties which the times require.
The world can testify this picture true;
From recent facts the muse her colours drew.
But ah! how soon those glowing colours fade!
The sons of Afric form a dismal shade:
Each southern state unnumber'd slaves commands,
Who steel their hearts, and enervate their hands.
There knotted whips in dreadful peals resound,
While blood and sweat flow mingled to the ground.
So fame reports, and rising in her ire
She adds, that some beneath the lash expire.
Ah stop! inhuman! why provoke the rod,

The dreadful vengeance of an angry God!
Behold with trembling the outstretched hand
Of incens'd justice lifted o'er the land!
For crimes like yours, and their pernicious brood,
(For these are parent-sins, and taint the blood)[10]
Malignant fevers through the land are sent,[11]
To punish sin, and lead us to repent;
But if these warnings we refuse to mind,
A train of evils follow close behind;
If we may credit God's eternal word,
And those examples left upon record.
Are these the blest abodes of liberty!
Is this the generous race that would be free!
The power to whom you fancied honours pay,
From scenes like these with horror turns away!
Wherever genuine liberty is found,
She copies heaven in shedding blessings round.
Should not this fruitful, this salubrious clime
Inspire us with the gen'rous and sublime?
Our hills appear for contemplation made,
Our lofty forests form a noble shade;
These seem the native haunts of liberty:
Was not the wild unletter'd Indian free?
Alas! the mournful truth must be confess'd,
Ferocious passions triumph'd in his breast;
There gloomy superstition's terrors reign'd;
Insidious wiles his manly courage stain'd;
While sloth and ignorance in fetters bind
The nobler workings of the savage mind.
See these by Europe's fairer sons displac'd,
With useful arts and polish'd manners grac'd!
Now sturdy labour, with incessant toil
Clears the rude wild, and cultivates the soil.
As art's first sample clapboard roofs appear;
But soon a neat convenient house they rear;

At length a stately dome attracts the eyes;
And seat with seat in taste and beauty vies.
Now liberal sciences the land pervade,
And philosophic musings court the shade.
The fairest traits of liberty we find,
Where equal laws to peace and order bind,
And true religion elevates the mind.
Oh, slavery! thou hell-engender'd crime!
Why spoil this beauteous country in her prime,
Corrupt her manners, enervate her youth!
Blast the fair buds of justice, mercy, truth!
But, Europe! know, to thy eternal shame,
From thee at first this foul contagion came;
Before we to a nation's stature grew,
We learn'd this trade, this barb'rous trade, from you:
Should not we now exert a noble pride,
And lay your follies, and your crimes, aside?
Yet not so vain, or self-sufficient be,
As not to copy excellence of thee.
How many futile reasons have been given
For mixing God and mammon,[12] sin and heaven!
Some say, they are of Canaan's cursed race,[13]
By God ordain'd to fill this servile place:
Was then their lineage fully ascertain'd,
Before they in the cruel hold were chain'd?
Before the tenderest ties of human life
Were torn asunder; the beloved wife
Dragged without mercy from her husband's breast,
And the sweet babes they mutually caress'd,
Carried like cattle;—(Let it not be told!)
By christians too, to be to christians sold?
Their lineage prov'd—it were of no avail;
Here all attempts at palliation fail.
In Joseph's case[14] we may a parallel see;
Sent into Egypt by divine decree,

His brethren's evil, God intends for good,
Yet they, as guilty, in his presence stood.
Some plead the precedent of former times,
And bring example in, to sanction crimes:
Greece had her Helots,[15] Gibeonites the Jew;[16]
Must then Columbia have her Negroes too!
By men who by his spirit were inspir'd,
To teach us what our blessed Lord requir'd,
Rules have been given to regulate our lives,
As subjects, husbands, parents, children, wives;
Masters and servants due directions have;[17]
But show a single lesson to a slave.
Those heavenly doctrines have a liberal aim,
And practis'd, soon would abrogate the name.
Our blessed Lord descended to unbind
Those chains of darkness which enslave the mind;
He draws the veil of prejudice aside,
To cure us of our selfishness and pride:
These once remov'd, then Afric's sable race
No more among the brutal herd we place:
Are they not blest with intellectual powers,
Which prove their souls are excellent as ours?
The same immortal hopes to all are given,
One common Saviour and one common heaven.
When these exalted views th'ascendant gain,
Fraternal love will form a silken chain,
Whose band, encircling all the human race,
Will join the species in one large embrace.

Notes

[1] James Beattie, "The Minstrel: Or, The Progress of Genius: A Poem. Book the First" (London: E.C. Dilly, 1771).

[2] "Therefore all things whatsoever ye would that men should do to you, do ye even so to them: for this is the law and the prophets." See Matthew 7:12. This and all subsequent Biblical references are from the Authorized (King James) Version of the Bible.

[3] See Matthew 5:14–16, in which Jesus says that His followers are the light of the world.

[4] The islands of the West Indies.

[5] Sugarcane, the dominant crop in the West Indies, cultivated by plantation slavery.

[6] Genesis 1:27 tells of how God created man in His image.

[7] Algeria, part of the Barbary States of North Africa. Captivity narratives of white slaves held in North Africa were well known during the late eighteenth and early nineteenth centuries.

[8] Another name for America, after Christopher Columbus.

[9] Inhabitants of Sparta, a city-state in southern Greece, were known for their austere lifestyles. Spartan girls engaged in the same physical training as boys, and Spartan women were held up as examples of motherhood in antiquity.

[10] Oliver refers to God's declaration in Exodus 34:7 that children will be punished for the sins of their parents.

[11] Oliver may be referring to the yellow fever and cholera epidemics that struck U.S. cities up and down the Atlantic seaboard. Yellow fever struck Philadelphia particularly hard in the 1790s with reports and death counts appearing in newspapers as far away as Boston.

[12] See Matthew 6:24 and Luke 16:13.

[13] See Genesis 9:19–29 in which Noah curses Canaan, Ham's son: "a servant of servants shall he be unto his brethren." Slavery's defenders used this story to argue that the Bible sanctions bondage, and claimed that blacks were the descendants of Canaan.

[14] Genesis 37–50. Joseph's brothers sold him into slavery in Egypt, but Pharaoh appointed him second in command. During a famine, Joseph's brothers came to Egypt for food, and did not recognize Joseph as governor and keeper of the granaries.

[15] Oliver refers to the Spartans' subjugation of the Messenians in the seventh and eighth centuries BCE: the Spartans turned the Messenians into helots, in a class only slightly better than slavery.

[16] Joshua 9. The Gibeonites tricked Joshua into forming a treaty, and when Joshua realized this, he made the Gibeonites serve his congregation.

[17] Oliver refers to passages such as Ephesians 5:22–33 and Colossians 3:18–4:1, in which wives, husbands, children, fathers, servants, and masters are instructed in how to treat one other.

AN ADDRESS

TO THE

INHABITANTS

OF

CHARLESTON,

SOUTH CAROLINA.

———

PHILADELPHIA:

PRINTED BY KIMBER, CONRAD, & CO.

———

1805.

AN ADDRESS
TO THE
INHABITANTS OF CHARLESTON,
SOUTH CAROLINA

SINGULAR as it may appear to many of you to be addressed by an unknown female, from a distant land, after this manner; I trust I am actuated therein by no other motives than the influence of that gospel love, shed abroad in my heart, which induces me, at times, with earnest solicitude, to crave the present and everlasting well-being of all my fellow-creatures. Impressed with these feelings, and an apprehension of duty, I have been engaged to leave divers of the nearest and tenderest connexions in life, for a season, to visit many of my friends, in religious profession, and others, on this continent, as my way opened. But not apprehending I am required to pay you a personal visit[1] (though I have felt my mind engaged on your behalf, in a very peculiar manner) I believe it right thus to call your attention to some considerations, which have appeared to me awfully important, as they regard your real interest, both in time and in eternity. In passing along through some of the southern states, my mind has been painfully affected at the sight of numbers of my fellow-creatures, of the African race, deprived of their natural liberty, and of almost every means of improvement of those faculties bestowed upon *them* as well as ourselves, for the noblest of purposes, by that all-wise and bountiful Creator, in whom "we live and move and have our being;"* and who, we are told by the great apostle of the Gentiles,[2] "hath made of one blood all nations of men, to dwell on all the face of the earth, and hath determined the times before appointed, and the bounds of their habitation."† For any of us, his dependent creatures, to force them from the place thus appointed by a gracious and superintending Providence, appears to be an infringement on the order and œconomy of this part of his rational creation, for which the aggressors must be accountable at his awful tribunal, who is infinite in justice as well as in mercy. I lament—exceedingly lament, that a custom, so barbarous as well as so repugnant to every principle of humanity and justice, as the

---

* Acts xvii. 28.   † Acts xvii. 26.

African Slave-Trade, should be continued in this or any other nation, and by involving them in the greatest of national crimes, lay them open to those national punishments, which must be expected, as a just retribution for the blood of thousands of those innocent people, which has long cried for vengeance, and whose cry has reached the ears of the Lord of Sabbaoth.[3] What then must be the expectation of those who support this horrid traffic, by purchasing and continuing in slavery those who have never forfeited that right of liberty they derive, with ourselves, from the one *Universal Parent?* What, but "a certain fearful looking for of judgment and fiery indignation,"[*] when he standeth up to plead who hath declared, that "for the oppression of the poor, for the sighing of the needy he will arise,"[†] who is undoubtedly able to deliver the oppressed from the hand of him that is mightier than he! While such also continue the profession of christianity, and are in the performance of what are deemed religious duties and ceremonies, may not these come under the same description as those spoken of by the prophet,[4] when he says, "ye fast for strife and debate, and to smite with the fist of wickedness!"[§] May all such, therefore, have their spiritual eyes so anointed, as clearly to discover that the fast which the Lord "hath chosen, is to loose the bands of wickedness, to undo the heavy burdens, and to let the oppressed go free, and that ye break every yoke: when thou seest the naked that thou cover him, and hide not thyself from thine own flesh: and if thou draw out thy soul to the hungry, and satisfy the afflicted soul, then shall thy light rise in obscurity, and thy darkness be as the noon-day."[‡] That this may become the engagement, and consequent experience of all those concerned in this sinful traffic, and of the inhabitants of Charleston in particular, that so you may "break off your sins by righteousness, and your iniquities by shewing mercy to the poor, if it may be a lengthening of your tranquillity,"[**] and the means of awful, and I apprehend, impending judgments *being averted,* is the sincere desire of one who wishes health and salvation to the souls of all mankind.

ANN ALEXANDER.

Philadelphia, 3d Mo. 1ˢᵗ, 1805.

---

[*] Heb. x. 27.   [†] Psal. xii. 5.   [§] Isa. lviii. 4.   [‡] Isa. lviii. 6, 7, 10.

[**] Dan. iv. 27.

Notes

[1] Alexander is known to have traveled to South Carolina, but her statement here suggests that she had not visited Charleston.

[2] The apostle Paul, author of the book of Acts.

[3] "Sabaoth" is a Hebrew word meaning "hosts."

[4] "The prophet" refers to Isaiah.

MINUTES

OF THE

PROCEEDINGS

OF A

Convention of Delegates

FROM THE

ABOLITION SOCIETIES

Eſtabliſhed in different Parts of the United States,

ASSEMBLED AT

PHILADELPHIA,

ON THE FIRST DAY OF JANUARY, ONE THOUSAND SEVEN
HUNDRED AND NINETY-FOUR, AND CONTINUED, BY
ADJOURNMENTS, UNTIL THE SEVENTH DAY
OF THE SAME MONTH, INCLUSIVE.

PHILADELPHIA:

PRINTED BY ZACHARIAH POULSON, JUNR. NUMBER EIGHTY,
CHESNUT-STREET, EIGHT DOORS BELOW THIRD-STREET.

M DCC XCIV.

[8]

A CONVENTION OF DELEGATES FROM
THE ABOLITION SOCIETIES

Introduction by Jennifer Randazzo, University of Notre Dame

In the minds of many people, the story of America's abolition movement originates in the nineteenth century with William Lloyd Garrison. The radical sense of immediacy that defined the Garrisonians has been allowed to characterize the whole of the American abolition movement, from its beginnings up through the Civil War. The *Minutes of the Proceedings of a Convention of Delegates from the Abolition Societies* challenges this traditional narrative. The 1794 publication shows that American abolitionism has roots that stretch back much further than the nineteenth century, and that in the early years the movement was characterized by a variety of approaches ranging from immediate emancipation to various states of gradualism. By recording the deliberations of representatives of nine different anti-slavery societies from six different states (Connecticut, Delaware, Maryland, New York, New Jersey, and Pennsylvania), meeting in a weeklong convention in 1794, this text provides a window in on the breadth and intensity of the anti-slavery activity in America in the 1790s.

The state abolition societies, which began to appear in the 1780s and 1790s, and which would endure well into the nineteenth century, played a vital role in publicizing and organizing the abolitionist cause in this early period of the movement. The first abolition society, and the model for the formation of subsequent societies, was founded in Pennsylvania in 1775. Though some prominent non-Quakers such as Benjamin Franklin and Benjamin Rush served as presidents of the Society, it was primarily a Quaker organization and had its roots in earlier Quaker efforts to protect freed slaves.[1] The Revolution forced the Society into a temporary hiatus, but in the mid-1780s, the suicides of two blacks who had been illegally enslaved led to the reactivation of what became the Pennsylvania Society, for Promoting the Abolition of Slavery, and the Relief of Free Negroes, Unlawfully Held in Bondage.

This group had a far-reaching impact on the larger abolition movement. The Pennsylvania Abolition Society (PAS) soon urged people in other states to form abolition societies of their own, and, because the PAS was the first such society, it set the precedent for what such organizations might look like, how they might conduct themselves, and what their goals might be. One of the defining characteristics of the PAS agenda was gradual rather than immediate emancipation. The term "abolition of slavery," as included in the official title of the resurrected PAS, was derived from a 1780 Pennsylvania law, which provided for mandatory gradual emancipation. The other state abolition societies followed suit in adopting this gradualist stance. By influencing the other state abolition societies in this way, Pennsylvania set the tone for the entire eighteenth-century abolition movement.

In 1793, the New York Manumission Society proposed that all abolition societies send delegates to a convention so that an anti-slavery petition might be prepared and sent to Congress. The convention took place the following year, January 1–7, 1794. Delegates representing nine abolition societies, from six states (a tenth society, in Virginia, asked to be represented by delegates from Pennsylvania), assembled in Philadelphia with the aim of producing a united voice against slavery that would be heard by Congress, the state legislatures, and the citizens of the United States. Like the model PAS, the delegates' aims for the convention had to balance moral urgency and political practicalities. The result, inevitably, was an overarching sense of moderation. The convention's primary demand of Congress involved prohibiting the trafficking of slaves from U.S. seaports, but the delegates recognized (and accepted) that Congress did not possess the power to prohibit the importation of slaves into the United States.[2]

During the four years preceding the convention, abolition societies had been devoting much time and energy to preparing petitions for Congress, encouraging the legislative body to use its powers to restrict the slave trade. This focus on petitioning Congress as a technique of political action was a result of a 1790 report that had clarified the receptiveness of the House of Representatives to petitions dealing with slavery. In the 1790 episode, Quakers from Pennsylvania and New York had petitioned Congress to take action against the slave trade. Hostilities from Southern congressmen led the petitions to be laid aside, but the legislators were soon overwhelmed by an even more vehement petition from the PAS, signed by Benjamin Franklin. The House voted 43 to 14 to send both petitions to a select committee, which, significantly, included no representatives from the deep South. Three weeks later, the committee presented a report, which in its final revised form as accepted by the committee of the whole, essentially defined the federal government's power with respect to slavery.[3] Like the Constitution, the report maintained that Congress could not place prohibitions on the slave trade before 1808. It also stated that Congress could not "interfere in the emancipation of slaves, or in the treatment of them within any of the States."

Though the report limited congressional power in these ways, it also asserted three powers of Congress: first, Congress could restrain American citizens from supplying foreign lands with slaves from Africa; second, it could prohibit foreigners from fitting out slave trade vessels in American ports; and third, it could regulate the shipboard treatment of any slaves imported into the United States. Moreover, though it had no binding effect since the Senate refused even to consider the anti-slavery petitions, the House report of 1790 encouraged Quakers and other abolitionists to continue sending petitions to Congress, urging it to make full use of the powers asserted in the report.[4] It was on these grounds that the 1794 convention of delegates appealed to Congress, affirming that they, as anti-slavery activists, would "not exceed the constitutional powers of Congress" in shaping and articulating their demands.

The results of the 1794 abolitionist convention were mixed. Its greatest success, according to a report published the following year, was that in March of 1794, Congress passed "An Act to Prohibit the Carrying on of the Slave-Trade from the United States to Any Foreign Place or Country."[5] At the state level a qualified success was that Connecticut's House of Representatives passed a bill to abolish slavery. However, the bill did not obtain a majority in the legislative council, and did not ultimately pass into law. Still more disappointingly, petitions sent to the Delaware, New York, Maryland, and Virginia legislatures had no apparent effect.[6]

The minutes of this 1794 Philadelphia convention attest to the existence of a nationally based anti-slavery organization decades before the more widely recognized abolition movement of the nineteenth century spearheaded by William Lloyd Garrison, Frederick Douglass, and so many others. That six of the thirteen states (and two of them southern states) sent delegates to the convention testifies to the vitality of the abolition movement in the eighteenth century. This pamphlet enables us to examine closely the specific ideals and aims of eighteenth-century abolitionists who, however frustrated in the short term, pursued a vision of America that would not materialize in any meaningful degree until 1865.

Notes

[1] David Brion Davis, *The Problem of Slavery in the Age of Revolution* (New York: Oxford University Press, 1999), 216.

[2] Leo H. Hirsch Jr. "New York and the National Slavery Problem," *The Journal of Negro History* 16, no. 4 (October 1931): 454.

[3] Don Edward Fehrenbacher, *The Slaveholding Republic: An Account of the United States Government's Relations to Slavery*, ed. Ward M. McAfee (New York: Oxford University Press, 2001), 138.

[4] Fehrenbacher, 139.

[5] *Minutes of the Proceedings of the Second Convention of Delegates from the Abolition Societies Established in Different Parts of the United States, Assembled at Philadelphia, on the Seventh Day of January, One Thousand Seven Hundred and Ninety-Five, and Continued, by Adjournments, until the Fourteenth Day of the Same Month, Inclusive* (Philadelphia: Zachariah Poulson, 1795), Manuscripts, Archives and Rare Books Division, Schomburg Center for Research in Black Culture (hereafter cited as American Convention for Promoting the Abolition of Slavery).

[6] American Convention for Promoting the Abolition of Slavery, 17.

MINUTES

OF THE

PROCEEDINGS

OF A

Convention of Delegates

FROM THE

ABOLITION SOCIETIES

Established in different Parts of the United States,

ASSEMBLED AT

PHILADELPHIA,

ON THE FIRST DAY OF JANUARY, ONE THOUSAND SEVEN
HUNDRED AND NINETY-FOUR, AND CONTINUED, BY
ADJOURNMENTS, UNTIL THE SEVENTH DAY
OF THE SAME MONTH, INCLUSIVE.

———

PHILADELPHIA:

PRINTED BY ZACHARIAH POULSON, JUNR.[1] NUMBER EIGHTY,
CHESNUT-STREET, EIGHT DOORS BELOW THIRD-STREET.

M DCC XCIV.

MINUTES

OF THE

PROCEEDINGS

OF A

Convention of Delegates.

In Convention of Delegates, from the Societies established, in different parts of the United States, for promoting the abolition of slavery, assembled at the City Hall, in the city of Philadelphia, January 1, 1794, it appeared, by the credentials delivered in, that the following persons had been duly appointed to represent their respective Societies in this Convention:

Connecticut Society. [2]
Uriah Tracy.[3]

New-York Society. [4]
Peter Jay Munro,[5]
Moses Rogers,
Thomas Franklin, junior,
William Dunlap.

New-Jersey Society. [6]
Joseph Bloomfield,[7]
William Coxe, junior,
John Wistar,[8]
Robert Pearson,
Franklin Davenport.[9]

Pennsylvania Society [10]
William Rogers,[11]
William Rawle,[12]
Samuel Powel Griffitts,[13]
Robert Patterson,[14]
Samuel Coates,[15]
Benjamin Rush.[16]

Delaware Society.[17]
Warner Mifflin,[18]
Isaiah Rowland,
Joseph Hodgson,
John Pemberton.[19]

Wilmington Society (State of Delaware.)[20]
Joseph Warner,
Isaac H. Starr,
Robert Coram.

Maryland Society.[21]
Samuel Sterett,
James Winchester,[22]
Joseph Townsend,[23]
Adam Fonerdon,
Jesse Hollingsworth.

Chester-town Society (State of Maryland.)[24]
Joseph Wilkinson,
James Maslin,
Abraham Ridgely.

Of whom the following appeared and took their seats, *viz.*
Uriah Tracy,
Thomas Franklin, junior,
William Dunlap,
Joseph Bloomfield,
William Coxe, junior,
Robert Pearson,
William Rogers,
William Rawle,
Samuel Powel Griffitts,
Robert Patterson,
Samuel Coates,
Benjamin Rush,
Warner Mifflin,

> Isaiah Rowland,
> Joseph Hodgson,
> John Pemberton,
> Joseph Warner,
> Isaac H. Starr,
> Samuel Sterett,
> Joseph Townsend,
> Joseph Wilkinson,
> Abraham Ridgely.

Joseph Bloomfield was elected President of the Convention.

John McCree, one of the Secretaries of the Pennsylvania Abolition Society, was appointed Secretary, and Joseph Fry, Doorkeeper.

Agreed, That all questions, which shall come before this Convention, be decided by a majority of the votes of the members present.

Benjamin Rush, William Dunlap, Samuel Sterett, William Rawle, and Warner Mifflin, were appointed a committee to report the objects proper for the consideration of this Convention, and the best plan for carrying the same into execution.

Adjourned.

JANUARY SECOND.

Adam Fonerdon and Jesse Hollingsworth, two of the Delegates from the Maryland Society, appeared and took their seats

Absalom Baird, delegated to represent the Washington Society in Pennsylvania,[25] appeared, produced his credentials, and took his seat.

A letter, directed to the Convention, from Robert Pleasants, Chairman of the committee of correspondence of the Virginia Society,[26] was presented and read. By this letter it appears, that Samuel Pleasants and Israel Pleasants, of the city of Philadelphia, were appointed to represent that Society, in this Convention; or, in case of their declining or being prevented from acting, the Convention were left at liberty to nominate two other members as their representatives.

Whereupon,

Resolved, That as information, and an unreserved comparison of one another's sentiments, relative to the important cause in which we are severally engaged, are our principal objects; and as the persons appointed by the Virginia Society, are not citizens of that state, nor members of that Society—to admit them, or, according to their proposal, for us to elect others as their representatives, would be highly improper.

In this letter was enclosed an authentic account of several vessels lately fitted out in Virginia, for the African slave-trade.

The President was directed to acknowledge the receipt of this letter, to inform the Virginia Society of the resolution of the Convention thereon, and to thank them for the above interesting information.

Benjamin Rush, from the committee appointed to bring in a report on the objects proper for the consideration of this Convention, and the best plan for carrying the same into execution, produced one, which was being considered and amended, was adopted as follows, *viz.*

First, That a memorial be presented to Congress, praying that Body to prohibit, by law, the citizens of the United States, from carrying on a commerce, in slaves, for the supply of foreign nations; and, also, to prohibit foreigners from fitting their ships in the ports of the United States, for the purpose of carrying on the slave-trade.

Second, That memorials and petitions be presented to the Legislatures of such of the states as have not yet passed laws to prohibit the importation of slaves—to enact laws for that purpose; and, also, to the Legislatures of the individual states—to prevent slaves from being forcibly carried away; and to grant to such of them as have been, or may be emancipated, such a participation in civil privileges, as, by the diffusion of knowledge among them, they may, from time to time, be qualified to enjoy.

Third, That addresses be sent to the different Abolition Societies, recommending to them to continue their zeal and exertions, in behalf of such of our African brethren as are yet in bondage; also, to use their utmost endeavours to have the children of the free and other Africans, instructed in common literature—in the principles of virtue and religion, and afterwards in useful mechanical arts; thereby to prepare them for becoming good citizens of the United States.

Fourth, That an address be written, and published to the citizens of the

United States, to impress upon them, in the most forcible manner, the obligations of justice, humanity and benevolence towards our African brethren, whether in bondage or free, and to request their concurrence with us in all the objects of the present Convention.

Fifth, That it be recommended to the different Abolition Societies, to appoint Delegates to meet in Convention, at Philadelphia, on the first Wednesday of January, 1795, and on the same day, in every year afterwards, until the great objects of their original association be accomplished.[27]

The following committees were then appointed, *viz.*

William Rawle, William Rogers, and William Dunlap, to prepare a memorial to Congress, as proposed in the first section of the above report.

Samuel Sterett, William Rawle, and William Dunlap, to prepare memorials to the different Legislatures, as proposed in the second section.

Samuel P. Griffitts, William Coxe, junior, and Abraham Ridgely, to prepare addresses to the several Abolition Societies, as proposed in the third section.

Benjamin Rush, Warner Mifflin, and Isaac H. Starr, to prepare an address to the citizens of the United States, as proposed in the fourth section.

Adjourned.

JANUARY THIRD.

Samuel Sterett, from the committee appointed to prepare memorials to the Legislatures of the different states, presented two essays; one to be presented to the Legislatures of such of the states, as have not passed laws to prohibit the importation of slaves; and the other to be presented to the Legislatures of the individual states, who have not abolished domestic slavery; which were read, and ordered to lie on the table.[28]

Adjourned.

JANUARY FOURTH.

SAMUEL P. Griffitts, from the committee appointed for the purpose, reported an address to the different Abolition Societies; which was read, and ordered to lie on the table.

Benjamin Rush, from the committee appointed for the purpose, reported an address to the citizens of the United States; which was read, and ordered to lie on the table.

The memorial, addressed to the states who have not enacted laws to prohibit the importation of slaves, was read a second time, and, being considered, was, after some amendments, agreed to as follows, *viz.*

To the   *of the*
State of

The memorial and petition of the Delegates, from the several Societies, formed in different parts of the United States, for promoting the abolition of slavery, in Convention assembled at Philadelphia, on the first day of January, 1794.

Respectfully shew,

That, actuated by a desire to vindicate the honour of the United States, the rights of man, and the dignity of human nature, the Abolition Societies, in various and distant parts of the Union, have delegated your memorialists, to consider of, and endeavour to promote, such plans as may tend to diminish the number of slaves in the United States, meliorate their situation, and eventually eradicate an evil, entailed upon us by our ancestors; which must, as long as it exists, be considered as a dishonourable stain upon a country, the basis of whole political happiness is man's equal rights.

We, therefore, earnestly entreat you, to take into consideration the propriety and necessity of enacting laws, to prohibit the importation of slaves into your state, from any foreign country, or from any neighbouring state.

We presume not here to expatiate, to the Representatives of an enlightened people, on the injustice, immorality, and dreadful tendency of the slave-trade; fully persuaded that men, in your respectable situation, are thinking men, and that all who reflect on this subject must have been long convinced of these truths. But, Gentlemen, the evil exists, and surely it is well worthy of your consideration; it is an evil of great magnitude, and to prevent its growth, and gradually to destroy it, is an object of weighty import.

Permit us then respectfully to suggest, that the first step to be taken is to prohibit an accumulation of the evil, by any further importation. Many of your sister states have adopted this measure, and have not found any disadvantages arising therefrom. On the contrary, they have shewn their approbation of the measure, on trial, by enacting subsequent laws, giving to the first additional force and efficacy.

Your memorialists therefore hope, that, on consideration, you will add your state to the number of those which prohibit the importation of slaves; and thus contribute to abolish a practice, no less destructive to the interests of the United States, than to the general cause of humanity.

Instead of the last paragraph, the following was agreed to be substituted in the memorial to be presented to the Legislature of South Carolina, *viz.*

Your memorialists therefore hope, that, on consideration, you will make perpetual the law which you have already enacted for the above purpose; thereby adding your state to the number of those which totally prohibit the importation of slaves, and thus contribute to abolish a practice, no less destructive to the interests of the United States, than to the general cause of humanity.

The memorial addressed to the individual states, who have not yet abolished domestic slavery, was read a second time; and, being considered and amended, was agreed to as follows, *viz.*

To the   of the
        State of

The memorial and petition of the Delegates from the several Societies, formed in different parts of the United States, for promoting the abolition of slavery, in Convention assembled at Philadelphia, on the first day of January, 1794.

Respectfully shew,

THAT, having been appointed and convened for the general purposes of considering and endeavouring to suggest the most eligible plans for promoting the abolition of slavery; and, where its suppression cannot be obtained, to effect its alleviation, they have been unavoidably led to contemplate, how much remains in the power of the Legislature to perform.

It has, therefore, become their duty, respectfully to represent to your House, some of those evils which are still permitted to continue; and, in the name of fellow-men, to solicit its protection, its assistance, and its justice.

Some of the principal evils, foremost in the group of calamities, incident to the practice of slavery, your memorialists take the liberty of specifying.

Negroes, considered merely as subjects of property, are frequently carried off, by force, from their dearest connections, and transported to places, where even the severity of their former bondage is encreased; where a new climate, rigid laws, and despotic manners, render their despair complete.

As subjects of property, they likewise become the objects of plunder; and the evils already mentioned, are aggravated by the violence with which they are executed.

Until a radical abolition of slavery itself, by exploding the general opinion, that the colour of a man is evidence of his deprivation of the rights of man, shall afford more effectual security, it is presumed, that the legislative protection of absolute prohibitions, and of adequate penalties, may be reasonably expected.

The voice of reason, and the impulse of humanity, always at war with injustice, gradually tend to the emancipation of slaves; but laws, often made in earlier times, or for different objects, occasionally interpose between the intention and the act. To enumerate those obstacles to individual emancipation which still remain, sometimes obvious, and sometimes concealed in the mass of municipal regulations, would exceed the reasonable bounds of the present application; but, with a knowledge of their existence, and a sense of their injustice, your memorialists respectfully unite a request, that individual emancipation may, if not promoted by encouragements, at least be relieved from incidental penalties.

Yet, in breaking the fetters, and removing the sorrows of slavery, what do we effect, if the new-made man is relieved from the power of one, only to be sensible of his hopeless inferiority to all? As the opinions of men continue to be regulated, we know, that the negro has little to expect from the distribution of public functions;—still there are certain rights, not privileges, certain claims, not favours, to which, we conceive, legislative justice might safely admit him.

Of what use is his hard-earned property, if the law does not spread its defence around him? Or, how is his liberty secured, if he loses little more than the name of a slave? Donations so ineffectual, and benevolence so incomplete, can only excite dissatisfaction, and suppress industry. To acquire an useful member of the community, we should hold up to his view a participation in its privileges. We promote industry, by rewarding it, and encourage knowledge, by rendering it the means of perceiving happiness.

In addition to the objects already mentioned, your memorialists, therefore, respectfully solicit the Legislature to grant to such as have been, or may be emancipated, such a participation in civil privileges, as, by the diffusion of knowledge among them, they may, from time to time, be qualified to enjoy.

Instead of the three last paragraphs, the following was agreed to be substituted, in the memorial to be presented to the several Legislatures of the states of Delaware, New-Jersey, New-York, Connecticut, and Rhode-Island, *viz.*[99]

Our present application to the Legislature of terminates with these requests:

We have observed, and we acknowledge, with pleasure, the liberality of its constitution, and the humanity of its laws.

As the prejudices, which those laws were originally intended to combat, are gradually dispelled, their useful effects will become more obvious and permanent. Liberality and humanity will extend from the archives of your state to the practice of your citizens. It will be confessed, that none of your provisions, avowing and securing the rights of fellow-creatures, ought to excite repentance or discourage imitation. It will be found, that an increase of the useful qualities of the African citizen, will keep pace with the kindness and protection of which he partakes; and, in future, the dignified office of the Legislature, will not be to repeal or refrain, but to enlarge and enforce, the provisions in his favour.

And in the memorial to be presented to the Legislature of the state of Pennsylvania, the following paragraph was agreed to be substituted, *viz.*

To the Legislature of *that state* which, in favour of the unhappy African, first dispelled the clouds of prejudice, and first extended the hand of consolation, no further request, on our part, at present, remains. We have observed, and we acknowledge with pleasure, the liberality of its constitution, and the humanity of its laws. We have seen that the effect of none of their provisions, avowing and securing the rights of fellow-creatures, has excited repentance, or discouraged imitation; we have witnessed an increase of the useful qualities in the African citizen, keeping pace with the kindness and protection of which he partakes; and we have found the legislative attention employed, not in repealing and restraining, but in enlarging and enforcing, its former provisions in his favour.

JANUARY SIXTH.

William Rogers, from the committee appointed for the purpose, reported a memorial to Congress, which was read, and ordered to lie on the table.

The address to the Abolition Societies was read a second time, and, being considered and amended, was agreed to as follows, *viz.*

To the   *Society for promoting the abolition of Slavery, &c.*

I T is with peculiar pleasure we inform you, that the Convention of Delegates, from most of the Abolition Societies formed in the United States, met in this city, have, with much unanimity, gone through the business which came before them. The advantages to be derived from this meeting are so evident, that we have agreed earnestly to recommend to you, that a similar meeting be annually convened, until the great object of our association—the liberty of our fellowmen—shall be fully and unequivocally established.

To obtain this important end, we conceive that it is proper, constantly to have in view the necessity of using our utmost and unremitting endeavours to abolish slavery, and to protect and meliorate the condition of the enslaved, and of the emancipated. The irresistible, though silent progress of the principles of true philosophy, will do much for us;

but, placed in a situation well adapted to promote these principles, it surely becomes us to improve every occasion of forwarding the great designs of our institutions. For this purpose, we think it proper to request you to unite with us, in the most strenuous exertions, to effect a compliance with the laws in favour of emancipation; and, where these laws are deficient, respectful applications to the State-Legislatures should not be discontinued, however unsuccessful they may prove.—Let us remember, for our consolation and encouragement in these cases, that, although interest and prejudice may oppose, yet the fundamental principles of our government, as well as the progressive and rapid influence of reason and religion, are in our favour—and let us never be discouraged by a fear of the event, from performing any task of duty, when clearly pointed out; for it is an undoubted truth—that no good effort can ever be entirely lost.

While contemplating the great principles of our associations, we cannot refrain from recommending to your attention the propriety of using your endeavours to form, as circumstances may require, Abolition Societies in your own, and in the neighbouring states; as, for want of the concurrence of others, the good intentions and efforts of many an honest and zealous individual, are often defeated.

But, while we wish to draw your attention to these objects, there is another which we cannot pass over. We are all too much accustomed to the reproaches of the enemies of our cause, on the subject of the ignorance and crimes of the Blacks, not to wish that they were ill-founded. And though, to us, it is sufficiently apparent, that this ignorance, and these crimes, are owing to the degrading state of slavery; yet, may we not, with confidence, attempt to do away the reproach?—Let us use our endeavours to have the children of the emancipated, and even of the enslaved Africans, instructed in common literature—in the principles of virtue and religion, and in those mechanic arts which will keep them most constantly employed, and, of course, will less subject them to idleness and debauchery; and thus prepare them for becoming good citizens of the United States: a privilege and elevation to which we look forward with pleasure, and which we believe can be best merited by habits of industry and virtue.

We shall transmit you an exact copy of our proceedings, with the different memorials and addresses which to us have appeared necessary at this time; and would recommend to you the propriety of giving full powers to the Delegates who are to meet in the year 1795; believing, that the business of that Convention will be rendered more easy and more extensively useful, if you send, by your Representatives, certified copies of the constitution and laws of your Society, and of all the laws existing in your state concerning slavery, with such facts relative to this business, as may ascertain the respective situation of slavery, and of the Blacks in general.

———————

The address to the citizens of the United States was read a second time, and, being considered and amended, was agreed to as follows, *viz.*

To the Citizens of the United States.

The address of the Delegates from the several Societies, formed in different parts of the United States, for promoting the abolition of slavery, in Convention assembled at Philadelphia, on the first day of January, 1794.

Friends and Fellow-citizens,

UNITED to you by the ties of citizenship, and partakers with you of the blessings of a free government, we take the liberty of addressing you upon a subject, highly interesting to the credit and prosperity of the United States.

It is the glory of our country to have originated a system of opposition to the commerce in that part of our fellow-creatures, who compose the nations of Africa.

Much has been done by the citizens of some of the states to abolish this disgraceful traffic, and to improve the condition of those unhappy people, whom the ignorance, or the avarice of our ancestors had bequeathed to us as slaves; but the evil still continues, and our country is yet disgraced by laws and practices, which level the creature man with a part of the brute creation.

Many reasons concur in persuading us to abolish domestic slavery in our country. It is inconsistent with the safety of the liberties of the United States.

Freedom and slavery cannot long exist together. An unlimited power over the time, labour, and posterity of our follow-creatures, necessarily unfits men for discharging the public and private duties of citizens of a republic.

It is inconsistent with found policy; in exposing the states which permit it, to all those evils which insurrections, and the most resentful war have introduced into one of the richest islands in the West-Indies.

It is unfriendly to the present exertions of the inhabitants of Europe, in favour of liberty. What people will advocate freedom, with a zeal proportioned to its blessings, while they view the purest republic in the world tolerating in its bosom a body of slaves?

In vain has the tyranny of kings been rejected, while we permit in our country a domestic despotism, which involves, in its nature, most of the vices and miseries that we have endeavoured to avoid.

It is degrading to our rank as men in the scale of being. Let us use our reason and social affections for the purposes for which they were given, or cease to boast a pre-eminence over animals, that are unpolluted with our crimes.

But higher motives to justice and humanity towards our fellow-creatures remain yet to be mentioned.

Domestic slavery is repugnant to the principles of Christianity. It prostrates every benevolent and just principle of action in the human heart. It is rebellion against the authority of a common FATHER. It is a practical denial of the extent and efficacy of the death of a common SAVIOUR. It is an usurpation of the prerogative of the GREAT SOVEREIGN of the universe, who has solemnly claimed an exclusive property in the souls of men.

But if this view of the enormity of the evil of domestic slavery should not affect us, there is one consideration more which ought to alarm and impress us, especially at the present juncture.

It is a violation of a divine precept of universal justice, which has, in no instance, escaped with impunity.

The crimes of nations, as well as of individuals, are often designated in their punishments; and we conceive it to be no forced construction, of some of the calamities which now distress or impend our country, to believe that they are the measure of evils, which we have meted to others.

The ravages committed upon many of our fellow-citizens by the Indians, and the depredations upon the liberty and commerce of others of the citizens of the United States by the Algerines, both unite in proclaiming to us, in the most forcible language, "to loose the bands of wickedness, to break every yoke, to undo heavy burthens, and to let the oppressed go free."[30]

We shall conclude this address by recommending to you,

First, To refrain immediately from that species of rapine and murder which has improperly been softened with the name of the African trade. It is Indian cruelty, and Algerine piracy, in another form.[31]

Secondly, To form Societies, in every state, for the purpose of promoting the abolition of the slave-trade, of domestic slavery, the relief of persons unlawfully held in bondage, and for the improvement of the condition of Africans, and their descendants amongst us.

The Societies, which we represent, have beheld, with triumph, the success of their exertions, in many instances, in favour of their African brethren; and, in a full reliance upon the continuance of divine support and direction, they humbly hope, their labours will never cease, while there exists a single slave in the United States.

JANUARY SEVENTH.

The memorial to Congress was read a second time, and, being considered and amended, was agreed as follows, *viz.*

To the Senate and House of Representatives of the United States in Congress assembled.

The memorial and petition of the Delegates from the several Societies, formed in different parts of the United States, for promoting the abolition of slavery, in Convention assembled at Philadelphia, on the first day of January, 1794.

Respectfully shew,

THAT your memorialists, having been appointed, by various Societies, in different parts of the Union, for the benevolent purpose of endeavouring to alleviate or suppress some of the miseries of their fellow-creatures, deem it their duty to approach the Congress of the United States with a respectful representation of certain evils,—the unauthorized acts of a few, but injurious to the interest and reputation of all.

America, dignified by being the first in modern times, to assert and defend the equal rights of man, suffers her fame to be tarnished, and her example to be weakened, by a cruel commerce, carried on from some of her ports, for the supply of foreign nations with African slaves.

To enumerate the horrors incident to this inhuman traffic, of which all the worst passions of mankind form the principal materials, would be unnecessary, when we offer to prove its existence.

Nor is it requisite to consume much of your valuable time in the endeavour to prove it a national injury.

While it exposes the lives and the morals of our seamen to peculiar danger, it renders all complaints of retaliation unjust; for those who deprive others of their liberty, for the benefit of foreign countries, cannot reasonably murmur, if, by other foreign nations, they are deprived of their own.

True it is, that the captivity at Algiers is not without a hope, and that the slavery of the West-Indies terminates only with existence; but, in proportion as that to which we are accessary is more severe, the duty of desisting from it becomes more urgent.

Your memorialists observe, and mention with pleasure, that this venal cruelty is at present confined to a few ports, and a few persons. Hence it becomes more easy to destroy a degrading exception from the general dignity of our commerce, and to restore our citizens to their former fame, of preferring the spirit of freedom to the delusions of interest.

An additional reason for the legislative interference, now requested, arises from the natural consequence of the facts already suggested.

Foreigners, seduced by the example, and believing that they may commit without reproach, what American citizens commit with impunity, avail themselves of our ports to fit out their vessels for the same traffic. Thus we become the accomplices of their offences, and partake of the guilt without the miserable consolation of sharing its profits.

Your memorialists, therefore, trusting that a compliance with their request, will not exceed the constitutional powers of Congress, nor injure the interests or disturb the tranquillity of any part of the Union, respectfully pray, that a law may be passed, prohibiting the traffic carried on by citizens of the United States for the supply of slaves to foreign nations, and preventing foreigners from fitting out vessels for the slave-trade in the ports of the United States.

Resolved, That the President do transmit to Granville Sharpe,[32] Chairman of the Committee of the London Society, formed for the purpose of effecting the abolition of the slave-trade, a copy of the proceedings of this Convention.

That the address directed to be presented to Congress, be signed by the President of this Convention, and attested by the Secretary; and that the same be transmitted, by the President, to the Speaker of the House of Representatives.

That the addresses to the several Legislatures, be signed and attested as above mentioned; and be transmitted to the respective Presidents, or Speakers, of one branch of the Legislature, or laid before the respective Houses, in such manner as the President of this Convention shall find expedient.

That the address to the people of the United States, be signed and attested as above mentioned; and that the same be published in one or more of the news-papers in each state; and that Uriah Tracy, William Dunlap, William Coxe, junior, Samuel Coates, Joseph Warner, Abraham Ridgley, and Joseph Townsend, be a committee to procure the publication thereof, and to transmit the addresses to the Abolition Societies.

That one thousand five hundred copies of the minutes and proceedings of the Convention be printed; that one hundred copies be sent to each of the Abolition Societies now established; and that Samuel Coates, Samuel P. Griffitts, and Robert Patterson, be a committee to superintend the publication and distribution of the proceedings of this Convention.

Published by order of the Convention,

JOHN McCREE, *Secretary.*

Philadelphia, January 7ᵗʰ. 1794.

Notes

[1] Zachariah Poulson was a member of the Pennsylvania Abolitionist Society. He served as printer to the Senate of Pennsylvania for many years, issued *Poulson's Town and Country Almanac,* and published the *American Daily Advertiser*. He was also a director of the Library Company of Philadelphia for thirty-one years, serving as its actual librarian for twenty-one.

[2] The Connecticut Society for the Promotion of Freedom and for the Relief of Persons Unlawfully Holden in Bondage, founded circa 1790.

[3] Uriah Tracy (1755–1807): Lawyer and politician who served on the Connecticut General Assembly from 1788 until 1793, when he was elected to the U. S. House of Representatives. In 1794, he rose to the rank of major general in the state militia.

[4] The New York Society for Promoting the Manumission of Slaves and Protecting Such of Them as Have Been or May Be Liberated was founded in 1785 with John Jay as its president.

[5] For Peter Jay Munro, as well as sixteen other individuals named in this pamphlet, no information could be found. Endnotes are provided only for those individuals about whom biographical information could be located.

[6] The New Jersey Society for Promoting the Abolition of Slavery was formed at Burlington in 1793, with the encouragement of the Pennsylvania Abolition Society.

[7] Joseph Bloomfield (1753–1823): Lawyer, soldier, and politician who served as captain in the Third New Jersey Regiment during the Revolutionary War.

[8] John Wistar (1759–1815): Member of a well known New Jersey Quaker family.

[9] Franklin Davenport (1755–1832): Pennsylvania-born lawyer, and nephew of Benjamin Franklin. Davenport served in the New Jersey militia during the Revolution, and was a member of the New Jersey Legislature, a U.S. Senator (1789–1799), and a U.S. Representative from New Jersey (1799–1801).

[10] The Pennsylvania Abolition Society, founded in 1775 largely by Quakers, was the nation's first state abolition society, and served as the model for subsequent abolition societies.

[11] William Rogers (1751–1824): Rhode Island-born clergyman and educator who, after working as a pastor and college professor in Philadelphia, was chosen as the Pennsylvania Abolition Society's president in 1790.

[12] William Rawle (1759–?): Philadelphia lawyer who founded Rawle and Henderson, today the law firm with the longest-operating practice in the United States. In 1789 Rawle was elected to the state legislative assembly, and in 1791 was appointed United States Attorney for Pennsylvania by George Washington.

[13] Samuel Powel Griffitts (1759–?): Philadelphia doctor who founded the Philadelphia Dispensary in 1786, and served as its staff physician for seven years. During 1793 and 1794, he was active in relieving and aiding destitute French

emigrants from St. Domingo (Haiti). In the 1800s, he went on to serve as director of the U.S. Mint and as an advisor to Meriwether Lewis in preparation for his famous expedition with William Clark.

[14] Robert Patterson (1743–1824): Irish-born mathematician, educator, and public official who immigrated to America in 1768. He served in the Delaware militia during the Revolutionary War, and, at the time of the 1794 convention, was an active member of the American Philosophical Society and the Select Council of Philadelphia.

[15] Samuel Coates (1748–1830): Philadelphia Quaker merchant who served as manager of the Pennsylvania Hospital, and as a director of the First Bank of the United States.

[16] Benjamin Rush (1746–1813): Respected physician and major political figure. Rush represented Pennsylvania at the Second Continental Congress, signed the Declaration of Independence, and was elected to the Pennsylvania ratifying convention for the new U.S. Constitution. As a physician he served as surgeon general of the Middle Department of the Continental Army, worked as surgeon to the Pennsylvania Hospital, and founded the Philadelphia Dispensary—the first institution in America to provide medical care for the poor.

[17] The Delaware Abolition Society, founded in 1788 by a group of Quakers.

[18] Warner Mifflin (1745–1798): Despite his lifelong anti-slavery stance, Mifflin came from a slave-owning family and himself became a slave owner through his wife's inheritance. Mifflin freed all his slaves in 1774–1775, and his father followed the son's example. Later, as an elder of the Society of Friends, Mifflin traveled from state to state preaching anti-slavery ideas, and was instrumental in the passing of the 1782 Virginia law allowing for private manumission.

[19] John Pemberton (1727–1795): Philadelphia-born Quaker leader who devoted much of his time to the Society of Friends, serving on many committees and in many offices as he campaigned against slavery.

[20] The Delaware Society for the Gradual Abolition of Slavery was founded circa 1789 in Wilmington and was entirely distinct from the Delaware Abolition Society in its headquarters and membership. The "Wilmington society" dissolved for a few months at the beginning of 1800 and was re-established on December 12, 1800, as the Delaware Society for the Abolition of Slavery and for Relief and Protection of Free Blacks and People of Colour, Unlawfully Held in Bondage or Otherwise Oppressed.

[21] The Maryland Society for Promoting the Abolition of Slavery, and the Relief of Free Negroes, and Others, Unlawfully Held in Bondage was founded in 1789.

[22] James Winchester (1752–1826): Maryland-born soldier and planter who, after purchasing land in Tennessee, became involved in frontier government and military service. When Tennessee became a state in 1796, he was promoted to brigadier general of the state militia and also became speaker of the state Senate.

[23] Joseph Townsend (1739–1816): Methodist clergyman who had originally studied medicine. He helped develop the population theories that would later be systematized by Malthus.

[24] The Chester-Town Society, for Promoting the Abolition of Slavery, and the Relief of Free Negroes, and Others, Unlawfully Held in Bondage was founded in 1791 and remained distinct from the Maryland Abolition Society, which had been founded two years earlier.

[25] With the arrival of a representative from the Washington Abolition Society (in Pennsylvania), the number of societies represented at the convention rose to nine.

[26] The Virginia Abolition Society was formed in Richmond, in 1790, eight years after the Virginia law allowing private manumissions went into effect. The Society was organized by Robert Pleasants, a wealthy Quaker planter and the leading abolitionist in Virginia, and Samuel and Israel Pleasants of Philadelphia were undoubtedly his relatives. Their authorization to represent the Virginia society, had it been accepted by the convention, would have brought the number of official delegations to ten.

[27] Delegates met annually in conventions from 1794 until 1803, with the exceptions of 1799 and 1802.

[28] By 1794, Pennsylvania, Connecticut, and Rhode Island had adopted gradual emancipation laws, and ten years later, New York and New Jersey would follow suit. Although no emancipation laws existed in the Southern states, Virginia, Delaware, and Maryland had all passed acts allowing private manumission by deed or will.

[29] All of these states had passed legislation that liberalized manumission policies or established emancipation laws. Connecticut and Rhode Island passed laws in 1784 that provided for gradual emancipation, though in the end no slaves were actually freed by them. In 1787 Delaware passed an act that allowed private manumissions.

[30] Isaiah 58:6. This Biblical reference is from the Authorized (King James) Version of the Bible.

[31] "Indian cruelty" refers to the treatment of European settlers in America by Native Americans, which was reputed to be harsh and inhumane. "Algerine piracy" refers to the thousands of white captives who were abducted and held as slaves by black masters in Algiers and elsewhere in North Africa in the late eighteenth century.

[32] Granville Sharp (1735–1813): Abolitionist, philanthropist, and author of the first major anti-slavery work by a British writer, *A Representation of the Injustice and Dangerous Tendency of Tolerating Slavery* (1769). With abolitionists Thomas Clarkson, William Wilberforce, and others, Sharp led the first sustained campaign against British slavery.

No 3

THE

American in Algiers,

OR THE

PATRIOT OF *SEVENTY-SIX*

IN

CAPTIVITY.

A POEM,

IN TWO CANTOS.

When God from Chaos gave this world to be,
Man then he form'd, and form'd him to be free.

FRENEAU.

New-York :

Printed and Sold by J. Buel, N°. 153, Water-
Street, corner of Fly-Market.
M,DCC,XCVII.

[9]
THE AMERICAN IN ALGIERS

Introduction by J. Micah Guster, Tennessee State University

The poem *The American in Algiers or the Patriot of Seventy-Six in Captivity*, originally published in 1797 and reprinted here in full for the first time in 200 years, tells the stories of two characters who undergo harrowing ordeals of capture and enslavement. In canto I, a Boston-born white American recounts his life. Raised in an affluent household, he fought in the American Revolution for eight years. Upon his return from the war, he married and had two children. When he met with financial hardship, he sought work on a merchant ship headed for Genoa. His woes intensified when the ship was captured in the Mediterranean by Barbary pirates and he was sold into slavery in Algeria, in which hapless situation he offers the lines of the poem. In canto II, a new speaker is introduced, a self-described black poet ("sable bard") who gives an account of his capture in Africa and his transportation to Baltimore where he was sold into slavery. He details how he was torn from his idyllic African home and made to endure the horrors of the middle passage. The author juxtaposes the stories of these two men from such very different backgrounds, now both held in bondage, to highlight the hypocrisy of Americans, who were outraged by the enslavement of their fellow citizens in Algeria in the late eighteenth century, while they continued to accept the slavery of blacks at home.

The history of discord between America and Algeria went back to the 1600s. When America had been a colony, its ships had been protected by Great Britain. However, after America became an independent country, it lost that British protection, and without its own navy to provide security on the open seas, its ships became more vulnerable to Barbary pirates from North Africa (Tunis, Tripoli, Morocco, and Algeria), who roamed the Mediterranean and the Atlantic in search of prey. In the summer of 1785, the United States had its first clash with Algerian pirates, who seized two U.S. ships, the *Maria* and the *Dauphin*, enslaving all on board.[1] The threat Algerian pirates posed to American ships increased in 1793, when Great Britain negotiated a peace treaty between Portugal and Algeria that allowed Algerian pirate ships to sail out of the Mediterranean Sea into the Atlantic Ocean.[2] America had depended on Portugal to confine Algerian ships to the Mediterranean. Now freer to roam, pirates captured eleven American ships in 1793 and enslaved all the crewmembers.

Americans at home heard much of the crisis and the abuse of the enslaved Americans through accounts published in newspapers and pamphlets, which provided graphic descriptions of the cruel treatment American slaves received at the hands of their Algerian captors. Slaves who were ill were often forced to go back to work before they were fully well, which sometimes resulted in death. Slaves were reportedly beheaded, set on fire, and impaled on rods that extended up through their buttocks and out through their necks. They were thrown off cliffs that had hooks, and if their skin caught on the hooks, they would hang there in agony until dead. Tigers, lions, and other animals were set loose in the prisons where the slaves were kept. The Dey of Algeria was even alleged to have committed sexual assaults against American captives.[3]

As the accounts detailing the horrors of the American captives were being published in newspapers in the United States,[4] outrage grew among the country's citizenry and leaders. Secretary of State Thomas Jefferson and Senate committees discussed possible methods for gaining the release of the American captives. President Washington sent David Humphreys as an ambassador to Algeria. Humphreys wrote home in 1794 that Americans needed to devise more strategies that might help free American captives. Churches became increasingly involved in raising public awareness about the crisis. Ministers preached about the issue to their congregations and church meetings were held to discuss possible methods for freeing the enslaved Americans. Churches began collecting money from among their parishioners to support various schemes to ransom the captives.

In 1796, Humphreys and Joel Barlow, a prominent American, drafted a peace treaty and created a tribute system, in which the United States would pay Algeria a sum equal to about one sixth of the federal budget in exchange for freeing the Americans in captivity and securing the safety of American ships. During the summer of 1796, more than 120 Americans were freed from slavery in Algeria and made their way back home, which in turn generated more published accounts of what had occurred in Algeria.

The American in Algiers, published in 1797, was no doubt inspired by the captivity narratives that were so prevalent at the time.[5] In the first canto, the white narrator tells of his experience as a slave in Algeria:

> My naked back oft' feels with keenest smart
> The pow'rful lash that pierces to the heart;
> Laborious days, and restless nights, in tears,
> Chained in a dungeon, wear away my years.

The poet then goes on, in the second canto, to describe, in similar harrowing detail, the experience of an African slave on a ship bound for America:

> Here groans of anguish, screams, and dismal cries,
> Forth from the deep and noxious hole arise;
> Lashes, and oaths, and threats, and clanking chains,
> Form the hoarse music of those curs'd domains;
> Hundreds of human beings here confin'd,
> In liquid torrents melt away their mind.

In juxtaposing these two experiences of slavery, the author seeks to show that the Algerian and American slave systems are equally cruel, and that America is no more justified in practicing slavery than Algeria.

The anonymous author is almost certainly of European descent, but in canto II he chooses to use the voice of an African narrator for effect. Probably because he lacked any first hand experience of African life, the narrator's cultural frame of reference seems indistinguishable from a typical European American's. For example, here is the author's description of a wedding in Africa that differs in no detail from a European wedding:

> The guests attend, the rev'rend priest appears,
> The vet'ran cook the costly feast prepares;
> All things in readiness, upright we stand,

And strait are link'd in wedlock's holy band;
Eager, anon, we to the banquet hie,
And all was mirth, festivity and joy,
Swift flew the glasses fill'd with cheering wine,
And ev'ry guest seem'd anx'ous to entwine
Venus' myrtle with old Bachus' vine.

Nonetheless, the author succeeds in such passages in humanizing the Africans by presenting descriptions of their familial and social activities.

The author implores his white American readers to examine their consciences and to recognize the hypocrisy in fighting for their freedom from Great Britain and condemning the slavery of Americans abroad while, at the same time, continuing to allow the importation of millions of Africans into the United States:

Thus freedom's sons, who once a despot spurn'd,
Now plac'd in pow'r have equal despots turn'd,
Rul'd by the Deamon of inconstancy,
They fought for freedom, yet enslave the free.

The poem was published in New York (by J. Buel) at a time when some civic groups in New York State were raising funds to free American captives in Algeria while the institution of African slavery itself remained legal in the state. In 1795, a church in Albany, N.Y., had taken pride in the fact that its members had been among the first to pay the sum necessary for freeing American captives. Yet, at the same time, New York State remained one of the last states in the North to still allow slavery. The double standard also existed at the highest level of American leadership. Thomas Jefferson and George Washington, who at the time of the Algerian crisis had worked so hard to secure the Americans' release, both themselves owned slaves, and of course, slavery was tolerated by the U.S. Constitution from 1788 to 1865.

The poet paraphrases the Declaration of Independence to stress the contradiction of fighting for freedom from British tyranny while, at the same time, holding slaves:

Read that first of laws,
The Manifesto of Columbia's cause;
'Tis your own act, on which you found your claim
Thro' endless ages to unrival'd fame;
Whose well form'd sentences thus spread abroad
The Rights of Nature, and the Gift of God:
"We hold these Truths self-evident to be
All men are Equal and created Free;
Endow'd with Rights, no Law can e'er suppress,
Life, Liberty, Pursuit of Happiness."

Other authors of the time used the Algerian crisis to highlight the hypocrisy of Americans on the slavery issue. Benjamin Franklin, in one of his later writings—a response to a pro-slavery speech that was presented in Congress in 1790—assumed the voice of an upper-level Algerian official and satirically mouthed a stream of pro-slavery rhetoric to deliver his underlying message that slavery is wrong. Others, too, felt that lessons could be learned from the Algerian crisis. The Pennsylvania Society for Promoting the Abolition of Slavery declared in a petition sent to Congress in 1787 that enslavement of Americans by Algerians was a sign from God intended to awaken Americans to the issue of slavery, not only in Algeria, but in America as well.[6]

Of course, there were many who continued to defend slavery, particularly Southerners or those who sympathized with the Southern cause. A good example might be James Madison, a Virginian, who, while troubled by the Algerian crisis, saw no reason to end slavery at home. Like many others, Madison, in the 1790s, professed an aversion to slavery but exerted his efforts politically to avoid having the issue brought to a vote.

The ten-line epilogue to the poem, "A Word of Comfort to the Author," poses still more interpretive challenges. In it, the speaker addresses himself to the "sable bard" of canto II, telling him to be optimistic:

Anon Columbia'll rouse, from prej'dice freed, . . .
E'er long (to set no more) shall Freedom rise,
Emancipate the world, and glad the skies.

He calls on Americans to follow their French brethren, who had proclaimed the end of slavery in 1794, an edict that would be reversed by Napoleon in 1802. *The American in Algiers* makes clear the contradictions that existed in America at this time. While Americans were eager for the release of their fellow citizens enslaved in Algeria, they were reluctant to end slavery in America. By showing that Algerian slavery and American slavery were equally barbaric and unjust, the author hopes to awaken his readers and spur them to action against slavery. The poem is unique for its deployment of these two distinct voices—one black and one white—to illustrate the horrors of slavery at home and abroad.

Notes

[1] Paul Baepler, *White Slaves, African Masters: An Anthology of Captivity Accounts* (Chicago: University of Chicago Press, 1999), 8, 76.

[2] Baepler, 8.

[3] Baepler, 76.

[4] For such an account, see "From the Minerva," *Columbian Gazetteer,* Oct. 30, 1794.

[5] Between 1788 and 1800, at least seven separate captivity accounts were published in the United States, most going through multiple editions. Baepler, 303–307.

[6] "The Memorial of the Pennsylvania Society for Promoting the Abolition of Slavery, and the Relief of Free Negroes Unlawfully Held in Bondage," *The Pennsylvania Gazette* (June 1787).

THE

American in Algiers,

OR THE

PATRIOT OF *SEVENTY-SIX*

IN

CAPTIVITY

A POEM,

IN TWO CANTOS.

When God from Chaos gave this world to be,
Man then he form'd, and form'd him to be free.

FRENEAU.[1]

New- York:

Printed and Sold by J. BUEL, N⁰· 153, WATER-
STREET, corner of FLY-MARKET

M,DCC,XCVII.

ARGUMENT PROPOSED.

INVOCATION—American Captive's address to his Countrymen—His happiness at home—Commencement of the American Revolution—Battle of Bunker's Hill—Death of Gen. Warren—Battle of Long-Island—Death of Gen. Mercer—Surrender of Burgoyne—The fatigues of war, and the American's return home—His misfortunes—He embarks for Genoa—His arrival and debarkation for home—A storm—Taken by an Algerine Corsair—Sea-fight between the Corsair and a French man of war—Arrival at Algiers—The American Captive is carried before the Dey, and offered pardon upon renouncing his religion—He rejects the proposition—Is sold at auction—His sufferings.

THE

American in Algiers, &c.

CANTO I.

Bless'd truth from heaven, descend in rains sublime,
To trump the ills of this despotic clime;
To rouse *Columbia*[2] from her torpid dream,
And bid her every free-born son reclaim;
The fate of Slavery's hapless sons to scan,
And haste the triumph of the rights of man,

While you my countrymen each blessing share,
I claim the gen'rous sympathetic tear,
While free as wind you rove from pole to pole,
(No locks, nor bars, nor dungeons to control)
Trembling I bend beneath a tyrants rod,
Or meet the vengeance of an earthly god,
Whose pride and cruelty to Pluto equal,
Shall stand recorded in my story's sequel:
While you enjoy prosperity and ease;

Live without care and taste the sweets of peace,
From me that birthright of Columbia's sons;
Deserv'd by virtue and by valor won,
For which they bade their warlike thunders roar,
And drench'd their native soil in kindred gore;
My much lov'd mistress, Liberty has flown,
And with her all the sweets of life are gone:
While unconsol'd the mighty loss I mourn,
A slave forgotten and a wretch forlorn.
Ye sons of ease, your ears attentive lend,
And while I sing of griefs, your joys suspend.
Attentive list while I a tale unfold,
"Whose lightest word shall harrow up the soul,"
Bolt upright set each scattering tuft of hair,
Chill the warm blood of each kind hearted fair,
And make each freeman with amazement stare.

    That place where first fair freedom made her stand,
And bade her genial rays o'er earth expand;
Whose hardy sons, first taught proud Albion's race[3]
To turn their backs where they should turn their face[*]
Where num'rous domes emit the lofty spire,
And social lasses grace the winters fire;
Thy pride *Columbia*, and thy queen O earth,
Britain thy scourge, fair Boston gave me birth;
Here joyful days and pleasant nights I spent,
Free from ambition, care or discontent;
Ceres with plenty crown'd my father's board,
And Pluto's bounty well his coffer stor'd,
Days, months and years in swift succession move,
And doubly blest I ask'd no more of Jove;
But when at Lexington the dread alarms,[4]
Loud sounding calls each citizen to arms,
And *Britain*'s sons with brutal pride display'd
Their thorough knowledge of the butcher's trade:

---

[*] Towards their enemies.

I flew to guard my injured country's right,
And arm'd and mingled in the bloody fight;
There untaught striplings fought in freedom's cause,
And wond'ring nations crown'd them with applause.
I saw that day *Britannia's* warlike sons,
Routed by sticks, by clubs and pebble-stones,
Surpass'd in bravery, and in feats undone
By country boys, who scarce could wield a gun;
From crimson fields in haste they fled away,
Scatter'd by discord, terror and dismay,
Like hen-roost thieves, their flight was urg'd with speed,
And the best fellow had the foremost lead:
Then read vile scourges of the human race,
These lines the hist'ry of that day's disgrace;
For while I live my tongue shall loud proclaim
Columbia's triumph, and Britannia's shame;
Next on that day that led the tyrant Gage,[5]
'Gainst Charlestown heights, a flaming* war to wage,
Where Mars in triumph roll'd his thund'ring car,
On Bunker's-Hill, I brav'd the bolts of war;[6]
Here I beheld destruction hurl'd around,
And dying heroes strew'd upon the ground;
Smoke and confusion veil the angry sky,
And deadly balls in swift succession fly:
Here WARREN fell[7], of all our host the pride,
In freedom's cause he fought, and bled, and dy'd;
In private life, each virtue he possess'd,
The first of heroes, and of men the best;
In him the world sustain'd a loss indeed,
And freedom's cause from every vein did bleed:
Oh had I found like him that day a grave,
I'd dy'd a freeman, and not liv'd a slave,
Nor heard the direful clanking of my chain,
Insult the sacred long lost rights of man.
The heights of Brooklyn fresh to mem'ry rise,[8]

---

* Charlestown, near Boston, was burnt by the British, June 17, 1775.

And fill my ears with wounded heroes cries,
There fell Virginia's patriotic band,*
Whose blood e'en fertiliz'd the barren sand;
Where Hudson's craggy shores enclose his flood,†
I saw the earth besmear'd with human blood;
The grim look'd king of terrors stalk around,
And dying warriors bite the sordid ground;
Cæcaria's crimson fields, full well I know,
Where oft I fac'd the bold terrific foe;
Witness where Princeton's gentle ascents swell,
Close by my side the gallant MERCER fell⁹,
Belov'd like WARREN, and like him renown'd,
He fell like him with deathless honor crown'd;
Again where Monmouth's fertile plains are spread,¹⁰
These eyes have seen full many a hero bleed:
Nor here alone, at *Saratoga's* field,
I saw the great Burgoyne compell'd to yield,¹¹
To own the prowess of our rising States,
And lay his laurels at the feet of Gates.¹²

    To trace each scene of sufferings and alarms,
For eight long years amidst the din of arms,
Would swell my tale beyond its proper size,
And draw soft tears of pity from your eyes;
Suffice to say, expos'd to cold and rain,
I suffer'd hunger, thirst, distress and pain,
The earth's damp surface, form'd my healthless bed,
And heav'n's vast concave, canopy'd my head;
Full oft a winter's march through ice and snows,
Have I perform'd, with neither coat nor shoes;
And oft been plac'd thus on a midnight post,
Expos'd to tempests and congealing frost,
That eight long years the threat'ning hostile flood

---

* At the battle on Long-Island, a company of Virginians, chiefly planter's sons, were slain with a few exceptions.
† The battle of the White Plains.

I brav'd, and purchas'd freedom with my blood;
This mangled body now with chains opprest,
As wounds and prison-ships can well attest,
Whene'er I fought, I fought for freedom's sake,
And hop'd her promis'd blessings to partake;
Nor dream'd, I serv'd my country eight long years
To end my days in slavery in Algiers.
When bravery broke the British tyrant's chains,
And hostile bands, forsook my native plains;
Weary of war I sought my native home.
Resolv'd abroad, henceforth no more to roam.
Prompted by love, I chose myself a bride,
Rosina fair, of all her sex the pride;
Who e'er twelve months, to crown my promis'd joy,
Dubb'd me the father of a lovely boy!
A female pledge, of mutual love sincere,
Next grac'd our arms, before another year.

   But now dread poverty drew on apace,
And stern misfortune star'd me in the face;—
Some daring villains with unfeeling soul,
Near all my father's property had stole;
My eight years' earnings in the hostile field,
Their real value scarce one tenth would yield;
Yet as no choice my wretched state could grant,
I sacrific'd them to the present want;
And now embrace vile slavery's iron chains,
While splendor round the sunshine patriot reigns,
To see my wife and children thus distress'd,
Fill'd with remorse my sympathetic breast;
I sought the means long time, but sought in vain,
To snatch them both from poverty and pain.
In Boston port a gallant ship was found
Well man'd and laden, to Genoa bound;
A birth lucrative here I soon did gain,
And left my home to plough the raging main;

That home which sire nor husband saw not since,
Ten years ago the breezes bore him thence;
To aid my fortune, one kind hearted friend,
His little all in cash to me did lend:
For which (to pay in twelve months time) I pawn'd
My household furniture, and gave a bond.
The anchor weigh'd, the wide spread canvas sails
Receive the tribute of the western gales;
Full oft' I saw our ship with gallant pride
O'er cloud cap'd waves majestically ride,
'Till past the realms of ocean's wat'ry god,
We safely anchor'd in the wish'd for road;
One cargo sold, and strait another bought,
Our bus'ness to a happy issue brought:
The nimble seamen quick unfurl the sails,
And spread their canvas to the fav'ring gales.
Thus on we drove 'till past the narrow streights,
O'er hung on either side with rocky heights,
Still urg'd our way, our native port to gain,
And thought ourselves secure from slavery's chain:
With fortune flush'd, and free from all alarms,
I long'd to fold Rosina in my arms
My new made treasure in her lap to pour,
And clasp my infant boy and girl once more;
My heart anticipated more than joy,
And future pleasure sparkled in my eye;
What secret pleasure in my bosom dwelt,
No one can tell, but who the like has felt.

But now head winds less rapid progress gave,
The ship hard lab'ring through the adverse wave,
A storm arose—and just beneath the deck
Our main-mast went, and left our ship a wreck.
Rude Boreas[13] blust'ring from the angry skies,
Caus'd vales to sink and mountain waves to rise;
Three days and nights heav'ns awful thunders roar'd,

Loud howl'd the winds, and all was grief on board:
Yet this was happiness, compar'd to those
Unhappy scenes my tale shall yet disclose.

   The storm now ceas'd, the weather-beaten crew
Their wanted voyage preparing to pursue;
When from the fore-mast's tall top gallant height
A distant sail salutes the seaman's sight;
Wide from her yards her canvas wings were spread,
And western breezes waft her on with speed,
Near and more near she wings her rapid way,
And full to view her bloody flags display;
Now consternation fills each mind with pain,
All cry for mercy, but all cry in vain.
Rang'd along side, the lordly pirate cries,
"Strike, or be sunk this instant, d—n your eyes."
Nor had his tongue pronounced the threat'ning word,
E'er a full broadside on our ship he pour'd;
Swift came the boats with fierce barbarians mann'd,
Took full possession, and the crew enchain'd;
A barb'rous wretch whose heart ne'er sympathiz'd,
Than whom the tyger is more civiliz'd,
A wretch through fear (and not respect) obey'd
This hoard of pirates train'd to plunder—led.
Meantime a torpid frenzy seiz'd my mind,
While pious Musselmen my limbs confin'd,
Then as unfeeling butchers handle goats,
But with less care, they threw us in their boats;
Close to the lofty hostile frigate row'd,
And there in haste their fetter'd slaves unload.
When sense return'd, I try'd to contemplate
The four-fold mis'ries of my present state.
Broad on my back, and fetter'd to the deck,
Huge iron chains embrac'd hands, feet and neck;
While from the zenith Sol's bright burning rays
Pour'd unobstructed full upon my face;

Now two long days and nights a prey to grief,
Food, drink, nor sleep, ne'er came to my relief,
'Till one more kind, with scanty crust of bread
My craving appetite in mercy fed.
Thus three whole weeks I journey'd on the main
Scorch'd by the sun and deluged by the rain,
Until full fraught with wealth, toward Algiers
With flowing sails at length the frigate steers.
Now as we roll'd, our grief afflicted eyes,
Which bolts and chains had fix'd upon the skies,
Far in the east upon the azure tide,
In hostile pomp, a lofty ship espy'd,
From whose tall mizzen-yard, than snow more white
A Gaulic ensign was unfurl'd to sight;
Now transient pleasure beam'd in ev'ry eye,
And whisper'd, wish'd for liberty was nigh;
Transient indeed—sent only to prepare
Our hapless minds for more complete despair.
The boatswain's pipe convey'd the shrill alarms,
And call'd each bloody Mussulman to arms;
Urg'd by the gale the ships each other near'd,
Alike for battle, and for blood prepar'd;
In warlike pomp they o'er the billows ride,
And place anon their thunders side by side,
With mutual fury each the foe attacks,
And kill'd and wounded soon bestrew the decks,
Broadside on broadside, each incessant pour'd
And one continued peal of thunder roar'd,
Round, grape, and langrage, bar, and chain shot too
From cannon's mouths in swift succession flew;
Heads, legs, and arms in wild confusion lay,
And clouds of smoke obscur'd the face of day;
Each fore and aft the foe alternate swept,
And crimson tears the full fraught scuppers wept.
Here death in hideous aspect stalk'd about,
Review'd the lines, and mark'd his victims out;

At length (by hell assisted) in the 'fray,
The pirate cut each Gaulic mast away;
And fore and aft for three long hours and more,
His utmost vengeance on the wreck did pour;
Whose boatswain's mate led on the gallant crew,
Amounting now to only thirty-two,
Who all resistance now conceiving vain,
And death preferring to a tyrant's chain,
Seiz'd the last sad resource, that deep despair
Had left, and blew the frigate in the air.

   Meantime confusion walk'd the pirate's deck,
His men half slain, his ship a scatter'd wreck:
Here lay a sail, and there a top-sail-yard,
And dying groans throughout the ship were heard;
While fetter'd slaves grew frantic with the fright,
Expos'd unshielded to this dreadful fight,
Of all our hapless crew to grief a prey,
Myself alone surviv'd the dismal day;
And even I, since liberty has fled,
Would freely have been number'd with the dead.
But why should I the mournful tale prolong,
And tire the Muse thus with a pensive song?
Suffice to say, from all her rubbish clear'd,
With rigging temporarily repair'd,
For Barbary's coast once more the frigate steer'd.
The winds were prosp'rous, and within a week
In Algiers' port the pirates moor'd the wreck.

   Now thro' the streets insulted all the way,
In rat'ling chains they led me to the Dey;[14]
A wretch austere! whose haughty looks, denote
A soul more savage than the forest brute;
With scornful visage and insulting mein,
"Vile wretch, (said he) *my* subjects rule the main;
My God commanded, and Mahomet gave
Full leave to make each Infidel a slave;

But if you'll turn Mahometan at once,
And all your former principles renounce,
Swear by that God who reigns in paradise,
You hate a Christian, and a Jew despise;
That Mah'met is the prophet of the Lord,
The blest revealer of his Holy Word;
My princely favor shall to you extend,
And break the chains that o'er your limbs impend."

"Proud Turk, (said I) e'er I abjure my faith,
I dare the utmost vigor of your wrath;
E'er I the Saviour of this world deny,
In chains, and racks, and gibbets let me die."

"I'll curb thy insolence, the Dey replies,
Since you my proffer'd lenity despise:
Guards to the market bear th' insulting slave,
That the best bidder may the villain have."

Follow'd by crouds, on change I next appear'd,
Where boys huzza'd and men and women jeer'd.
And as hogs, sheep, or oxen oft' are sold
To him who pays the weightiest mass of gold,
So was Columbia's son to market bro't,
And by a Moor[15] at public auction bought;
In whose dark bosom all the vices reign,
The vilest despot and the worst of men.
Naked and hungry, days, and months, and years,
I've serv'd this thankless tyrant in Algiers;
My naked back oft' feels with keenest smart
The pow'rful lash that pierces to the heart;
Laborious days, and restless nights, in tears,
Chain'd in a dungeon, wear away my years;
My nightly cell is hung with cobwebs round,
A stone my pillow, and my bed the ground;
Absorb'd in grief, I spend each hapless hour,
Sigh for lost friends, and my sad fate deplore:

My lov'd Rosina, and my infants, Oh!
My soul runs frantic when I think of you;
I rave with madness, and attempt in vain,
By dint of strength, to break my galling chain.
Thus to nocturnal woes I constant yield,
'Till day-light calls me to the busy field,
When locks resound, and bolts and massy bars
Bid me for toil and tyranny prepare;
Urg'd by the driver, whose unfeeling lash
Extorts the blood that trickles from the gash.

    And does Columbia still disdain to own
A well try'd Patriot and a free born son?
And has she means within her pow'r to save
Her num'rous offspring from becoming slaves?
She does—and has—and Oh! my country hear
Thy offcast son, prefer his humble pray'r:
"Where grows the lively oak or sturdy pine,
Or where are seaman half compar'd with thine?
Rouse! rouse! my country, from thy torpid dream,
Unsheath thy sword, let vengeance be thy theme;
Thy long triumphant flag once more unfurl,
And on piratic fleets thy thunders hurl;
Then steer the hostile prow to Barb'ry's shores,
Release thy sons, and humble Afric's pow'rs.
Secure old Janus' doors with double bars,*
And free the world from massacres and wars.
If thou, my country, deign'st to hear my prayer,
I live to breath thy vivifying air;
If not, adieu my much lov'd native plains,
The curtain falls, and I expire in chains;
The silent grave shall hide me from thy sight,
And wrap me in the chaos of eternal night."

    END OF THE FIRST CANTO.

---

* The shutting up the temple of Janus by the Romans was the emblem of universal peace.

ARGUMENT PROPOSED.

ADDRESS to the Reader—Effects of the Sugar-Cane—On the Declaration of American Independence—Address to the Congress of 1776—Inconsistency of African Slavery—A Tribute to Washington—Domestic Slavery Delineated—The African's Complaint—His captivity—His arrival in America—Himself and family sold—Worn out with servitude—Conclusion.

THE

𝔄merican in 𝔄lgiers, &c.

CANTO II.

NOW gentle reader, think thy task not hard
Awhile to listen to a sable bard,
Whose pen undaunted thus shall dare address
A world of critics, and her thoughts express,
Th' envenom'd source of every ill to trace,
That preys incessant on his hapless race;
And trump the inconsistency of those
Feign'd friends to liberty, feign'd slavery's foes;
From that piratic coast where slavery reigns,
And freedom's champions wear despotic chains;
Turn to Columbia—cross the western waves,
And view her wide spread empire throng'd with slaves;
Whose wrongs unmerited, shall blast with shame
Her boasted rights, and prove them but a name.

To call forth all the vices of the cane,
Confusion's sire, and friendship's mortal bane;*

---

* If we trace matters to their source, we shall find that the cultivation of the Cane has been productive of more bloodshed and misery to mankind, than any other

To introduce luxurious rules of art,
To sink the genius and enslave the heart,
To make mankind in vicious habits bold,
By bart'ring virtue for the love of gold.
For these, old Europe's fleets first cross'd the flood,
And bath'd the coast of Africa in blood;
For these, her sons have rob'd the world of peace,
And sluic'd the veins of half the human race;[*]
For these, Hispania's pious children hurl'd
Death and destruction round the western world;[†]
For these, Britannia loos'd the dogs of war,
And pour'd her vengeance from Belona's[16] carr;
For these, French, Dutch, and Portuguese, and Danes,
Have slaughter'd millions on Columbia's plains;
And with our sable sons the place supply'd
Of tribes less suited to sustain their pride.[§]

---

modern circumstance. In order to attain this object, the thick settled Indies were depopulated, to make room for a race of slaves obtained by exciting wars, massacres, and every species of devastation among the quiet inhabitants on the coast of Africa. Thousands of those have perished on their passage; other thousands after their arrival; and what was wanting to fill up the measure of iniquity, has been supplied by whipping and starvation. And when to these, we add the numerous instances of women being reduced to beggary, children to want, and men to brutes, by the pernicious use of spirituous liquors, drawn from the same source (the sugar cane.) Stoicism itself, must shudder. Of the legal trade of kidnapping, the humane treatment on board guineamen, and the sympathetic conduct of whippers, overseers, &c. I shall have occasion to speak hereafter.

[*] Witness millions of the natives of both Indies, wantonly sacrificed by the Spaniards, French, Dutch, Portuguese and British. To say nothing of the unhappy Africans, whose seacoasts have for more than two hundred years been the theatre of wars, massacres, &c. instigated by speculators in flesh and blood for the sole purpose of procuring slaves, by purchasing prisoners from all parties; yet the perpetrators of those enormities, their heirs and assigns, appeal to the mandates of heaven for justification.

[†] See the Spanish conquests in America.

[§] The natives of America are of so turbulent a disposition as to render abortive every effort to enslave them and it is this together with their inability of body to

Such are the boasted virtues that possess
These pious scourgers of the human race;
Their title such, to fair unsullied fame,
Which zones and climes, and distant realms proclaim;
Such are the murders—such the deeds of blood,
Vile Christians perpetrate to serve their God;
Who ne'er taught men his brother to enslave,
But dy'd, they boast, all human kind to save.
A God of wisdom, justice, mercy, peace!
Whose word (constru'd by potentees of grace)*
Breathes death and vengeance to the human race.

I pause to freedom's sons—my lays belong,
And hence to *them* I consecrate my song:
Rulers and rul'd in turn, shall share my rhyme,
Well made, and suited to Columbia's clime.

Ye rev'rend Sages! who first fram'd the plan,
And rear'd the fabric of the rights of man,†
To you I speak, in truth's undaunted tone,
And plead the cause of Afric's injur'd sons.
Say then, ye Sires! who, by a just decree,
O'erturned a *throne*, and made a nation *free*,
Does not that Sacred Instrument contain
The Laws of Nature, and the Rights of Man?
If so—from whence did you the right obtain
To bind our Africans in slav'ry's chain?
To scourge the back, or wound the bleeding heart,
By all the base tyrannic rules of art?
Nature ne'er gave it.—Read that first of laws,
The Manifesto of Columbia's cause;

---

withstand the fatigues of constant manual labour, that accounts why the Europeans chose to extirpate them, and fill up their places with slaves brought 5000 miles.

* Let the reader see the pious conduct of the Spanish priests in America, and he will forgive the above expressions.

† The Declaration of Independence.

'Tis your own act, on which you found your claim
Thro' endless ages to unrival'd fame;
Whose well form'd sentences thus spread abroad
The Rights of Nature, and the Gift of God:
"We hold these Truths self-evident to be
All men are Equal and created Free;
Endow'd with Rights, no Law can e'er suppress,
Life, Liberty, Pursuit of Happiness."*
Recall the feelings of each Patriot mind,
When first this mighty Instrument was sign'd,
Hear the loud echoes rend the distant sky,
And *death*, or *freedom*, was the general cry.

What then, and are all men created free,
And Afric's sons continue slaves to be,
And shall that hue our native climates gave,
Our birthright forfeit, and ourselves enslave?
Are we not made like you of flesh and blood,
Like you some wise, some fools, some bad, some good?
In short, are we not men? and if we be,
By your own declaration we are free.
Forbear then sires to boast your glorious deed,
While yet humanity in torrents bleed,
Turn to your kitchens recognize your shame,
And cease to stun our ears with freedom's name:
The Spaniards say, that he's a silly dunce,
Whose house is glass, yet 'gins at throwing stones;
So he who lords it o'er his fellow man,
Should ne'er of wrongs or tyranny complain.

Great son of Mars,[17] with deathless honor crown'd,
Mount Vernon's pride o'er earth and seas renown'd,[18]
Freedom's first born, who stem'd the hostile flood,

---

* The precise words in the Declaration of Independence are, "We hold these Truths to be self-evident, that all men are created equal; that they are endowed by their Creator with certain unalienable rights; that among these are Life, Liberty, and the pursuit of Happiness."

And march'd to liberty through fields of blood;
Oh how my bowels yearn to see the brave,
The worthy WASHINGTON possess a slave;
If you whose sword still reeks with despots blood,
Have drench'd your fields with Afric's purple flood;
Sure some malicious fiend to blot your fame,
Has sanctioned usurpation with your name:
Look o'er your fields, and see them black with slaves,
Where freedom's flag in boasted triumph waves,
Nor let your soul despotic laws despise,
Since as despotic ones yourself devise,
And now convert to slavery's galling chain,
That sword you drew to aid the rights of man:
Such mighty chieftain is thy portrait drawn,
By one who knows not basely how to fawn.

    I now address a much respected band,
And bid my lays to ev'ry heart expand;
You who have triumph'd in the field of mars,
And led whole squadrons to the din of wars:
And you brave patriots who in private ranks,
Laid claims well founded to your country's thanks;
Who now the last, o'er trembling slaves extend,
And insult daily with oppression blend;
Kings of your kitchens, say tyrannic lords,
What impulse prompted to unsheath your swords,
'Midst toils and dangers eight long years to wield,
Each murd'rous weapon in th' embattled field;
If love of liberty impell'd the fight,
Why now deprive another of his right?
That very right for which you shed your blood,
And solemnly appeal'd to nature's God;
Where are the rights you once so fondly taught?
Or where the liberty for which you fought?
You say all men were first created free,
Whence then the right t' usurp their liberty?

Hath not the African as good a right,
Deriv'd from nature to enslave the white?
As whites to say the hue our climate gave,
Our rights shall forfeit and ourselves enslave?
Do we not see where'er we turn our view,
Throughout all nature's children different hues?
And do white hogs the unjust priv'lege claim,
To make the black ones root the ground for them?
Did e'er the whites among the feather'd brood,
Compel the blacks for them to gather food?
Think what an inconsistency 'twould be,
Such usurpation in the brutes to see:
As inconsistent are the steps you trace,
You conquer'd tyrants to supply their place.

    Thus freedom's sons, who once a despot spurn'd,
Now plac'd in pow'r have equal despots turn'd,
Rul'd by the Deamon of inconstancy,
They fought for freedom, yet enslave the free;
If in past ages steps you're now to tread,
In vain your vaunted heroes fought and bled;
In vain Montgomery,[19] Warren, Mercer fell;
In vain the World their wond'rous actions tell;
Because your fathers stole their neighbor's good,
Must you pursue the crooked paths they trod?
If rogues obtain our property by stealth,
Should that debar the owner from his wealth?
Your laws are strict—and woe to he or she
Who dares infringe the right of property!
'Tis a vast crime to steal man's worthless pelf,
But virtue rare to steal the man himself.
Such is your system which all good men curse,
The Theory is bad, the practice worse.

    And now all you whose stomachs gorge in food
Obtain'd by tyranny, and steep'd in blood,

Who boast of liberty and equal laws,
And croud your fields with slaves to damn your cause,
In undivided mass, Slave-holders, all,
Jointly, and severally, to you I call,
And crave attention, while the bard recites,
The usurpation of his country's rights;
Daring each artful sophist to confute
The stubborn truths his pen shall thunder out.

On yon wide plains, toward the rising sun,
(Lords of creation and the world their own)
Free as wild nature's self with guiltless souls,
Near where the Gambia's[20] mighty current rolls,
My ancestors from immemorial time
Had liv'd contented in old Afric's clime;
Here on the summit of a verdant hill,
That smil'd beneath his tender care and skill,
Facing rude Neptune's realm[21] of azure hue,
Where skies join seas to circumscribe the view,
My father liv'd—of all mankind the friend,
Whose constant care was virtue to defend,
And sweet relief to ev'ry want extend.
Of wealth possess'd, and to the needy free,
His heart ne'er knew ungenerosity.
Beneath this tender parent's fost'ring care,
My father's joy, my mother's only dear,
In youth's gay hours, I spent a joyous life,
Free from contention, care, or feudal strife;
Nurs'd in the lap of luxury and ease,
Nocturnal pleasures follow'd days of peace,
And life was one continued scene of bliss;
An only sister, virtuous, kind, and fair,
Partook my joys and all my pleasures shar'd.
To crown which pleasing scenes, love lent his aid,
And me a captive to fair Zephra made;
A lovely orphan by my father rear'd

Who with my sister half his favors shar'd:
Whose rare perfections ev'ry pen defy,
Nor can description half her worth convey;
(Nor here let scorn attempt the point to prove
That blacks ne'er feel the soft impulse of love;
If actions speak the feelings of the mind,
Whites have the bluntest of the human kind.)
This heav'nly maid on me bestow'd her heart,
And pleas'd me well, altho' I felt the smart;
In courtship's hours on Gambia's verdant banks,
Oft' have we sat and play'd our artless pranks,
'Till that wish'd mark arriv'd to make her mine,
And me the happiest of the human kind.
The guests attend, the rev'rend priest appears,
The vet'ran cook the costly feast prepares;
All things in readiness, upright we stand,
And strait are link'd in wedlock's holy band;
Eager, anon, we to the banquet hie,
And all was mirth, festivity and joy,
Swift flew the glasses fill'd with cheering wine,
And ev'ry guest seem'd anx'ous to entwine
Venus' myrtle with old Bachus' vine.[22]

But oh! what mis'ries tread on heels of joy!
How soon dark clouds oft' veil the beautious sky!
Roses with thorns are twin'd by native art,
And he who plucks them must expect the smart.
Sudden o'er distant waves appears a sail,
Whose canvas wings arrest the western gale,
Borne on by which, she nears our peaceful shore,
(Which ne'er beheld a hostile ship before,)
And here secure from ev'ry danger, moor;
Swift to the shore a band of ruffians came
And wrap'd our peaceful mansion in a flame,
While unarm'd warriors met the desp'rate clan,
And fought impetuous for the rights of man,

But skill or bravery here could nought avail
'Gainst foes well arm'd, who ev'ry side assail;
Friends, children, lovers, age nor sex they spare,
But wife from husband, child from parent tear.
Fast lock'd in captive bands, the hapless few
Now bade to blythe festivity, adieu;
With burning rage I saw my lovely bride,
By ruffian hands, insulted, seiz'd, and ty'd;
Rage nought avail'd—myself, and all my friends
Meantime were fetter'd by their impious hands;
In haste the monsters now their pris'ners strip,
And with a lash more keen than phæton's²³ whip,
Drive them unfeelingly toward the ship.

　My much lov'd sister and my new made bride,
Scourg'd by the hands of insolence and pride;
Fainting beneath the deep afflicting wound,
Victims to grief, fell senseless on the ground;
But soon reviv'd to feel the lash again,
And recognize in tears their galling chain;
Welt'ring in blood and petrify'd with fear,
On board the ship at length we all appear.

　A faint description of which floating hell,
Aid me, ye heav'nly muses, to reveal.
Here groans of anguish, screams, and dismal cries,
Forth from the deep and noxious hole arise;
Lashes, and oaths, and threats, and clanking chains,
Form the hoarse music of those curs'd domains;
Hundreds of human beings here confin'd,
In liquid torrents melt away their mind;
While savage seamen with ferocious pride,
Damn, huff, and beat, the slaves on ev'ry side;
For eight long weeks amidst this doleful scene,
I liv'd confin'd upon the boist'rous main;
Parching with thirst, and threat'ned with starvation;

Nor in that time beheld the fair I prize,
Though oft' I heard her agonizing cries.

    At length in sight Columbia's shores appear,
Where Baltimore her lofty turrets rear,
And Albion's flag in haughty triumph wav'd,
The pround insignia of a world enslav'd.
Now money'd crouds advance with eager pace
To cull this cargo of the human race;
With caution great, and scrutinizing eyes,
Each jockey views the slaves before he buys;
Tears from one family a tender mother,
A father, wife, or sister from another;
A father, mother, sister, self, and wife,
To diff'rent ones were sold, and sold for life.

    One short embrace we crave, this they refuse—
The drivers lash precludes all interviews;
By vi'lence parted, each reluctant mov'd
With tardy steps from objects so belov'd.
Since which, the earth has round yon central sun
Full five and twenty times her orbit run;
Yet where those friends, to me than life more dear,
Drag out their wretched days, I ne'er could hear.

    Suffice to say, 'gainst me all ills combin'd,
Enerv'd my body, and unhing'd my mind;
The galling whip unceasing greets my ears,
Wielded by savage brutes and overseers;
Its constant echo rends my bleeding heart,
Alike men, women, children, feel its smart.
To heat, to cold, and nakedness I yield,
And brave half starv'd the labours of the field;
When languishing with sickness no kind friend
With soothing hand his gen'rous service lend:
In leaky hutt, all comfortless I lie,
Left there alone in solitude to die.

Eternal God! and is this freedom's land,
Where the whip is law, and mis'ries wings expand?
Are these the men who spurn'd despotic power?
And drench'd their swords in haughty Albion's gore?
Freedom, avaunt! your sweets I'll never crave,
If this is Liberty, oh! let me be a slave.

I'm now worn out with servitude and woe,
And patient wait for death to strike the blow
That ends each care, each suffering and dread,
Lets drop the curtain of oblivion's shade,
And sends me headlong to the silent dead.
Yet apprehensions haunt my wretched mind,
To think I leave so many friends behind.

And now base tyrants, who no mercy shew,
I crave no sympathetic tears from you;
Callous to every feeling of the heart,
Language must fail, your baseness to impart.
But you, whose breasts with warm affections glow,
Whose ears are open to the tale of woe,
Whose softer bosoms feel paternal care,
Fraternal love or filial duty share;
And you whose hearts, a tender passion warms,
Who know the pow'r of love's ten thousand charms,
To hearts like yours, which soft impressions feel,
Of Afric's race, I make the just appeal;
And leave the portrait which my pen has drawn,
A short, concise, and comprehensive one.

CONCLUSION.

A WORD OF COMFORT TO THE AUTHOR.

Hapless descendant of old Afric's race,
Check the big tear that damps thy aged face;
See o'er the south, the Gaulic flag unfurl'd,*
Proclaiming peace and freedom to the world:
The splendid sun that gilds the Indian isles,
On tyrants frown, but on your brethren smiles;
Anon Columbia'll rouse, from prej'dice freed,
To share the glories of that godlike deed;
E'er long (to set no more) shall Freedom rise,
Emancipate the world, and glad the skies.

———

FINIS.

---

* The French have declared all their negroes in the West-Indies free.

273

Notes

[1] From "American Independence, an Everlasting Deliverance from British Tyranny. A Poem, by Philip Freneau," published in *The Travels of the Imagination; a True Journey from Newcastle to London,* by James Murray (Philadelphia: Robert Bell, 1778).

[2] The United States of America. The name dates back to attempts to have the New World named after Christopher Columbus.

[3] Albion is an archaic term for England.

[4] The battle fought at Lexington on April 19, 1775, was traditionally regarded as the starting point of the American Revolution.

[5] General Thomas Gage was the British military governor of Massachusetts.

[6] The battle of Bunker Hill, actually fought at Breed's Hill, took place outside Boston on June 17, 1775. The rebel forces thoroughly destroyed British forces, but retreated because they had run out of ammunition and their troops were depleted.

[7] Joseph Warren, a prominent spokesman and doctor, was killed instantly when he was shot in the head at the battle of Bunker Hill.

[8] The battle of Brooklyn, fought at Brooklyn Heights in New York, August 17, 1775, a thorough defeat for the Continental Army.

[9] Brigadier General Hugh Mercer was wounded in the battle of Princeton, January 3, 1777, and died nine days later. The battle was a victory for General George Washington.

[10] Battle of Monmouth, June 28, 1778. Neither the British nor Americans won a decisive victory.

[11] At the battle of Saratoga, on October 17, 1777, the British general John Burgoyne was defeated.

[12] General Horatio Gates was the commanding American general at the battle of Saratoga.

[13] Boreas: Greek god of the north wind.

[14] The absolute monarch of Algiers.

[15] A Muslim or North African.

[16] Bellona: Roman goddess of war.

[17] Mars: Roman god of war.

[18] George Washington, here associated with his home at Mount Vernon, Virginia.

[19] American brigadier general Richard Montgomery was killed on December 31, 1775, while attempting to capture Quebec—an effort that ultimately failed.

[20] The river Gambia in West Africa.

[21] The sea, so called for Neptune, the Roman god of the sea.

[22] Venus is the Roman goddess of love and beauty, and Bacchus is the Greek god of wine.

[23] A Greek word for a chariot driver.

AN

ORATION

ON THE

Abolition of the Slave Trade;

DELIVERED

IN

THE AFRICAN CHURCH,

IN

THE CITY OF NEW-YORK,

January 2, 1809.

By HENRY SIPKINS,
A DESCENDANT OF AFRICA.

New-York:

PRINTED BY JOHN C. TOTTEN,
No. 155 CHATHAM-STREET.

1809.

[10]

AN ORATION ON THE ABOLITION
OF THE SLAVE TRADE
by Henry Sipkins

Introduction by Laura Ferguson, Oregon State University

In March 1807, the United States passed a law ending the slave trade, which became effective (in tandem with similar legislation passed in Great Britain) January 1, 1808. This monumental event in the campaign against slavery inaugurated a period of celebration, especially for communities of abolitionists and free blacks in the United States. As part of these celebrations, black speakers, such as Henry Sipkins (1788–1838), gave orations about the opportunities and challenges facing African Americans, both enslaved and free. In annual celebrations that took place commemorating the end of the slave trade, Sipkins delivered his *Oration on the Abolition of the Slave Trade* when he was just 20 years old, on January 2, 1809, in the African Methodist Episcopal Zion Church of New York City. The *Oration* was published in pamphlet form later that month.

In stepping forward with his *Oration*, the young Sipkins was taking his place among other black community leaders in New York, such as William Hamilton and Joseph Sidney, in using these opportunities to present a state-of-the-people address about the black community at that time.[1] In his *Oration,* Sipkins delves into the origins of the slave trade and the cruel realties of slavery, praises those who had been actively working for better conditions for free blacks, and expresses hope for a time when all people, regardless of race, will be able to enjoy liberty. He uses sentimental language and emphasizes the similarity of feelings and experiences between the races to create empathy in his audience: "Behold a mother with her helpless infant on her shoulders, a sufferer in these toilsome scenes, or, in despite of the overbearing impulse of maternal affection, forced to lay it on the ground." European writers had been the first to adopt this sentimental style, but by the end of the eighteenth century many American abolitionists, including Sipkins, had followed suit. Prior to the ascendancy of sentimentalism in the late eighteenth century, many abolitionists had drawn from Enlightenment thought and Revolutionary rhetoric to form arguments against slavery that emphasized equality and natural rights. Other abolitionists had relied primarily on religion to shape their anti-slavery appeals. While both religious and moral arguments remained a part of abolitionist language, the use of sentimentalism became increasingly prevalent among abolitionists. By appealing to people on an emotional rather than a rational level, Sipkins and others hoped to more effectively convey the terrible conditions of slavery.

The African Methodist Episcopal Zion Church (called the African Church of New York on the title page of this pamphlet), where Sipkins delivered his *Oration,* was the first black church in New York City. The Methodist church had long been popular with African Americans partly because of the anti-slavery stance of its founder, John Wesley. However, pressure from Southern Methodists had compelled the church to retract its anti-slavery position in 1785, and, as a result, blacks had slowly started to form their own churches. The African Methodist Episcopal Zion Church was formed in 1796, when Peter Williams Sr., a former slave, led a group of black men, Sipkins' father Thomas among them, to break away from John Street Methodist Episcopal Church to form their own church. Thomas Sipkins would be expelled from the Zion Church, in 1813, for "headstrong" and "ungovernable" behavior, and with the help of Reverend William Miller, would form the Asbury Methodist Episcopal Church in New York.[2] Eventually the Zion and Asbury churches completely broke away from the white Methodist Episcopal organization, giving these black churches the autonomy they desired.

Given Thomas Sipkins' involvement with the Methodist church, it is not surprising that the publisher of Henry Sipkins' *Oration,* John C. Totten, was closely affiliated with the Methodist church. Totten, who began printing in 1799, primarily published materials relating to Methodism, such as sermons, minutes from Methodist Episcopal meetings, collections of hymns, and biographies of John Wesley. Totten also printed grammar books for children, established a periodical called *New York Spy,* and owned a dry-goods store. In addition to Sipkins' *Oration*, Totten published a few slave narratives.

New York State had passed its gradual emancipation bill in 1799, much later than many other Northern states.[3] Sixteen years earlier, in

1783, it had appeared as though slavery in New York City might end when the British evacuated the city, their last outpost of the Revolutionary War, taking with them thousands of former slaves. But the temporary drop in the slave population did not fundamentally undermine the institution in the state. A gradual emancipation bill had been proposed in New York in 1785, but, with slavery firmly entrenched, abolitionists had found it increasingly difficult to pass even a gradual emancipation act. Three years later, the New York legislature passed a law making it illegal to sell New York slaves out of the state. By 1790, approximately one in five households owned slaves, reflecting the steady increase of slave ownership that took place through 1800.[4]

By 1799, when the power of legislators from Long Island and the Hudson Valley, strong slaveholding areas, had declined, and the legislature expanded to include representatives from frontier regions of New York that were less supportive of slavery, legislators were finally able to pass the gradual emancipation act. The act stipulated that children born on or after July 4, 1799, were free after serving their masters for a specified term—females received their freedom at the age of 24 and males at age 28. Although the gradual emancipation act had been in place for ten years at the time of Sipkins' oration, many slaves were either unaffected by the act because they were born before July 4, 1799, or they were fulfilling their service requirement into their adulthood. Thus, Sipkins' comments on the harsh conditions of slavery were still very relevant in his home state of New York. Eight years after his oration, in 1817, the legislature passed a law ensuring all slaves would receive their freedom by July 4, 1827. Even then, however, slavery did not cease altogether because nonresidents could hold slaves in New York for up to nine months, a loophole that was not closed until 1841.

The free black population grew faster than mandated by law, as manumitted slaves and runaways moved to New York City from other areas of the state, from New Jersey, and from as far away as the Caribbean. While some slaves grew tired of waiting for their freedom and ran away, others negotiated for their freedom at an earlier date than the gradual emancipation act stipulated. Some owners simply freed their slaves after the gradual emancipation act passed, since it was clear that slavery was going to end. In 1790 there were roughly 1,000 free blacks living in New York. That number grew to about 3,300 by 1800 and 7,400 by 1810.[5]

At the time of Sipkins' oration, free blacks in New York could vote, but just a few years later the New York Legislature began establishing limits, due to the successful efforts of Republicans (Thomas Jefferson's party), who resented blacks' strong support of the Federalists. States had the power to set eligibility requirements, and, in accordance with an 1811 New York State law, African Americans had to prove that they were not slaves in order to vote. Ten years later, the state reduced voting requirements for white voters, while requiring African Americans to own a minimum of $250 worth of property and to demonstrate three years of residency in the state. As a result, very few free blacks in New York City could vote. Long after his 1809 address, Sipkins would be disturbed about the disenfranchisement of blacks and, with several other free blacks, would circulate petitions and lobby the legislature to remove property qualifications. African Americans would not earn the right to vote on the same terms as white voters in New York until 1870.

While the abolition of slavery remained an important issue among free blacks, many were more concerned with improving their own marginal status and formed societies and organizations to meet these needs. Throughout his life, Sipkins was an active participant in many of these societies. He was an original member of the New York Society for Mutual Relief, founded in 1808 to support African Americans dealing with family sickness or death. He would also emerge as a leader of the Phoenix Society, which sought "to promote the improvement of the coloured people in Morals, Literature, and the Mechanic Arts."[6] The organization, founded in 1833, encouraged families to send their children to school, established circulating libraries for African Americans, organized lectures, and urged adults to attend school and go to church on the Sabbath. The group's goals were consistent with a movement of moral reformers who believed that through self-improvement African Americans would not only enhance their own lives, but would also demonstrate to white Americans that blacks deserved full citizenship.

Eliminating political apathy among the larger free black population was a primary goal for the societies dedicated to improving the conditions of free blacks. They held public meetings to foster activism in the black community. Sipkins, who had encouraged activism in his 1809 oration, would later serve as vice president of the New York Association for the Political Elevation and Improvement of the People of Colour, formed in 1838, which sought to adopt "immediate measures for bringing forth the active and decisive exertions and energies of the Colored people, both in this city and throughout the entire State, in regard to the all-absorbing subject of their political enfranchisement and improvement."[7]

In addition to his work in various societies, Sipkins would become involved in the Conventions for the Improvement of the Free People of Colour, the first of which was held in Philadelphia in 1831. Sipkins attended the first four conventions, serving as president at the fourth of them. The convention delegates emphasized the importance of moral reform and determined that education, temperance, and economy were the most important virtues for the elevation of free blacks. A controversial topic that came up at these conventions was that of colonization, an idea supported by blacks and whites who believed the races could not live together. Those advocating colonization felt the best solution was to return blacks to Africa. Setting aside the inherent immorality of forcing blacks to leave their homes, colonization plans were unfeasible as it was logistically impossible to move such a large population back to Africa. A few blacks did go to Africa, and others, fearful that they would never be able to achieve equality in the United States, did consider the possibility of creating a community in Canada. However, for the most part, free blacks were strongly opposed to the idea of colonization, and each year, the delegates at the convention made a statement opposing the American Colonization Society.

After a committed career of activism, Sipkins died suddenly on September 30, 1838, shortly before his fiftieth birthday, when he fell from a rocky ledge along the Harlem railroad line. In a eulogy, Thomas L. Jinnings (or Jennings), a fellow abolitionist, remembered Sipkins as "one of those independent minds who did not seek for popular favor, but was guided more by principle than from any other consideration. In his manner he was unassuming, quiet and modest—was a kind and affectionate husband, and sincere friend."[8] Throughout his life, Sipkins maintained the commitment to the abolition of slavery that he demonstrates in his 1809 *Oration*. He remained concerned about the conditions of free blacks and continued to work toward the ideals he had set out in his oration—to a time when all African Americans would find "protection under the fostering wing of LIBERTY."

Notes

[1] See William Hamilton, *An Address to the New York African Society, for the Mutual Relief, Delivered in the Universalist Church, January 2, 1809* (New York, 1809) and Joseph Sidney, *An Oration Commemorative of the Abolition of the Slave Trade in the United States; Delivered before the Wilberforce Philanthropic Association. In the City of New-York, on the Second of January, 1809* (New York, 1809).

[2] Christopher Rush and George Collins, *A Short Account of the Rise and Progress of the African M. E. Church in America* (New York: J. J. Zuille, 1866), 28.

[3] Vermont and Massachusetts ended slavery through their state constitutions, in 1777 and 1780, respectively. In 1780, Pennsylvania was the first state to pass a gradual emancipation law, which served as a model for other Northern states. New Hampshire's Declaration of Rights ended slavery in 1783. New Jersey passed a gradual emancipation act in 1804, much later than New York.

[4] Shane White, *Somewhat More Independent: The End of Slavery in New York City, 1770–1810* (Athens: University of Georgia Press, 1991), 5, 27.

[5] White, 156.

[6] *Minutes and Proceedings of the Third Annual Convention for the Improvement of the Free People of Colour in These United States, Held by Adjournments in the City of Philadelphia, from the 3d to the 13th of June, Inclusive, 1833* (New York, Published by order of the convention, 1833).

[7] *The Colored American*, June 16, 1838.

[8] *The Colored American*, Nov. 24, 1838.

AN

ORATION

ON THE

𝕬𝖇𝖔𝖑𝖎𝖙𝖎𝖔𝖓 𝖔𝖋 𝖙𝖍𝖊 𝕾𝖑𝖆𝖛𝖊 𝕿𝖗𝖆𝖉𝖊;

DELIVERED

IN

THE AFRICAN CHURCH.

IN

THE CITY OF NEW-YORK,

January 2, 1809.

By HENRY SIPKINS,

A DESCENDANT OF AFRICA.[1]

𝕹𝖊𝖜-𝖄𝖔𝖗𝖐:

PRINTED BY JOHN C. TOTTEN,

No. 155 CHATHAM-STREET.

1809.

District of New-York, 88.

BE IT REMEMBERED, that on the thirteenth day of January, in the thirty-third year of the Independence of the United States of America, HENRY SIPKINS, of the said district, hath deposited in this office the title of a book, the right whereof he claims as Author, in the words and figure following, to wit:

> "An Oration of the Abolition of the Slave trade; delivered in the African Church, in the City of New-York, January 2, 1809, by Henry Sipkins, a descendant of Africa."

In conformity to the Act of the Congress of the United States, entitled, "An Act for the encouragement of learning, by securing the copies of maps, charts, and books, to the authors and proprietors of such copies during the times therein mentioned," and also to an act, entitled "An Act supplementary to an Act, entitled an Act for the encouragement of learning by securing the copies of maps, charts, and books, to the authors and proprietors of such copies during the times therein mentioned, and extending the benefits thereof, to the arts of designing, engraving, and etching historical and other prints."[2]

CHAR: CLINTON,
Clerk of the District of New-York.

To HENRY SIPKINS.

SIR,

WE, the Committee of Arrangement for celebrating the first Anniversary of the Abolition of the Slave Trade, highly gratified with your performance in the African Church, on the 2d day of January, 1809; in concurrence with the wish of many of our friends, and also believing it may be useful, solicit a copy of the Oration for publication.

THOMAS MILLER, sen.[3]
Chairman.

New-York, January 4, 1808.[4]

284

ORDER OF THE DAY.

FORENOON SERVICE.

1. A Prayer by Mr. Thomas Miller, sen.
2. A hymn under the direction of Thomas W. Commeraw.[5]
3. The Act, with an Introductory Address, by Henry Johnson.
4. Singing, by Thomas W. Commeraw.
5. The Oration, by Henry Sipkins.
6. A Hymn, by Thomas W. Commeraw.
7. A Prayer, by the Rev. June Scott.[6]

AFTERNOON SERVICE.

1. A hymn under the direction of Thomas W. Commeraw.
2. A Prayer and Sermon by the Rev. Abraham Thompson.[7]
3. Singing.
4. A Prayer by the Rev. Abraham Thompson.

THIS ORATION

is

HUMBLY INSCRIBED

TO THE

FRIENDS OF HUMANITY,

WHOSE

ASSIDUITY, AND DISINTERESTED PHILANTHROPY,

HAVE BEEN CONSPICUOUS

IN THE

PROPAGATION

OF

EMANCIPATION.

INTRODUCTORY ADDRESS
BY HENRY JOHNSON.

Fathers and Brethren,

THE attentive seriousness, the respectable appearance of this crowded audience; and the grandeur that I behold in the countenance of so many in this great assembly: and the solemnity of the cause for which we are this day met together, joined to the consideration of the part that I am to take in the important business of this day, increase the sense which I have had of my unworthiness of gracing this sacred stage.

And now let us Africans and descendants of Africans, with uplifted hands and bended knees make daily prayers and expressions of gratitude to God, for the long lives of those benevolent men who have been so arduously engaged in the abolition of the slave trade. And may that Almighty being mercifully dwell in all our councils; and may he direct us to such proceedings as he himself shall approve and be pleased to bless. And may we ever be favoured of him. And may the whole world be a world of liberty, the seat of virtue, and a refuge for the oppressed. And then will the poor African no longer have to exclaim:

> I long to lay this painful head,
>   And aching heart, beneath the soil;
> To slumber in that dreamless bed,
>   From all my toil.
>
> For misery stole me at my birth,
>   And cast me naked on the wild,
> I perish, O my mother earth;
>   Take home thy child.[8]

ORATION.

Brethren and Fellow-Citizens,

WE are again assembled to tender our sincere thanks, to recount the beneficial exertions of humane men, to venerate the beneficence of the Almighty Father of the universe, and to commemorate the return of a day that has, in some degree, restored the long-lost tranquility of the once happy inhabitants of Africa.

The prohibition of the Slave-Trade, which is the momentous occasion of our convention, is perhaps equal to any inscribed in the page of history. No event therein occurs, that so conspicuously points out the magnanimity of spirit, by which the advocates of its annihilation were stimulated, whose venerable names will be perpetuated to latest posterity, and receive from them a tribute of unfeigned gratitude; while the exposed pusillanimity of their predecessors and opponents, meet its merited reproach, and indignation from all upright persons. By means of this nefarious traffic, the delectable scenes of our parent-country have been immersed in the blood of our ancestors. This flagitious infringement on human rights was not confined within the sphere of a single province; its rage was not exhausted by reducing one or two tribes to the most unparalleled miseries; but, clothed in the habiliments of destruction, it spread its unlimited cruelties over the wide-expanded realms of Africa.

The most sanguinary massacres, committed by the nations of antiquity, at the taking or subversion of Troy, Babylon, or Jerusalem, notwithstanding their enormous horrors, at which the blood of every thing, animated by rational feelings, is appalled; yet, when we revert our thoughts to the productive inseparable evils, attendant on the Slave Trade, we are compelled to attribute to it unequalled cruelty, barbarity and injustice.

Let us for a moment take a retrospective view of Africa in its primitive state.

It exhibits the most blissful regions, productive of all the necessaries and even luxuries of life, almost independent of the arm of husbandry. Its innocent inhabitants regardless of, or unacquainted with the concerns of busy life, enjoyed with uninterrupted pleasure the state in which, by the beneficent hand of nature, they were placed.

But, ah! sad reverse. By this abominable trade they have been forced to bid adieu to their serenity and happiness.

When this envenomed monster of misery explored the passage to their fertile shore, when it reared its hideous head on their luxuriant plains; when with all its dismal concomitants it approached their peaceful abodes, all was consternation and woe.

It owes its being to the Portuguese, who, in the year 1508, by basely kidnapping numbers of the inhabitants, made the first import into the island of Hispaniola, for the purpose of cultivating the possessions of the Spaniards.[9] It owes its rise to the fostering hand of other nations, who, as they acquired settlements in America, adopted the execrable practice, which the Spaniards had tolerated. And it owes its maturity to the increasing avarice of all Europeans, who conceived it the most conducive to the enlarging of their fortunes out of the inexhaustible treasures which the new world unfolded.

Although conscious of the turpitude of destroying the liberties of the Africans, which they knew to be as inherent in them, as in the Europeans, length of time lead them to view it as a matter of right; and no sooner was it so conceived, than it was prosecuted to the greatest possible extent.

It was not until the year 1551, that the English commenced trading to Africa for gold, ivory, &c. And in 1556, Sir John Hawkins[10] sent on shore a number of men to take and enslave the inhabitants.

But, being defeated in the attack, dropt down the river, where he recommended the enforcing of his inhuman plan; and the better to effect it, burnt the towns.

After repeated efforts, he procured his number and proceeded to the West-Indies, where he exposed them for sale. After this, his first adventure, he was pleased with the success of this base employ, from the sight of which human nature revolts with terror. But alas, such was his depravity, as with the utmost composure, to see them linger out a miserable existence.

Hearing that the Africans were a valuable commodity in Hispaniola, he readily expressed his sentiments to his most intimate friends, who promised him their utmost endeavours to facilitate his design.

But finding the slaves purchased at too dear a price, being often at the expence of many lives, he thought it advisable to resort to other means of obtaining them; and conceived it the most effectual by instilling into them a spirit of avarice, and love of luxury. The gratification of which soon became the most powerful incentives to a speedy dissolution. Fatal, indeed, to the peace of Africa was this divised plan.

The harmless Africans, who had ever been strangers to the arts of deception, and unsuspicious of treachery in the bosoms of others, gratefully received the proffers of friendship from their cruel invaders, and consequently became an easy prey to European wiles.

Stimulated by the promised rewards of the Europeans, and in some cases intoxicated by the excessive use of spirituous liquors, joined them in their cruel depradations against their unhappy countrymen.

Once disunited, and the same stimulous ever remaining, eminently conduced to the waging of perpetual war.

Hence, no sooner than a slave ship presented itself to the view of the inhabitants bordering on the coast, than they beat to arms, and regardless of age, or sex, with unequalled violence attacked their neighbouring friends, to whom but a few minutes before they evinced the most amicable disposition.

In some of their hostilities, when they have been obstinately opposed, have been so heated with revenge, as to become insensible of the dictates of avarice, and indiscriminately murder men, women and children.

Notwithstanding the depredations of these intestine broils, the horrid desolation and ravages which are their constant attendants, yet far is their misery from being at its summit.

Augmented much are their sorrows on board the slave ship, almost inconceptionable must be their sufferings.

Confined in these caverns of despair, their tender limbs in weighty shackles bound, without the most distant hope of release, is truly miserable.

Torn from their native land, the endearing bonds of society are broken by the remorseless hearts of their assailants, whose insatiate thirst for sordid treasure dooms them victims to the most abject slavery.

But here their miseries do not cease. Still are they advancing toward maturity. Once brought into port a new and unbounded field of oppression presents itself to their view.

Here the most relentless tyranny on them is inflicted.

In this scene of their torture is summoned the aggregate distresses of both the former.

The day of sale at length arrives, they are now driven from this abode of distress? the ties of relation and friendship are now dissolved, which were the more strongly cemented by being fellow-sufferers for several months.

Severed from their native shore, and after enduring the pain of a long voyage, they are now the victims of a second parting. The sale now over, perhaps without taking the last tender embraces of an eternal separation, they are precipitantly hurried to the estates of their various purchasers. They now become witnesses of scenes the most direful. They are now the subjects of miseries the most replete.

The plantation bell summonses them to the incessant fatigues of the day.

One moment's delay subjects them to the malevolence of their revengeful overseers.

The scorching sun now rising to its high noon meridian, and pouring its intolerable radiance on them, and they languishing under the labour of the field, if they chance to fall a little behind their fellow-sufferers, they are reminded of their indolence by the stripes of their brutal drivers.

Nor are these the duties and punishments of the men only; but even feminine weakness and juvenile years are not exempted.

Behold a mother with her helpless infant on her shoulders, a sufferer in these toilsome scenes, or, in despite of the overbearing impulse of maternal affection, forced to lay it on the ground.

Night now approaches, but instead of retiring to habitations to enjoy a frugal repast, to support almost exhausted nature, or to recline their wearied frames on even their sheaf of straw, they are obliged to appropriate part of this cessation from the labour of the field, to the gathering of grass for the cattle.

But why attempt to pourtray, in their true colours, scenes of oppression, which language the most descriptive is inadequate to delineate: or why any longer expatiate on a subject of such complicated misery.

Suffice it to say, that to this deplorable situation, my brethren, descendants of Africans, have millions of our forefathers, and brethren fell victims. In this state of hopeless servitude, do many yet remain, who look forward with pleasing expectation to the termination of their lives, as the only possible means of emancipating them from servile despotism.

At the bare thought of such unexampled debasement of part of mankind, humanity shudders. The slave trade, in its every stage, unfolds to the view of every beholder, in whose heart glows the most latent particle of sympathy, scenes of woe and detestation. For the destruction of this almost inexhaustible magazine of cruelty, much thanks, my brethren, from us are due. In producing which, America boasts the unrivalled exertions of Woolman[11] and Benezet[12], whose boundless services in the cause of emancipation have been viewed with admiration by a surrounding world. Wheresoever they turned their eyes, discouraging obstacles presented their withering frowns; but emboldened by a consciousness of rectitude, they resolved to persevere. Also the venerable names of Dillwyn,[13] Sharp,[14] and many others, will ever resplendently embelish the historic page—will ever receive from us the most grateful homage, and will by posterity be heard of with peculiar satisfaction. We can pleasantly anticipate the gratulation with which their virtues will be received.[15] *Oh, our most worthy advocates! we humbly beg you to accept our grateful thanks for your disinterested, indefatigable exertions to ameliorate our state. When we were under the iron hand of oppression, you did generously step forward to ease our burthen. When we trembled at the haughty mandates of imperious tyrants, your consoling whispers offered some shelter. When sinking under the weighty shackles of slavery to the most consummate despondency, with unremitting zeal you flew to our relief.—These, my brethren, are but a few of innumerable instances in which they have proved our strenuous beneficial advocates. It was their ineffable delight to see mankind restored to primative parity. And for it the voice of justice and humanity were heard in the Congress of these United States and the British Parliament. At this despair seemed to erect her appalling brow; but, by their dauntless spirits, she was quickly repelled. Their prayers, though often discarded, did not intimidate them. Still was their ardour invigorated—still they remained the firm champions of our cause.

To these philanthropic exertions, my African brethren, we are indebted for our present happiness and prosperity. To these we owe our preser-

---

*Addressed to the Friends.

vation from a second bondage; and on these depend the prospect of future felicity. Their ever-memorable acts were such as the paternal hand rearing its tender offspring to mature years, and planning for it the edifice of virtue and happiness. By their unabating energy they accomplished the long sought conquest; at which the votaries of liberty shouted their congratulations; she waved in extacies her tallest standards; and calling to the drooping captives of slavery, bade them behold and admire! They disdained the stimulous of pecuniary gains, and felt themselves amply compensated by the smiles of an approving conscience.

My beloved Africans, let us by an upright and steady deportment merit a continuance of former favours, and evince to the world our high sense of gratitude. Eminent respect should, perhaps, be engraven on our hearts for the distinguished lustre with which our advocates, in these United States, have shone. These to their honour have it in their power to boast the first seminary[16] for the cultivation of our understanding, and advancing us in morals. And they have had the gratification to see some make considerable attainments in literature, and become worthy members of civil society.

The benevolent exertions of the persons, who are the subjects of the foregoing thanks, although worthy the highest eulogiums of terrestrial praise, can only be considered a secondary cause in the completion of this incomparable epoch. If these merit the greatest encomiums; how infinitely small must be our means of fixing the properties of respect, which infallibly belong to a primary cause? Stunned with astonishment we stand when contemplating the goodness of the divine majesty of heaven, who of his wonderful providence summoned our votaries by a voice of humanity to espouse the cause of the injured African race. In the moments of deliberate reflection on the causes, tending to produce this memorable era, we are ingulped in the amazing labyrinth of his unfathomable condescention. Our hearts are lost in the maze of his incalculable benignity. Let us however endeavour to offer our indispensible obligations of unfeigned gratitude to eternal goodness—let us pay our greatest veneration to his matchless beneficence, and impel it loudly to re-echo through the regions of eternity. By his august decree the grossest debasement of mortals was abjured. He saw with piteous eyes our wretched state, and sent his guardian angels to rescue us from our distressed condition. Oh our heavenly Father! deign we beseech thee to accept the thanks of thy humble supplicants. In commiseration to our state thou didst inspire, by the dictates of humanity, men who became the vigilant exterminators of that commerce, which has much depopulated the land of our nativity. And which has reduced its inhabitants with all their progeny under the sentence of perpetual bondage.

But rejoice, my brethren, through the efficiency of the friends of humanity this fell sentence has now subsided. It is absorbed in the refulgence of that memorable day, which announced the Abolition of the Slave Trade, the return of which we now celebrate. That day which caused our hearts to dilate with the ideal hope of future bliss.

This day completes the first anniversary of the suspension of the facinerious[17] traffic, which has made the most indelible blot in the history of nations. May it ever be held as a monument of contempt by rising generations. Rejoice that its baneful effects shall no longer be seen in these United States, nor the British colonies. No longer shall the shores of Africa be drenched with human gore. No longer shall its inhabitants be torn from their native soil; no longer shall they be brought on cruel shipboard, weighed down in chains; nor shall we any longer hear the dreadful recital of their mutilated, fettered limbs; nor shall the dismal groans of dying captives intercept our ears. No longer shall we witness the woeful prospect of an unnatural separation of a loving husband, an affectionate wife; nor a darling child cling to its fond parents, imploring their protection from the impending fury of their merciless owners. Rejoice, that no longer shall the sons of Africa become the subjects of such inhuman drudgery. Rejoice, my brethren; descendants of Africans, that the exiles of our race are emerging from the depths of forlorn slavery, in which they have been environed. The thick fogs of ignorance, that have ever encompassed their gloomy mansions, are gradually vanishing, they have been dissipated by the superior radiance of increasing knowledge.

But let not our expressions of joy suppress the inestimable obligations of gratitude due to our patrons. For on the most transient survey of our past condition, you must manifestly discover the unshaken constancy with which they have persevered to have established us in our present improved state. Beset with the most insuperable difficulties, arising from the strong imbibed opinions of our inferiority, they nevertheless, with that fortitude which characterizes true worth, stemmed the torrent of popular prejudice. May it no longer shed on the mind its wizard darkness; nor the false tongue of envy envenom it by its beguiling insinuations.

But may the long wished for time soon arrive when slavery of every species shall be destroyed—when despotism and oppression shall forever cease—when the Africans shall be reinstated in their former joys—when the exulting shouts of Princes, embracing their long lost oppressed subjects, shall reverberate on our ears—when the bursting acclamations of approbation shall resound from the tombs of our worthy departed ancestors; and all find protection under the fostering wing of LIBERTY.

FINIS.

Notes

[1] For details about Henry Sipkins' life, see the introduction. Sipkins' identification of himself on the title page as a descendent of Africa (i.e. an African American) is remarkable for the author's public identification of himself in terms of his race, a gesture that few writers made in the early 1800s.

[2] These acts, passed in 1790 and extended in 1802, gave authors and publishers exclusive rights to the printing and reprinting of their documents for fourteen years. It was fairly common practice to print the law at the beginning of publications.

[3] Thomas Miller: Minister involved in the formation of the African Methodist Episcopal Zion Church (A.M.E. Zion Church) in New York City who served as treasurer in 1799, when construction of the church was underway, and subsequently in other offices and committees of the church.

[4] "1808" is an obvious misprint for 1809.

[5] For Thomas W. Commeraw, no information could be found. Notes are provided only for those individuals about whom biographical information could be located.

[6] June Scott: Minister at the A.M.E. Zion Church who had been involved in the church's establishment. Years after Sipkins' oration, Scott and Reverend Abraham Thompson, another founder of the A.M.E. Zion Church, left to form the Union Society with John Edwards, who had been expelled from the Friends Society. Later, Reverend Abraham Thompson ended his alliance with the Union Society and returned to the A.M.E. Zion Church. Scott remained a part of the Union Society until it eventually went bankrupt.

[7] Abraham Thompson: A founder of the A.M.E. Zion Church, who, after returning from an interlude in another church, became an active leader of the A.M.E. and worked to fully separate the A.M.E. Zion and Asbury Churches from the white Methodist Episcopal organization.

[8] From "The Grave" (1804), by James Montgomery, an early nineteenth-century Romantic and a leading anti-slavery poet.

[9] Europeans first took slaves from the west coast of Africa in the 1440s, but the slave trade did not become a major economic venture until the European colonization of the Americas. The Portuguese, who began the Atlantic slave trade, took Africans to the island of Hispaniola (today divided between Haiti and the Dominican Republic) to work on sugar plantations because the indigenous population had been decimated by disease and violence.

[10] John Hawkins (1532?–1595): English naval commander, who, with the support of Queen Elizabeth I, engaged in the slave trade, making three expeditions between 1562 and 1567. "1556" may be a typographical error as Sipkins is undoubtedly referring to events that took place during one of the three trips between 1562 and 1567.

[11] John Woolman (1720–1772): Quaker abolitionist who worked to end slave ownership within the Society of Friends. He believed that slavery was inconsistent with Christian teachings and harmful to both slaves and their owners.

[12] Anthony Benezet (1713–1783): Abolitionist, education advocate, and Quaker, who, through his anti-slavery pamphlets, sought to persuade fellow Quakers to emancipate their slaves. He opened schools for children who might not have otherwise received an education, including a school for black students.

[13] William Dillwyn (1743–1824): Philadelphia-born Quaker who spent most of his adult life in England, where he was an important organizer of the abolition movement.

[14] Granville Sharp (1735–1813): English writer and abolitionist whose exertions led to the landmark Somerset case of 1772 by which no slave could be forcibly removed from England once he had landed there.

[15] The Society of Friends, another name for Quakers, one of the earliest religious groups to oppose slavery. The Quakers began by encouraging their members to treat slaves in a Christian manner and then ruled, in 1776, that members could no longer own slaves.

[16] The African Free School, founded by the New York Manumission Society, was the first school for black children in New York. The records and files of the New York African Free School today reside in the archives of the New-York Historical Society in New York City.

[17] Variant of "facinorous," meaning extremely wicked, grossly criminal, atrocious, infamous, vile.

LETTERS

FROM

A MAN OF COLOUR,

ON

A LATE BILL BEFORE THE SENATE OF PENNSYLVANIA.

Letter I.

O Liberty! thou power supremely bright,
Profuse of bliss and pregnant with delight,
Perpetual pleasures in thy presence reign,
And smiling Plenty leads thy wanton train.

ADDISON.

WE hold this truth to be self-evident, that GOD created all men equal, and is one of the most prominent features in the Declaration of Independence, and in that glorious fabrick of collected wisdom, our noble Constitution. This idea embraces the Indian and the European, the Savage and the Saint, the Peruvian and the Laplander, the white Man and the African, and whatever measures are adopted subversive of this inestimable privilege, are in direct violation of the letter and spirit of our Constitution, and become subject to the animadversion of all, particularly those who are deeply interested in the measure.

These thoughts were suggested by the promulgation of a late bill, before the Senate of Pennsylvania, to prevent the emigration of people of colour into this state. It was not passed into a law at this session and must in consequence lay over until the next, before when we sincerely hope, the white men, whom we should look upon as our protectors, will have become convinced of the inhumanity and impolicy of such a measure, and forbear to deprive us of those inestimable treasures, Liberty and Independence. This is almost the only

A

11

LETTERS FROM A MAN OF COLOUR
[by James Forten?]

Introduction by Nicholas Osborne, Johns Hopkins University

Letters from a Man of Colour, on a Late Bill Before the Senate of Pennsylvania (1813) is at first glance a conservative document. Far from being an indictment of the entire system of race relations in the United States, it presents itself as an attempt to stem the tide of increased legal racial discrimination by focusing on protecting what legal rights free African Americans had in 1813 Pennsylvania. Written in response to a proposed state law that would have abridged those rights, it is an attempt to protect specifically such rights as freedom of movement and protection of property, which, while not equally enjoyed by African Americans and whites, were generally acknowledged in principle.[1] At the same time, *Letters from a Man of Colour* is emblematic of a progressive chapter in the early history of the United States—one in which African Americans led the fight to defend what basic rights they had and subtly agitated for an expansion of them. This series of letters is a prime example of contemporary passionate pleas for Americans to finally incorporate their patriotic rhetoric of freedom and equality into an *actual* society without regard to race.

Letters from a Man of Colour was published anonymously as a privately printed pamphlet in 1813. The author simply signed himself "A Man of Colour." When *Freedom's Journal* (the first black-owned and -operated newspaper in the United States) reprinted the document in February and March 1828,[2] the paper's editors introduced the author with the equally cryptic "one of our most intelligent and respectable citizens of Colour in the United States." Despite the author's concealed identity, the essays are almost universally accepted as the work of James Forten (1766–1842), "a man of colour" who considered himself just as American as those who would restrict his rights and those to whom he was appealing.[3]

Forten's audience was first and foremost the legislators in the Pennsylvania General Assembly. While Pennsylvania was one of the most progressive states in its treatment of blacks—in 1780 it had been the first state to pass a gradual emancipation law,[4] and it had crafted a race-neutral state constitution in 1790[5]—it still had serious legislative and popular impediments to black equality. As early as 1712, the colony of Pennsylvania had imposed a tax with the purpose of "discouraging the Importation of *Negroes*" into its domain, in an attempt to limit the African-American population.[6] Ultimately, this policy was overruled by the British government. Although slavery had flourished in Pennsylvania (primarily Philadelphia) for a brief time in the mid-eighteenth century, it was in rapid decline by the end of the century, mainly as a result of a low rate of importation of new slaves and a low reproduction rate among established slaves.[7] The comparatively small impact of private manumissions in the mid-eighteenth century[8] suggests that despite various progressive developments, there were those who took a radically different view of emancipation.

Perhaps the apparent contradiction of racial animosity and laws protecting the rights of African Americans in Pennsylvania can be explained as a case of the government not adjusting to the decline of slavery—as the old institution began to fade, new laws to restrict the rights of free African Americans didn't arise for a few years. Alternatively, perhaps it was the result of having a few key anti-slavery Pennsylvanians in power when the original laws were being drafted, despite popular feeling against such laws. In each case, by the time *Letters from a Man of Colour* was published, a climate of racial animosity predominated. Particularly in Philadelphia— one of the largest cities in the United States and the hub of Pennsylvania society, and which was approximately ten percent African-American in the 1810s[9]—this climate was virulent enough to lead to the formation on January 18, 1813, of a committee of the state House of Representatives "to inquire into the expediency of prohibiting by law, the emigration of people of colour into the commonwealth of Pennsylvania."[10]

The proposed law hinged on its requirement that all "people of colour," regardless of whether they were permanent residents of Pennsylvania, register with the state—facing jail and possibly sale into slavery if they were found without documentation. Following this potential legislative endorsement of racial discrimination, a series of petitions arrived in the state capital from both inhabitants and elected officials in favor of legislation restricting the flow of African Americans into the state. Less than two weeks after the second of these petitions was presented, the Pennsylvania Abolition Society presented a remonstrance against the enactment of any legislation to bar black migration into the state. The next day another remonstrance "from sundry free people of color of the city and county of Philadelphia" was also filed. Interestingly, the petitions against the anti-migration legislation were presented to the legislature by the same representative from Philadelphia, Thomas Sergeant, who had earlier presented petitions calling for a ban on migration[11]—demonstrating the pivotal influence of Philadelphia on this issue.

Ultimately the 1813 push to bar African-American immigration into Pennsylvania died without ever coming to a vote in the state legislature, though the issue itself was far from over. As late as 1831, Pennsylvania, like other states, was still consistently introducing bills with the intent of severely limiting black movement into and within the commonwealth.[12] For example, Maryland and Virginia were considering legislation in 1831 that would expel free blacks from their states, which was used as part of the justification for Pennsylvania's proposed parallel measure,[13] and Illinois was actually successful in banning black immigration in its 1848 constitution.[14]

Despite its ultimate failure to pass, the anti-African-American-migration law was symbolic of a racial tension that existed not only in Pennsylvania, but in most states, both North and South. While the parliamentary maneuvers of both sides of the legislation were unfolding, Forten decided that the proposed legislation posed a significant threat to certain African-American rights and took the opportunity to argue for a broader acceptance of blacks as equal citizens of the United States.

Forten, as a second generation free black, was already a rarity in his time. His family found the resources to allow him several years of education at the Friends' African School, where the prominent Quaker abolitionist Anthony Benezet was an advisor.[15] In 1781, Forten enlisted aboard an American privateer sailing the East Coast in search of British ships (serving in the dangerous role of powderboy) and later became a prisoner of war. After being released and serving as a merchant sailor, Forten returned to Philadelphia, where he took up sail making and eventually became one of the wealthiest residents of Philadelphia.[16]

Forten was particularly proud of his military service. He had fought in the Revolutionary War—and continued to fight in spirit in such documents as *Letters from a Man of Colour*—for the ideals of liberty and equality that he felt the United States, as well as the state of Pennsylvania, were supposed to represent. *Letters from a Man of Colour* begins by invoking the lofty rhetoric of the Declaration of Independence and the Constitution. His reference to "our noble constitution" is perhaps ambiguous; it does not specify whether he is referring to the United States Constitution, which forbore using the word "slave," or to the more radical Pennsylvania constitution of 1790, which used no racial modifiers whatsoever.

The ideals of the country's founding documents pervade *Letters from a Man of Colour*—as in the fifth and final section, when he echoes them in the phrase "Civil Liberty, and sacred Justice . . . [for] all." The use of such phrases was one of the most common rhetorical tools in African-American and early abolitionist pamphleteering, when the ideologies that produced American independence were still fresh in everyone's mind, especially the minds of the five thousand blacks who fought for independence and the thousands more who won their freedom by escaping during the war.[17] *Letters from a Man of Colour* reiterates the pervasive belief that the freedom Americans sought from Britain should apply also to American slaves.

Forten's appeal to patriotism—as well as his assertion that a true American patriot is one who embraces equality for all citizens—is more stirring when considered in the context of the War of 1812, which had been going on for less than a year when *Letters from a Man of Colour* was published. Scattered throughout the document are disparaging comments about "European despotism," of which he claims the proposed legislation to restrict African American rights is a comparable evil. In many ways, the War of 1812 served rhetorically as a continuation of the Revolutionary War. It appeared to be a final test of whether the young United States and its experiment of democracy could succeed. Forten capitalized on the atmosphere of the war by highlighting the rhetoric of American independence in terms that were suddenly relevant not only to those who had lived through the Revolution, but to all those who were now living through a parallel struggle. The War of 1812 reinvigorated Forten's patriotism, and in 1814–1815 he was asked by Philadelphia's Vigilance Committee to rally free African Americans in the city to the U.S. military cause, to help ready Philadelphia's defenses against the British army.[18] In general, blacks played an important part in the new war—for example, approximately ten percent of troops in the navy that sailed the Great Lakes were black.[19] Perhaps Forten thought that this time such service from African Americans might actually win concessions from the government.

Letters from a Man of Colour is emblematic of African-American pamphlets of the time because it publicly posits a rational disputation of racism. Forten argues about the unconstitutionality of the proposed legislation, in a way that almost completely separates the issue from the moral evils of racism and slavery.[20] In a society where African Americans were largely unable to vote or to serve in public office or practice law, the pamphlet served as a vehicle to comment on legal matters and to attempt to influence policy. Forten references the raging debate over how to interpret the U.S. Constitution on matters of race, arguing that racist legislation violates both "the letter and spirit" of the law, and weighs in on the matter of whether African Americans were covered by the use of the word "man" in the Pennsylvania Constitution. Such questions were of utmost importance on both a local and national level in the early decades of the new republic.

The limited demands that Forten makes show an approach that emphasized logical debate and rationality, and appealed to the principles and rhetoric of independence and equality, not simply to the morality involved in humanely treating one's fellow man. It is important to note that *Letters from a Man of Colour,* while clearly an anti-slavery document, makes no explicit demands for slavery's abolition. Nor does it demand full equality for free African Americans. Rather, from the moderate position it takes, *Letters from a Man of Colour* is an attempt to conserve the rights that free blacks already enjoyed in 1813 Pennsylvania. While it is rich in slavery metaphors (especially in its analogy of the colonial British relationship with America as that of a slave and a master), that part of the work primarily operates on an emotional level, suggesting that slavery is wrong without actually asking for the institution of slavery to change.

Certainly there are moral overtones in Forten's writing. He was a devout Episcopalian, serving in the vestry of his church for many years. There are several biblical references sprinkled throughout the text, as well as a passing call for temperance when he writes of the rowdy Independence Day celebrations. The hints of a more emotional moral argument, despite the obvious stress on a rational approach, do mark *Letters from a Man of Colour* as a kind of bridge document between the early and later abolitionist movements: it broadens slightly the typical argument of his time without going as far as the later abolitionist movement of the 1820s and beyond.

Letters from a Man of Colour is a contribution to a public debate that affected American society at a specific place and time. It is doubtful that it had much, if any, impact on the fate of the proposed legislation that gave birth to it, because similar legislation continued to be introduced. The disfranchisement of blacks under the 1838 Pennsylvania constitution demonstrates that despite Forten's pleas, the state and the country were moving not toward further equality, nor maintaining the status quo—but toward restricting the rights of African Americans even more than they already were.

However, the fact that *Letters from a Man of Colour* was deemed important enough to be reprinted fifteen years after it first appeared—in *Freedom's Journal*, the centrally important newspaper in the African-American community—suggests that it had lasting meaning, especially in the minds of African Americans. Its dominant themes of liberty and equality and its arguments against racially motivated policies resonated with a large segment of the early abolitionist and civil rights movements. In those ways, Forten successfully questioned a society that treated a "man of colour" as being something other than simply a "man"—and his refutation of such a distinction is perhaps the work's lasting legacy.

Notes

[1] The Fugitive Slave Law of 1793 authorizing the recovery of runaway slaves across state lines underscores the difficulty, regardless of the general sentiments and laws of the populace of Pennsylvania in 1813, of treating African Americans on a truly equal footing with whites. See David Brion Davis, *The Problem of Slavery in*

the *Age of Revolution: 1770-1823* (Ithaca, N.Y.: Cornell University Press, 1975), 133-134.

[2] [unsigned], *Freedom's Journal*, New York, Feb. 22, 1828. (Reproduced in "Accessible Archives CD-ROM Edition: The African-American Newspapers: the 19th Century," item #839.)

[3] One of the main reasons for ascribing authorship to Forten, apart from his relative prominence in Philadelphia, where the pamphlet first appeared, is that he is known to have used the pseudonym "A man of colour" in others of his publications. See Julie Winch, *A Gentleman of Color: The Life of James Forten* (New York: Oxford University Press, 2002), 7, 169.

[4] Under the law, all slaves would be emancipated by 1808. This ultimately led to a large free African-American population in Pennsylvania, particularly in Philadelphia. See Davis, 87; Winch, 129.

[5] For the full text of the 1790 Pennsylvania constitution, see Francis Newton Thorpe, ed., *The Federal and State Constitutions, Colonial Charters, and Other Organic Laws of the States, Territories, and Colonies Now or Heretofore Forming the United States of America*, vol. 5 (St. Clair Shores, Mich.: Scholarly Press, 1977), 3092-3103.

[6] Anonymous petition to the General Assembly of the colony of Pennsylvania, quoted in Kenneth L. Carroll, "William Southeby, Antislavery Writer," *Pennsylvania Magazine of History and Biography* 89 , no. 4 (1965): 423-424.

[7] Gary B. Nash, "Slaves and Slave Owners in Colonial Philadelphia," *African Americans in Pennsylvania: Shifting Historical Perspectives*, ed. Joe William Trotter Jr. and Eric Ledell Smith (University Park: Pennsylvania State University Press, 1997), 45-47, 50-52.

[8] Nash, 50, 60-62.

[9] Winch, 129.

[10] Pennsylvania General Assembly, *Journal of the Twenty Third House of Representatives of the Commonwealth of Pennsylvania* (Harrisburg, Pa: J. Peacock, Market Street, 1812 [1813]), 216.

[11] Pennsylvania General Assembly, *Journal of the Twenty Third House of Representatives of the Commonwealth of Pennsylvania*, 417, 481, 566-567, 588-589.

[12] Winch, 284-285.

[13] Winch, 284-287.

[14] William Cheek and Aimee Lee Cheek, *John Mercer Langston and the Fight for Black Freedom: 1829-1865* (Urbana: University of Illinois Press, 1996), 152.

[15] Winch, 24-25.

[16] The only full-length biography of James Forten remains Winch's *Gentleman of Color*. The discussion here draws especially on chapters 2–4.

[17] For information concerning trends in early African-American pamphleteering, as well as Forten's exemplification of them, see Richard Newman, Patrick Rael, and Philip Lapansky, *Pamphlets of Protest: An Anthology of Early African-American Protest Literature, 1790–1860* (New York: Routledge, 2001), 8–11. For statistics on African-American soldiers, see John Hope Franklin, *From Slavery to Freedom: A History of American Negroes* (New York: Knopf, 1947), 125–138.

[18] Winch, 174–176.

[19] Franklin, 123.

[20] Newman, Rael, and Lapansky, 10–14. The divergence between deep moral issues of equality and the sometimes selective rhetorical arguments of anti-slavery publications, and the evolution from eighteenth-century political legalistic arguments to more all-encompassing moral and theological arguments of the nineteenth century, are issues that continue to challenge students of American history today.

LETTERS

FROM

A MAN OF COLOUR,[1]

ON

A LATE BILL BEFORE THE SENATE OF PENNSYLVANIA.

Letter I.

O Liberty! thou power supremely bright,
Profuse of bliss and pregnant with delight,
Perpetual pleasures in thy presence reign,
And smiling Plenty leads thy wanton train.

ADDISON.[2]

WE hold this truth to be self-evident, that GOD created all men equal, and is one of the most prominent features in the Declaration of Independence, and in that glorious fabrick of collected wisdom, our noble Constitution. This idea embraces the Indian and the European, the Savage and the Saint, the Peruvian and the Laplander, the white Man and the African, and whatever measures are adopted subversive of this inestimable privilege, are in direct violation of the letter and spirit of our Constitution, and become subject to the animadversion of all, particularly those who are deeply interested in the measure.

These thoughts were suggested by the promulgation of a late bill, before the Senate of Pennsylvania, to prevent the emigration of people of colour[3] into this state. It was not passed into a law at this session and must in consequence lay over until the next, before when we sincerely hope, the white men, whom we should look upon as our protectors, will have become convinced of the inhumanity and impolicy of such a measure, and forbear to deprive us of those inestimable treasures, Liberty and Independence. This is almost the only state in the Union wherein the

305

African race have justly boasted of rational liberty and the protection of the laws, and shall it now be said they have been deprived of that liberty, and publickly exposed for sale to the highest bidder? Shall colonial inhumanity that has marked many of us with shameful stripes, become the practice of the people of Pennsylvania, while Mercy stands weeping at the miserable spectacle? People of Pennsylvania, descendants of the immortal Penn,[4] doom us not to the unhappy fate of thousands of our countrymen in the Southern States and the West Indies; despise the traffick in blood, and the blessing of the African will for ever be around you. Many of us are men of property, for the security of which, we have hitherto looked to the laws of our blessed state, but should this become a law, our property is jeopardized, since the same power which can expose to sale an unfortunate fellow creature, can wrest from him those estates, which years of honest industry have accumulated. Where shall the poor African look for protection, should the people of Pennsylvania consent to oppress him? We grant there are a number of worthless men belonging to our colour, but there are laws of sufficient rigour for their punishment, if properly and duly enforced. We wish not to screen the guilty from punishment, but with the guilty do not permit the innocent to suffer. If there are worthless men, there are also men of merit among the African race, who are useful members of Society. The truth of this let their benevolent institutions and the numbers clothed and fed by them witness. Punish the guilty man of colour to the utmost limit of the laws, but sell him not to slavery! If he is in danger of becoming a publick charge prevent him! If he is too indolent to labour for his own subsistence, compel him to do so; but sell him not to slavery. By selling him you do not make him better, but commit a wrong, without benefitting the object of it or society at large. Many of our ancestors were brought here more than one hundred years ago; many of our fathers, many of ourselves, have fought and bled for the Independence of our country. Do not then expose us to sale. Let not the spirit of the father behold the son robbed of that Liberty which he died to establish, but let the motto of our Legislators be: "The Law knows no distinction."

These are only a few desultory remarks on the subject, and intend to succeed this effervescence of feeling, by a series of essays, tending to prove the impolicy and unconstitutionality of the law in question.

For the present, I leave the publick to the consideration of the above observations, in which I hope they will see so much truth, that they will never consent to sell to slavery

A MAN OF COLOUR.

APRIL, 1813.

———

Letter II.

THOSE patriotick citizens, who, after resting from the toils of an arduous war, which achieved our Independence and laid the foundation of the only reasonable Republick upon earth, associated together, and for the protection of those inestimable rights for the establishment of which they had exhausted their blood and treasure, framed the Constitution of Pennsylvania, have by the ninth article, declared; that "All men are born equally free and independent, and have certain inherent and indefeasible rights, among which are those of enjoying life and liberty."[5] Under the restraint of wise and well administered laws, we cordially unite in the above glorious sentiment, but by the bill upon which we have been remarking, it appears as if the committee who drew it up mistook the sentiment expressed in this article, and do not consider us as men, or that those enlightened statesmen who formed the constitution upon the basis of experience, intended to exclude us from its blessings and protection. If the former, why are we not to be considered as men. Has the GOD who made the white man and the black, left any record declaring us a different species. Are we not sustained by the same power, supported by the same food, hurt by the same wounds, wounded by the same wrongs, pleased with the same delights, and propagated by the same means. And should we not then enjoy the same liberty, and be protected by the same laws.—We wish not to legislate, for our means of information and the acquisition of knowledge are, in the nature of things, so circumscribed, that we must consider ourselves incompetent to the task; but let us, in legislation, be considered as men. It cannot be that the authors of our

Constitution intended to exclude us from its benefits, for just emerging from unjust and cruel mancipation, their souls were too much affected with their own deprivations to commence the reign of terrour over others. They knew we were deeper skinned than they were, but they acknowledged us as men, and found that many an honest heart beat beneath a dusky bosom. They felt that they had no more authority to enslave us, than England had to tyrannize over them. They were convinced that if amenable to the same laws in our actions, we should be protected by the same laws in our rights and privileges. Actuated by these sentiments they adopted the glorious fabrick of our liberties, and declaring "all men" free, they did not particularize white and black, because they never supposed it would be made a question whether *we were men or not.* Sacred be the ashes, and deathless be the memory of those heroes who are dead; and revered be the persons and the characters of those who still exist and lift the thunders of admonition against the traffick in blood. And here my brethren in colour, let the tear of gratitude and the sigh of regret break forth for that great and good man, who lately fell a victim to the promiscuous fury of death, in whom you have lost a zealous friend, a powerful, an herculean advocate; a sincere adviser, and one who spent many an hour of his life to break your fetters, and ameliorate your condition—I mean the ever to be lamented Dr. BENJAMIN RUSH.[6]

It seems almost incredible that the advocates of liberty, should conceive the idea of selling a fellow creature to slavery. It is like the heroes of the French Revolution, who cried "*Vive la Republick,*" while the decapitated Nun was precipitated into the general reservoir of death, and the palpitating embryo decorated the point of the bayonet. Ye, who should be our protectors, do not destroy.—We will cheerfully submit to the laws, and aid in bringing offenders against them of every colour to justice; but do not let the laws operate so severely, so degradingly, so unjustly against us alone.

Let us put a case, in which the law in question operates peculiarly hard and unjust.—I have a brother, perhaps, who resides in a distant part of the Union, and after a separation of years, actuated by the same fraternal affection which beats in the bosom of a white man, he comes to visit me. Unless that brother be registered in twenty four hours after, and be able to produce a certificate to that effect, he is liable, according to the second and third sections of the bill, to a fine of twenty dollars, to arrest, imprisonment and sale. Let the unprejudiced mind ponder upon this, and then pronounce it the justifiable act of a free people, if he can. To this we trust our case, without fear of the issue. The unprejudiced must pronounce any act tending to deprive a free man of his right, freedom and immunities, as not only cruel in the extreme, but decidedly unconstitutional both as regards the letter and spirit of that glorious instrument. The same power which protects the white man, should protect

A MAN OF COLOUR.

———

Letter III.

T H E evils arising from the bill before our Legislature, so fatal to the rights of freemen, and so characteristick of European despotism, are so numerous, that to consider them all, would extend these numbers further than time or my talent will permit me to carry them. The concluding paragraph of my last number, states a case of peculiar hardship, arising from the second section of this bill, upon which I cannot refrain from making a few more remarks. The man of colour receiving as a visiter any other person of colour, is bound to turn informer, and rudely report to the Register, that a friend and brother has come to visit him for a few days, whose name he must take within twenty four hours, or forfeit a sum which the iron hand of the law is authorized to rend from him, partly for the benefit of the REGISTER. Who is this Register? A man, and exercising an office, where ten dollars is the fee for each delinquent, will probably be a cruel man and find delinquents where they really do not exist. The poor black is left to the merciless gripe of an avaricious REGISTER, without an appeal, in the event, from his tyranny or oppression! O miserable race, born to the same hopes, created with the same feeling, and destined for the same goal, you are reduced by your fellow creatures below the brute. The dog is protected and pampered at the board of his master, while the poor African and his descendant, whether a Saint or a felon, is branded with infamy, registered as a slave, and we may expect shortly to find a law to prevent their increase, by taxing them according to numbers, and authorizing the Constables to seize and confine every one who dare to walk the streets without a collar on his neck!—What have the people of colour been guilty of, that they more than others, should be compelled to register their houses, lands, servants and *Children*. Yes, ye rulers of the black man's destiny, reflect upon this; our *Children* must be registered, and bear about them a certificate, or be subject to imprisonment and fine. You, who are perusing this effusion of feeling, are you a parent? Have you children around whom your affections are bound, by those delightful bonds which none but a parent can know? Are they the delight of your prosperity, and the solace of your afflictions? If all this be true, to you we submit our cause. The parent's feeling cannot err. By your verdict will we stand or fall—by your verdict, live slaves or freemen. It is said, that the bill does not extend to children, but the words of the bill are, "Whether as an *inmate, visiter, hireling, or tenant, in his or her house or room.*" Whether this does not embrace every soul that can be in a house, the reader is left to judge; and whether the father should be bound to register his child, even within the twenty four hours after it is brought into the world, let the father's feelings determine. This is the fact, and our children sent on our lawful business, not having sense enough to understand the meaning of such proceedings, must show their certificate of registry or be borne to prison. The bill specifies neither age nor sex—designates neither the honest man or the vagabond— but like the fretted porcupine, his quills aim its deadly shafts promiscuously at all.

For the honour and dignity of our native state, we wish not to see this bill pass into a law, as well as for its degrading tendency towards us; for although oppressed by those to whom we look for protection, our grievances are light compared with the load of reproach that must be heaped upon our commonwealth. The story will fly from the north to the south, and the advocates of slavery, the traders in human blood, will smile contemptuously at the once boasted moderation and humanity of Pennsylvania! What, that place, whose institutions for the prevention of Slavery, are the admiration of surrounding states and of Europe, become the advocate of mancipation and wrong, and the oppressor of the free and innocent!—Tell it not in Gath! publish it not in the streets of Askelon! lest the daughters of the Philistines rejoice! lest the children of the uncircumcised triumph![7]

It is to be hoped that in our Legislature there is patriotism, humanity, and mercy sufficient, to crush this attempt upon the civil liberty of freemen, and to prove that the enlightened body who have hitherto guarded their fellow creatures, without regard to the colour of the skin, will still stretch forth the wings of protection to that race, whose persons have been the scorn, and whose calamities have been the jest of the world for ages. We trust the time is at hand when this obnoxious Bill will receive its death warrant, and freedom still remain to cheer the bosom of

A MAN OF COLOUR.

———

Letter IV.

I PROCEED again to the consideration of the bill of *unalienable* rights belonging to black men, the passage of which will only tend to show, that the advocates of emancipation can enact laws more degrading to the free man, and more injurious to his feelings, than all the tyranny of slavery, or the shackles of infatuated despotism. And let me here remark, that this unfortunate race of humanity, although protected by our laws, are already subject to the fury and caprice of a certain set of men, who regard neither humanity, law nor privilege. They are already considered as a different species, and little above the brute creation. They are thought to be objects fit for nothing else than lordly men to vent the effervescence of their spleen upon, and to tyrannize over, like the beard-ed Musselman[8] over his horde of slaves. Nay, the Musselman thinks more of his horse, than the generality of people do of the despised black!—Are not men of colour sufficiently degraded? Why then increase their degradation. It is a well known fact, that black people, upon certain days of publick jubilee, dare not be seen after twelve o'clock in the day, upon the field to enjoy the times; for no sooner do the fumes of that potent devil, Liquor, mount into the brain, than the poor black is assailed like the destroying Hyena or the avaricious Wolf! I allude particularly to the FOURTH OF JULY!—Is it not wonderful, that the day set apart for the festival of Liberty, should be abused by the advocates of Freedom, in endeavouring to sully what they profess to adore. If men, though they know that the law protects all, will dare, in defiance of law, to execute their hatred upon the defenceless black, will they not by the passage of this bill, believe him still more a mark for their venom and spleen.—Will they not believe him completely deserted by authority, and subject to every outrage brutality can inflict—too surely they will, and the poor wretch will turn his eyes around to look in vain for protection. Pause, ye rulers of a free people, before you give us over to despair and violation— we implore you, for the sake of humanity, to snatch us from the pinnacle of ruin, from that gulph, which will swallow our rights, as fellow crea- tures; our privileges, as citizens; and our liberties, as men!

There are men among us of reputation and property, as good citizens as any men can be, and who, for their property, pay as heavy taxes as any citizens are compelled to pay. All taxes, except personal, fall upon them, and still even they are not exempted from this degrading bill. The vil- lainous part of the community, of all colours, we wish to see punished and retrieved as much as any people can. Enact laws to punish them severely, but do not let them operate against the innocent as well as the guilty. Can there be any generosity in this? Can there be any semblance of justice, or of that enlightened conduct which is ever the boasted pole star of freedom? By no means. This bill is nothing but the ignus fatuus[9] of mistaken policy!

I could write for ages on the subject of this unrighteous bill, but as I think enough has already been said, to convince every unprejudiced mind, of its unjust, degrading, undeserved tendency, one more number shall conclude the Letters from

A MAN OF COLOUR.

———

Letter V.

A FEW more remarks upon the bill which has been the subject of my preceding numbers, shall conclude these Letters, which have been written in my own cause as an individual, and my brethren as a part of the community. They are the simple dictates of nature and need no apology. They are not written in the gorgeous style of a scholar, nor dressed in the garments of literary perfection. They are the impulse of a mind formed, I trust, for feeling, and smarting under all the rigours which the bill is calculated to produce.

By the third section of this bill, which is its peculiar hardship, the police officers are authorized to apprehend any black, whether a vagrant or a man of reputable character, who cannot produce a Certificate that he has been registered. He is to be arrayed before a justice, who is thereupon to commit him to prison!—The jailor is to advertise a Freeman, and at the expiration of six months, if no owner appear for this degraded black, he is to be *exposed to sale*, and if not sold to be confined at hard labour for seven years!!—Man of feeling, read this!—No matter who, no matter where. The Constable, whose antipathy generally against the black is very great, will take every opportunity of hurting his feelings!—Perhaps, he sees him at a distance, and having a mind to raise the boys in hue and cry against him, exclaims, "Halloa! Stop the Negro!" The boys, delighting in the sport, immediately begin to hunt him, and immediately from a hundred tongues, is heard the cry—"*Hoa, Negro, where is your Certificate!*"—Can any thing be conceived more degrading to humanity!—Can any thing be done more shocking to the principles of Civil Liberty! A person arriving from another state, ignorant of the existence of such a law, may fall a victim to its cruel oppression. But he is to be advertised, and if no owner appear—How can an owner appear for a man who is free and belongs to no one!—If no owner appear, he is exposed for sale!—Oh, inhuman spectacle: found in no unjust act, convicted of no crime, he is barbarously sold, like the produce of the soil, to the highest bidder, or what is still worse, for no crimes, without the inestimable privilege of a trial by his peers, doomed to the dreary walls of a prison for the term of seven tedious years!—My God, what a situation is his. Search the legends of tyranny and find no precedent. No example can be found in all the reigns of violence and oppression, which have marked the lapse of time. It stands alone. It has been left for Pennsylvania, to raise her ponderous arm against the liberties of the black, whose greatest boast has been, that he resided in a State where Civil Liberty, and sacred Justice were administered alike to all.—What must be his reflections now, that the asylum he had left from mancipation has been destroyed, and that he is left to suffer, like Daniel[10] of old, with no one but his God to help him! Where is the bosom that does not heave a sigh for his fall, unless it be callous to every sentiment of humanity and mercy?

The fifth section of this bill, is also peculiarly hard, inasmuch as it prevents freemen from living where they please.—Pennsylvania has always been a refuge from slavery, and to this state the Southern black, when freed, has flown for safety. Why does he this! When masters in many of the Southern states, which they frequently do, free a particular black, unless the Black leaves the state in so many hours, any person resident of the said state, can have him arrested and again sold to Slavery:—The hunted black is obliged to flee, or remain and be again a Slave. I have known persons of this description sold three times after being first emancipated. Where shall he go? Shut every state against him, and, like Pharoah's kine,[11] drive him into the sea.—Is there no spot on earth that will protect him! Against their inclination, his ancestors were forced from their homes by traders in human flesh, and even under such circumstances, the wretched offspring are denied the protection you afford to brutes.

It is in vain that we are forming societies of different kinds to ameliorate the condition of our unfortunate brethren, to correct their morals and to render them not only honest but useful members to society. All our efforts, by this bill, are despised, and we are doomed to feel the lash of oppression:—As well may we be outlawed, as well may the glorious privileges of the Gospel, be denied us, and all endeavours used to cut us off from happiness hereafter as well as here!—The case is similar, and I am much deceived if this bill does not destroy the morals it is intended to produce.

I have done. My feelings are acute, and I have ventured to express them without intending either accusation or insult to any one. An appeal to the heart is my intention, and if I have failed, it is my great misfortune, not to have had a power of eloquence sufficient to convince. But I trust the eloquence of nature will succeed, and that the law-givers of this happy Commonwealth will yet remain the Black's friend, and the advocates of Freemen, is the sincere wish of

A MAN OF COLOUR.

Notes

[1] James Forten, a second generation free black in Philadelphia. For details, see the introduction.

[2] From "A Letter from Italy to the Right Honourable Charles Lord Halifax in the Year MDCCI"(1703), by the Whig poet and statesman Joseph Addison (1672–1719). The lines printed here had previously been used in other pamphlets and early celebrations of American independence.

[3] The phrase "people of colour" was used in the official journal of the Pennsylvania General Assembly in 1813 to refer to African Americans. Forten's use of this phrase, as opposed to "negro" (also an acceptable term at the time, but one that has no explicit declaration of the humanity of its subjects) is important in light of the argument that he lays out. One could argue that the Assembly's choice of the phrase "people of colour" makes explicit their humanity.

[4] William Penn (1644–1718), one of the leading members of the early Society of Friends, won a charter in 1681 to found the colony of Pennsylvania. Drawing on his vast resources, he attempted, in Pennsylvania, to build a new society based on moral uprightness and the radical ideals of the Quakers.

[5] From article 9, section 1 of the Pennsylvania Constitution of 1790, which reads: "That all men are born equally free and independent, and have certain inherent and indefeasible rights, among which are those of enjoying and defending life and liberty, of acquiring, possessing, and protecting property and reputation, and of pursuing their own happiness." A close variation appeared in the original state constitution of 1776, and the exact phrase survives in the current state constitution, established in 1874.

[6] Dr. Benjamin Rush (1746–1813): Leading medical doctor, chemist, and politician. In addition to holding a number of prominent medical and teaching positions, Rush helped to organize the early American government, and was a president of the Pennsylvania Abolition Society. Forten, a great admirer of Rush, also had a personal connection to him: his son, Richard Rush, represented Forten in a court case. Benjamin Rush died April 19, 1813, shortly before this document was printed, and his name was probably hastily added in tribute to his service to Philadelphia and to African Americans.

[7] 2 Samuel 1:20. This passage is a lament from David, king of Israel, on the deaths of Jonathan and Saul in battle. Gath and Askelon were Philistine cities. Forten alludes to the terrible reversals that the righteous (i.e. African Americans and their supporters) could suffer. This and all subsequent Biblical references are from the Authorized (King James) Version of the Bible.

[8] Variant of "Mussulman," or "Muslim."

[9] Variant of "ignis fatuus," which literally means "foolish fire" in Latin. The term, used to signify any misleading or deluding goal, originally denoted the phos-

phorescent glow sometimes seen at night above marshland, which misled travelers who were foolish enough to follow it.

[10] The Biblical Daniel of Judah survived a night sealed in a den of lions as a test of his faith and God's ability to protect him (Daniel 6:16–27).

[11] "Kine" is an archaic plural of "cow." Perhaps a reference to a Biblical allegory in which the Pharaoh has a dream that seven fat kine come out of a river, followed by seven lean and ill kine that devour the fat ones. The dream was interpreted by Joseph to be a warning from God that seven years of plenty would come to Egypt, followed by seven years of terrible famine (Genesis 41:1–36).

PAPERS

RELATIVE TO THE RESTRICTION OF

SLAVERY.

SPEECHES OF

Mr. KING,

IN THE SENATE,

AND OF

Messrs. TAYLOR & TALMADGE,

IN THE

HOUSE OF REPRESENTATIVES,

OF THE

UNITED STATES,

ON THE BILL FOR AUTHORISING THE PEOPLE OF THE TER-
RITORY OF MISSOURI TO FORM A CONSTITUTION
AND STATE GOVERNMENT, AND FOR THE
ADMISSION OF THE SAME INTO
THE UNION.

IN THE SESSION OF 1818—19.

WITH A

REPORT OF A COMMITTEE

OF THE

ABOLITION SOCIETY OF DELAWARE.

PHILADELPHIA:
PRINTED BY HALL & ATKINSON, 53, MARKET STREET.
....
1819.

12

PAPERS RELATIVE TO THE RESTRICTION OF SLAVERY
by Rufus King and John Jay

Introduction by Eric C. Steinhart, St. Olaf College

Writing in retirement in late April 1820, Thomas Jefferson remarked that the recently settled Missouri Controversy had "like a fire-bell in the night awakened and filled me with terror."[1] Jefferson's alarm was aroused by the previous year's heated congressional debates over whether to admit Missouri (as a slaveholding state) and the vehemence of Northern anti-slavery rhetoric that made it clear that slavery had emerged as the volatile fault line of the United States. This issue was by no means new. Indeed, it had arisen at the very formation of the new nation when article 1 of the U.S. Constitution provided representation for "three-fifths" of all unfree persons, giving slaveholding states an influence in national politics that was disproportionate to the size of their free populations. Many hoped that the "three-fifths compromise" would dampen debate on the issue, and it seemed to for most of three decades. However, the controversy, in 1818–1819, over the admission of Missouri marked a turning point at which westward expansion forced the federal government to confront the divisive issue of slavery more starkly than ever before. The texts reprinted here were published at just this crucial moment in history as part of a larger pamphlet entitled *Papers Relative to the Restriction of Slavery. Speeches of Mr. King, in the Senate, and of Messrs. Taylor & Talmadge, in the House of Representatives. Of the United States . . . in the Session of 1818–19. With a Report of a Committee of the Abolition Society of Delaware* (Philadelphia, 1819).[2] In addition to the speech by Rufus King (1755–1827) and the letter by John Jay (1745–1829)—the two texts reprinted here—the original pamphlet also contained anti-slavery speeches by John W. Taylor (1784–1854) and James Tallmadge Jr. (1788–1853), as well as a report made by a committee of the Abolition Society of Delaware.

The scale and acrimony of the Missouri dispute in 1818–1819 would probably have surprised most of the drafters of the U.S. Constitution who originally met in Philadelphia in 1787. In fact, during the 1780s and early 1790s, slaveholders—even those in the South—had actively contemplated the demise of the "peculiar institution."[3] In contrast to the furor that would erupt over the Missouri Controversy thirty years later, Congress had peacefully assented to the Northwest Ordinance of 1787, which banned slavery from the Old Northwest.[4] Eli Whitney's 1793 invention of the cotton gin, however, reenergized slavery by making slave-produced cash crops highly profitable. Thus slaveholders, who had once agreed to the restriction of slavery from the Old Northwest, reconsidered their attitudes about the expansion of slavery in the newly acquired Louisiana Territory. Put simply, following the renewed profitability of slavery, maintaining the dominance of slaveholding states in the national government became a matter of tremendous economic importance to those who stood to profit from it. Given that in 1818 the national government was roughly balanced between free and slaveholding states, it was clear to all concerned that the character of the new states carved from the Louisiana Territory would decide the ultimate control of the nation. According to the prophetic congressional speech of one Georgian in 1819, this crisis had ignited an inferno that "all the waters of the ocean could not extinguish. It would be extinguished only in blood!"[5]

The Missouri Territory's November 1818 petition for statehood kindled these embers of contention.[6] Following procedures established during the initial expansion westward, the Missouri Territory was required to petition the federal government for legislation enabling it to form a constitution and, thereby, to become part of the Union. The proposed Missouri Enabling Act rose to prominence in the debate over the expansion of slavery when, in February of 1819, Representative James Tallmadge Jr. of New York proposed an amendment to prohibit the further introduction of slaves into Missouri and to manumit all slaves born within the territory when they reached the age of twenty-five years.[7] Slaveholders reacted immediately to Tallmadge's proviso; indeed, John Scott, the territorial representative from Missouri, berated the New Yorker for "sowing the seeds of discord in this Union."[8] Tallmadge was unable to lead the charge in the House, due to his own illness and the unexpected death of his son, so following Tallmadge's opening volley, John W. Taylor, a fellow New Yorker, continued the anti-slavery sortie.[9] While Tallmadge eventually did address the House, the true oratorical masterpiece of the debates was rendered by Senator Rufus King of New York. The Senator's two speeches, which appear here as a single text, as they did for publication in 1819, represent the most forceful opposition from the free states to the admission of Missouri as a slave state.

The acrimonious debate over the future of Missouri's statehood would only be resolved after both Maine and Missouri were admitted to the Union in early March of the following year, thereby continuing the balance between free and slave states. Illinois Senator Jesse B. Thomas offered a territorial restriction clause, which, with the exception of the new state of Missouri, forever forbade slavery in the Louisiana Purchase above 36° 30' and provided a template for the further admission of Western territories into the Union. Nevertheless, what became known as the Missouri Compromise was a defeat for congressional restrictionists, who failed to prohibit slavery in the new state of Missouri.

Notwithstanding the heated congressional debates, until the late summer and early fall of 1819 public opinion in both the North and the South was largely apathetic regarding the potential admission of Missouri as a slave state. Beginning in the latter half of 1819, under the leadership of a former president of the Continental Congress, Elias Boudinot, anti-slavery societies established committees of correspondence and distributed circular letters in an effort to mobilize public opinion in favor of the Tallmadge anti-slavery amendment.[10] Thus, when Congress reconvened in December 1819, it faced a concerted and vocal effort to oppose the Missouri Enabling Act if it would not incorporate the Tallmadge amendment.[11]

During the height of the Missouri Controversy, between March and December 1819, anti-slavery organizations produced myriad pamphlets in an effort to break the congressional deadlock in favor of the restrictionist cause. Indeed, King's address, and the speeches of Taylor and Tallmadge, were all reproduced in many pamphlets during 1819. Although Taylor and Tallmadge delivered their orations in the House of Representatives, King published "the substance" of his speeches on the Tallmadge amendment in response to a request from a committee of correspondence.[12] Like King's address, Jay's epistle in favor of the Tallmadge amendment was written at the request of a Northern restrictionist organization, the Trenton Committee for the Missouri Bill, and signed by its chairman, Elias Boudinot.[13] Jay wrote his supporting letter in mid-November 1819, and within weeks Boudinot published it.[14] Thus, King's speeches and Jay's letter were widely read in the North.

The pamphlet's printer, Hall & Atkinson, originally founded by Benjamin Franklin in the mid-eighteenth century, by 1815 had passed to David Hall, the younger son of Franklin's former partner. It began to specialize in publications for anti-slavery organizations. Thus, it is perfectly typical of Hall's publications that King's speech and Jay's letter were published in a pamphlet that also included speeches by New York Representatives Taylor and Tallmadge, as well as a report made by a committee of the Abolition Society of Delaware.

It would be a mistake to understand King's and Jay's views on slavery as unequivocal simply because the publisher produced predominantly anti-slavery literature. King sorely disappointed the more fervent abolitionists by writing that his comments on the Missouri Bill were "confined to Missouri and other new States," and thus did not apply to the institution of slavery as a whole.[15] Despite King's endorsement of the British abolitionist William Wilberforce during his tenure as American Minister to London from 1796 to 1803, and Jay's service as a founding member and first president of the New York Manumission Society (from 1785), both men had been slaveholders,[16] but years before writing the texts reprinted here both had taken steps to manumit their slaves. As one historian writes of figures like King and Jay: "few of these men were abolitionists in the Garrisonian sense. They frequently viewed slavery as a misfortune and even as an injustice, but few of them viewed it as a sin."[17]

To be sure, there were differences between King and Jay. Whereas Jay objected to slavery largely on the grounds that it violated innate human rights, King viewed slavery as politically destructive to the country. Indeed, King's speech may be seen as an intellectual progenitor of the political doctrine of free soil. King's cry would be adopted by supporters of the Free Soil Party, which would reprint his address three decades later with the preface: "To vindicate the truth of history, and to restore to the honored dead the laurels in which the political harlequins of the hour are playing fantastic tricks, we reproduce the speeches by Rufus

King, in the U.S. Senate on the *Free Soil* question."[18] Although opposed to the admission of western territories as slave states, the free soil ideology eschewed the moral objections to slavery based upon universal human rights and focused instead on its ruinous implications for society at large.[19] That the following document reproduces two related, yet ultimately distinct forms of anti-slavery rhetoric speaks to the galvanizing impact of the Missouri Controversy, not only in the solidification of sectionalism, but also as a turning point in the anti-slavery movement.[20]

While the speech given by King served as a harbinger of future anti-slavery arguments, the impact of his address was far more immediate and violent in slaveholding states. Less than three years after the resolution of the Missouri Controversy, in the late spring of 1822, Denmark Vesey allegedly organized an abortive, although intricately planned, slave uprising in Charleston, South Carolina.[21] Subsequent investigation revealed that during the course of their preparations, literate slaves had publicly read portions of restrictionist speeches, including the one given by King. Following the trial of Vesey and his alleged co-conspirators, the ideas articulated in pamphlets such as the one in which King's speech appeared were so threatening to Southern politicians that they viewed the pamphlets' dissemination as tantamount to violent rebellion.[22] Thus, whereas in the North the pamphlet witnessed the blossoming of a new vein of anti-slavery polemic, in the South it represented a challenge to the very foundations of slaveholding society. Few, however, were as perceptive as Thomas Jefferson, who wrote: "It is hushed, indeed, for the moment. But this is a reprieve only, not a final sentence. A geographical line, coinciding with marked principle, moral and political, once conceived and held up to the angry passions of men, will never be obliterated; and every new irritation will mark it deeper and deeper."[23]

Notes

[1] *The Writings of Thomas Jefferson*, vol. 15, edited by Albert Ellery Bergh (Washington, D.C.: The Thomas Jefferson Memorial Association of the United States, 1907), 249.

[2] The original title of the pamphlet in full is *Papers Relative to the Restriction of Slavery. Speeches of Mr. King, in the Senate, and of Messrs. Taylor & Talmadge, in the*

House of Representatives. Of the United States, on the Bill for Authorizing the People of the Territory of Missouri to Form a Constitution and State Government, and for the Admission of the Same into the Union. In the Session of 1818–19. With a Report of a Committee of the Abolition Society of Delaware.

3 See Thomas Jefferson, *Notes on the State of Virginia* (New York: Harper Torchbooks, 1964). In 1781, Thomas Jefferson, who himself owned more than 200 slaves, theorized about the manumission and removal of slaves from the United States. Likewise, George Washington, one of the largest slaveholders in Virginia, made provisions in his will to manumit his slaves upon the death of his wife. As these examples suggest, manumission was relatively common in the upper South during the early years of the new nation.

4 See article 6 of the Ordinance of 1787; Clarence E. Carter, ed., *The Territory Northwest of the River Ohio, 1787–1803*, vol. 2, *The Territorial Papers of the United States* (Washington, D.C.: U.S. Government Printing Office, 1934), 49.

5 *Annals of Congress*, 15th Cong., 2d sess., *Debates and Proceedings in the Congress of the United States; with an Appendix, Containing Important State Papers and Public Documents, and All the Laws of a Public Nature; with a Copious Index, House of Representatives* (Washington: Gales and Seaton: 15th Congress, 2nd Session, 1855), 1437.

6 Glover Moore, *The Missouri Controversy 1819–1821* (Lexington: University of Kentucky Press, 1953), 34.

7 *Annals of Congress*, 1178.

8 *Annals of Congress*, 1203; Don E. Fehrenbacher, "The Missouri Controversy and the Sources of Southern Separatism," *Southern Review* 14, no. 4 (1978). Fehrenbacher suggests that the Missouri Controversy taught Southerners the efficacy of threatening disunion to achieve their sectional political goals.

9 Moore, 50.

10 Moore, 67–84; Edward Kenneth Spann, "John W. Taylor, the Reluctant Partisan, 1784–1854" (PhD diss., New York University, 1957), 200–201.

11 Duane Meyer, *The Heritage of Missouri: a History* (Saint Louis: State Publishing Co., 1967), 152; Spann, 201–202. With the exception of Missouri, slaveholding states were more concerned with the economic recession of 1819 than with Northern efforts to restrict the expansion of slavery. At a Fourth of July celebration held in St. Louis, Missourians drank a toast to: "Messrs. Tallmadge and Taylor—politically insane—May the next Congress appoint them a dark room, a straight waistcoat [straitjacket] and a thin water gruel diet."

12 Charles R. King, ed., *Rufus King, Life and Correspondence: Comprising His Letters, Private and Official, His Public Documents, and His Speeches*, vol. 4 (New York: G.P. Putnam's Sons, 1900), 233; Spann, 199. It appears that Taylor was not eager to reprint his congressional speeches until the autumn of 1819.

[13] Elias Boudinot to John Jay, *The John Jay Papers* (New York City: Columbia University Rare Books Collection: November 5, 1819); George Adams Boyd, *Elias Boudinot: Patriot and Statesman, 1740–1821* (Princeton: Princeton University Press, 1952), 289.

[14] Moore, 72–73.

[15] Charles R. King, ed., 236. There is wide scholarly consensus that King's opposition to the admission of Missouri as a slave state was motivated by political rather than humanitarian concerns. See Joseph L. Arbena, "Politics or Principle? Rufus King and the Opposition to Slavery, 1785–1825," *Essex Institute Historical Collections* 101, no. 1 (1965): 56; Robert Ernst, "Rufus King, Slavery, and the Missouri Crisis," *New York Historical Society Quarterly* 46, no. 4 (1962): 363; Homer C. Hockett, "Rufus King and the Missouri Compromise," *Missouri Historical Review* 2 (1908): 217. However, some argue that the Missouri Controversy was the intellectual progenitor to the "free soil" movement. See Joshua Michael Zeitz, "The Missouri Compromise Reconsidered: Rhetoric and the Emergence of the Free Labor Synthesis," *Journal of the Early Republic* 20, no. 3 (2000): 452.

[16] Arbena, 67; Ernst, "Rufus King, Slavery, and the Missouri Crisis," 58–59, 361; Daniel C. Littlefield, "John Jay, the Revolutionary Generation, and Slavery," *New York History* 81, no. 1 (2000): 94–95.

[17] Ernst, "Rufus King, Slavery, and the Missouri Crisis," 361–363; Littlefield, 103.

[18] Rufus King, *The True Advocate of Free Soil [the Substance of Two Speeches on the Missouri Bill Delivered in the Senate of the United States]* (Newark: Steam Power Press, [1848?]), 1; Robert Ernst, *Rufus King, American Federalist* (Chapel Hill: Published for the Institute of Early American History and Culture at Williamsburg, Va., by University of North Carolina Press, 1968), 375.

[19] Zeitz, 452.

[20] Moore, 348.

[21] Recent scholarship raises doubt about the existence of Vesey's conspiracy. See Michael P. Johnson, "Denmark Vesey and His Co-Conspirators," *William and Mary Quarterly* 58, no. 4 (2001). Regardless of whether or not an actual uprising was planned, Charlestonians nevertheless saw King as one of its intellectual progenitors.

[22] Thomas Bennett, "Servile Conspiracy in S. Carolina," *Niles' Weekly Register,* September 7, 1822, 11.

[23] *Writings of Thomas Jefferson*, vol. 15, 207.

PAPERS

RELATIVE TO THE RESTRICTION OF

SLAVERY.

═══════════════

SPEECHES OF

Mr. KING,[1]

IN THE SENATE,

AND OF

Messrs. TAYLOR.[2] & TALMADGE,[3]

IN THE

HOUSE OF REPRESENTATIVES.

OF THE

UNITED STATES,

ON THE BILL FOR AUTHORISING THE PEOPLE OF THE TER-
RITORY OF MISSOURI TO FORM A CONSTITUTION
AND STATE GOVERNMENT, AND FOR THE
ADMISSION OF THE SAME INTO
THE UNION.

IN THE SESSION OF 1818—19.

WITH A

REPORT OF A COMMITTEE

OF THE

ABOLITION SOCIETY OF DELAWARE.[4]

══════

PHILADELPHIA:

PRINTED BY HALL & ATKINSON, 53, MARKET STREET

1819.

327

OBSERVATIONS

OF

RUFUS KING,

ON THE MISSOURI BILL;

Being the substance of two Speeches delivered in the Senate of the United States, during the last session of Congress.

The constitution declares "that congress shall have power to dispose of, and make all needful rules and regulations respecting the territory and other property of the United States."[5] Under this power, congress have passed laws for the survey and sale of the public lands, for the division of the same into separate territories; and have ordained for each of them a constitution, a plan of temporary government, whereby the civil and political rights of the inhabitants are regulated, and the rights of conscience and other natural rights are protected.

The power to make all needful regulations, includes the power to determine what regulations are needful; and if a regulation prohibiting slavery within any territory of the United States be, as it has been, deemed needful, congress possess the power to make the same, and moreover to pass all laws necessary to carry this power into execution.

The territory of Missouri is a portion of Louisiana, which was purchased of France,[6] and belongs to the United States in full dominion; in the language of the constitution, Missouri is their territory or property, and is subject, like other territories of the United States, to the regulations and tempory government, which has been, or shall be prescribed by congress. The clause of the constitution, which grants this power to congress, is so comprehensive, and unambiguous, and its purpose so manifest, that commentary will not render the power, or the object of its establishment, more explicit or plain.

The constitution further provides, that "new states may be admitted by congress into the union."[7]—As this power is conferred without limitation, the time, terms, and circumstances of the admission of new states are referred to the discretion of congress; which may admit new states, but are not obliged to do so:—of right, no new state can demand admission into the union, unless such demand be founded upon some previous engagement of the United States.

When admitted by congress into the union, whether by compact or otherwise, the new state becomes entitled to the enjoyment of the same rights, and bound to perform the like duties as the other states—and its citizens will be entitled to all privileges and immunities of citizens in the several states.

The citizens of each state possess rights, and owe duties that are peculiar to, and arise out of the constitution and laws of the several states. These rights and duties differ from each other in the different states; and among these differences none is so remarkable or important as that which proceeds from the constitution and laws of the several states respecting slavery;—the same being permitted in some states, and forbidden in others.

The question respecting slavery in the old thirteen states had been decided and settled before the adoption of the constitution, which grants no power to congress to interfere with, or to change what had been so previously settled; the slave states therefore, are free to continue or to abolish slavery. Since the year 1808, congress have possessed power to prohibit and have prohibited the further migration or importation of slaves into any of the old thirteen states;[8] and at all times under the constitution have had power to prohibit such migration or importation into any of the new states, or territories of the United States.[9] The constitution contains no express provisions respecting slavery in a new state that may be admitted into the union; every regulation upon this subject belongs to the power whose consent is necessary to the formation and admission of such state. Congress may, therefore, make it a condition of the admission of a new state, that slavery shall be forever prohibited within the same. We may with the more confidence pronounce this to be the true construction of the constitution, as it has been so amply confirmed by the past decisions of congress.

Although the articles of confederation were drawn up and approved by the old congress in the year 1777, and soon afterwards were ratified by some of the states, their complete ratification did not take place until the year 1781.—The states which possessed small and already settled territory, withheld their ratification, in order to obtain from the large states a cession to the United States of a portion of their vacant territory. Without entering into the reasons on which this demand was urged, it is well known that they had an influence on Massachusetts, Connecticut, New York, and Virginia; which states ceded to the United States their respective claims to the territory lying north west of the river Ohio. This cession was made on the express condition, that the ceded territory should be sold for the common benefit of the United States; that it should be laid out into states, and that the states so laid out should form distinct republican states, and be admitted as members of the federal union, having the same rights of sovereignty, freedom and independence as the other states. Of the four states which made this cession, two permitted, and the other two prohibited slavery.

The United States having in this manner become proprietors of the extensive territory north west of the river Ohio, although the confederations contained no express provision upon the subject, congress, the only representation of the United States, assumed, as incident to their office, the power to dispose of this territory; and for this purpose, to divide the same into distinct states, to provide for the temporary government of the inhabitants thereof, and for their ultimate admission, as new states, into the federal union.

The ordinance for these purposes, which was passed by congress in 1787, contains certain articles which are called—"Articles of compact between the original states, and the people and states within the said territory, forever to remain unalterable unless by common consent." The sixth of those unalterable articles provides "that there shall be neither slavery nor involuntary servitude in the said territory."[10]

The constitution of the United States supplies the defect that existed in the articles of confederation; and has vested congress, as has been stated, with ample powers on this important subject. Accordingly, the ordinance of 1787, passed by the old congress, was ratified and confirmed by an act of the new congress, during their first session under the constitution.

The state of Virginia, which ceded to the United States her claims to this territory, consented by her delegates in the old congress, to this ordinance. Not only Virginia, but North Carolina, South Carolina, and Georgia, by the unanimous votes of their delegates in the old congress, approved of the ordinance of 1787 by which slavery is for ever abolished in the territory north west of the river Ohio. Without the votes of these states the ordinance could not have passed; and there is no recollection of an opposition from any of these states, to the act of confirmation passed under the actual constitution. Slavery had long been established in these states—the evil was felt in their institutions, laws and habits, and could not easily or at once be abolished. But these votes, so honourable to these states, satisfactorily demonstrate their unwillingness to permit the extension of slavery into the new states which might be admitted by congress into the union.

The states of Ohio, Indiana, and Illinois, on the north west of the river Ohio, have been admitted by congress into the union, on the condition and conformably to the articles of compact, contained in the ordinance of 1787, and by which it is declared that there shall be neither slavery nor involuntary servitude in any of the said states.

Although congress possess the power of making the exclusion of slavery a part or condition of the act admitting a new state into the union, they may in special cases, and for sufficient reasons, forbear to exercise this power. Thus Kentucky and Vermont were admitted as new states into the union, without making the abolition of slavery the condition of their admission. In Vermont slavery never existed; her laws excluding the same. Kentucky was formed out of and settled by Virginia; and the inhabitants of Kentucky equally with those of Virginia, by fair interpretation of the constitution, were exempt from all such interference of congress as might disturb or impair the security of their property in slaves. The western territory of North Carolina and Georgia, having been partially granted and erected under the authority of these states, before the cession thereof to the United States, and these states being original parties to the constitution, which recognizes the existence of slavery, no measure restraining slavery could be applied by congress to this territory.[11] But, to remove all doubts on this head, it was made a condition of the cession of this territory to the United States, that the ordinance of 1787, except the sixth article thereof, respecting slavery, should be applied to the same; and that the sixth article should not be so applied. Accordingly, the

states of Tennessee, Mississippi, and Alabama, comprehending the territory ceded to the United States by North Carolina and Georgia, have
been admitted, as new states, into the union, without a provision by
which slavery shall be excluded from the same.[12] According to this
abstract of the proceedings of congress in the admission of new states
into the union,—of the eight new states within the original limits of the
United States, four have been admitted without an article excluding slavery; three have been admitted on the condition that slavery should be
excluded; and one admitted without such condition. In the first four cases, congress were restrained from exercising the power to exclude slavery; in the next three, they exercised this power; and in the last, it was
unnecessary to do so,—slavery being excluded by the state constitution.

The province of Louisiana, soon after its cession to the United States,
was divided into two territories comprehending such parts thereof as
were contiguous to the river Mississippi; being the only parts of the
province that were inhabited.[13] The foreign language, laws, customs and
manners of the inhabitants, required the immediate and cautious attention of congress; which, instead of extending in the first instance, to
these territories the ordinance of 1787, ordained special regulations for
the government of the same. These regulations were from time to time
revised and altered, as observation and experience shewed to be expedient, and as was deemed most likely to encourage and promote those
changes which would soonest qualify the inhabitants for self-govern-
ment and admission into the union. When the United States took possession of the province of Louisiana, in 1804, it was estimated to contain
fifty thousand white inhabitants, forty thousand slaves, and two thousand
free persons of colour.*[14] More than four-fifths of the whites, and all the
slaves, except about thirteen hundred, inhabited New Orleans and the
adjacent territory: the residue, consisting of less than ten thousand
whites, and about thirteen hundred slaves, were dispersed throughout
the country now included in the Arkansas and Missouri territories. The
greater part of the thirteen hundred slaves were in the Missouri territo-

---

*This estimate was too high, as by the census of 1810, the whole province was
found to contain only 97,000 inhabitants, viz: – 51,000 whites, 37,000 slaves,
8,000 free persons of colour.

ry; some of them having been removed thither from the old French settlements on the east side of the Mississippi, after the passing of the ordinance of 1787, by which slavery in those settlements was abolished.

In 1812, the territory of New Orleans, to which the ordinance of
1787, with the exception of certain parts thereof, had been previously
extended, was permitted by congress to form a constitution and state
government; and admitted as a new state into the union, by the name of
Louisiana. The acts of congress for these purposes, in addition to sundry
important provisions respecting rivers and public lands, which are
declared to be irrevocable unless by common consent, annex other
terms and conditions whereby it is established, not only that the constitution of Louisiana should be republican, but that it should contain the
fundamental principles of civil and religious liberty;—that it should
secure to the citizens the trial by jury in all criminal cases, and the privilege of the writ of habeas corpus[15] according to the constitution of the
United States; and after its admission into the union, that the laws which
Louisiana might pass should be promulgated, its records of every
description preserved, and its judicial and legislative proceedings conducted, *in the language* in which the laws and judicial proceedings of the
United States are published and conducted.

Guards so friendly to the rights of the citizens, and restraints on the
state sovereignty so material to the gradual confirmation and security of
their liberties, demonstrate the extensive and parental power of congress:
powers, the wise exercise of which, on this occasion, is not confined to the
inhabitants of the new state, but reaches and protects the rights of the citizens of all the states. The habits of the people and the number of slaves
by whom the labour of the territory of New Orleans was performed, were
doubtless the reasons for the omission of an article in the act of admission, by which slavery should be excluded from the new state.

Having annexed these new and extraordinary conditions to the act
for the admission of Louisiana into the union, congress may, if they shall
deem it expedient, annex the like conditions to the act for the admission
of Missouri; and moreover, as in the case of Ohio, Indiana, and Illinois,
provide by an article for that purpose, that slavery shall not exist within
the same.

Admitting this construction of the constitution, it is alleged that the power by which congress excluded slavery from the states north west of the river Ohio, is suspended in respect to the states that may be formed in the province of Louisiana. The article of the treaty referred to declares, "That the inhabitants of the territory shall be incorporated in the union of the United States, and admitted as soon as possible, according to the principles of the federal constitution, to the enjoyment of all rights, advantages and immunities of citizens of the United States; and in the mean time, they shall be maintained and protected in the free enjoyment of their liberty, property, and the religion which they profess."[16]

Although there is a want of precision in the article, its scope and meaning cannot be misunderstood. It constitutes a stipulation by which the United States engage that the inhabitants of Louisiana should be formed into a state or states, and as soon as the provisions of the constitution permit, that they shall be admitted as new states into the union, on the footing of the other states;—and before such admission, and during their territorial government, that they shall be maintained and protected by congress in the enjoyment of their liberty, property and religion. The first clause of this stipulation will be executed by the admission of Missouri as a new state into the union; as such admission will impart to the inhabitants of Missouri, "all the rights, advantages, and immunities"[17] which citizens of the United States derive from the constitution thereof;—these rights may be denominated federal rights, are uniform throughout the union, and are common to all its citizens. But the rights derived from the constitution and laws of the states, which may be denominated state rights, in many particulars differ from each other. Thus, while the federal rights of the citizens of Massachusetts and Virginia are the same, their state rights are however dissimilar,—slavery being forbidden in one, and permitted in the other state. This difference arises out of the constitutions and laws of the two states, in the same manner as the difference in the rights of the citizens of these states to vote for representatives in congress arises out of the state laws and constitution: in Massachusetts, every person of lawful age and possessing property of any sort, of the value of two hundred dollars, may vote for representatives to congress;—in Virginia, no person can vote for representatives to congress unless he be a freeholder. As the admission of a new state into the union confers upon its citizens only the rights denominated federal, and as these are common to the citizens of all the states, as well of those in which slavery is prohibited, as of those in which it is allowed, it follows that the prohibition of slavery in Missouri will not impair the federal rights of its citizens; and that such prohibition is not restrained by the clause of the treaty which has been cited.

The remaining clause of the article is expressly confined to the period of the territorial government of Missouri—to the time between the first occupation of the country by the United States, and its admission as a new state into the union. Whatever may be its import it has no reference nor application to the terms of the admission, or to the condition of Missouri after it shall have been admitted into the union. The clause is but the common formula of treaties, by which inhabited territories are passed from one sovereign to another: its object is to secure to such inhabitants the permanent or temporary enjoyment of their former liberties, property and religion; leaving to the new sovereign, full power to make such regulations respecting the same, as may be thought expedient, provided these regulations be not incompatible with the stipulated security.

What were the liberties under the French government, the enjoyment of which under ours called for protection, we are unable to explain: As the United States have no power to prevent the free enjoyment of the Catholic religion, no stipulation against their interference to disturb it could be necessary; and the only part of the clause whose object can be readily understood, is that relative to "property."

As all nations do not permit slavery, the term property in its common and universal meaning, does not include or describe slaves. In treaties therefore between nations, and especially in those of the United States, whenever stipulations respecting slaves were to be made, the word "negroes," or "slaves," has been employed; and the omission of these words in this clause, increases the uncertainty whether by the term property, *slaves* were intended to be included. But admitting that such was the intention of the parties, the stipulation is not only temporary, but extends no further than to the property actually possessed by the inhabitants of Missouri, when it was first occupied by the United States: Property since acquired by them, and property acquired or possessed by the new inhabitants of Missouri, has in each case been acquired under the laws of the United States, and not during and under the laws of the province of Louisiana. Should, therefore, the future introduction of slaves into Missouri be forbidden, the feelings of the citizens would soon become reconciled to their exclusion; and the inconsiderable number of slaves owned by the inhabitants at the date of the cession of Louisiana, would be emancipated or sent for sale into states where slavery exists.

It is further objected, that the article of the act of admission into the union, by which slavery should be excluded from Missouri, would be nugatory, as the new state in virtue of its sovereignty, would be at liberty to revoke its consent and annul the article by which slavery should be excluded.

Such revocation would be contrary to the obligations of good faith, which enjoins the observance of our engagements—it would be repugnant to the principles upon which government itself is founded. Sovereignty in every lawful government is a limited power, and can do only what it is lawful to do—sovereigns, like individuals, are bound by their engagements, and have no moral power to break them. Treaties between nations repose on this principle. If the new state can revoke and annul an article concluded between itself and the United States, by which slavery is excluded from it, it may revoke and annul any other article of the compact: it may for example annul the article respecting public lands; and in virtue of its sovereignty, assume the right to tax and to sell the lands of the United States.

There is yet a more satisfactory answer to this objection. The judicial power of the United States is co-extensive with their legislative power; and every question arising under the constitution or laws of the United States, is cognizable by the judiciary thereof. Should the new state rescind any of the articles of compact contained in the act of admission into the union, that for example by which slavery is excluded, and should pass a law authorizing slavery, the judiciary of the United States, on proper application, would immediately deliver from bondage, any person detained as a slave in said state; and in like manner, in all instances affecting individuals, the judiciary might be employed to defeat every attempt to violate the constitution and laws of the United States.

If congress possesses the power to exclude slavery from Missouri, it still remains to be shewn that they ought to do so. The examination of this branch of the subject, for obvious reasons, is attended with peculiar difficulty, and cannot be made without passing over arguments which to some of us might appear to be decisive, but the use of which, in this place, would call up feelings, the influence of which would disturb, if not defeat the impartial consideration of the subject.

Slavery unhappily exists within the United States. Enlightened men in the states where it is permitted, and every where out of them, regret its existence among us, and seek for the means of limiting and of mitigating it. The first introduction of slaves, is not imputable to the present generation nor even to their ancestors. Before the year 1642, the trade and ports of the colonies were open to foreigners equally as those of the mother country; and as early as 1620, a few years only after the planting of the colony of Virginia, and the same year in which the first settlement was made in the old colony of Plymouth, a cargo of negroes was brought in and sold as slaves in Virginia, by a foreign ship.*[18] From this beginning the importation of slaves was continued for nearly two centuries.—To her honour, Virginia, while a colony, opposed the importation of slaves, and was the first state to prohibit the same, by a law passed for this purpose in 1778, thirty years before the general prohibition enacted by congress in 1808.[19] The laws and customs of the states in which slavery has existed for so long a period, must have had their influence on the opinions and habits of the citizens; which ought not to be disregarded on the present occasion.

Omitting therefore, the arguments which might be urged, and which by all of us might be deemed conclusive, were this an original question, the reasons which shall be offered in favor of the interposition of the power of congress to exclude slavery from Missouri, shall be only such as respect the common defence, the general welfare, and that wise administration of the government which as far as possible may produce the impartial distribution of benefits and burdens throughout the union.

---

* Stith's *History of Virginia.*

By the article of confederation, the common treasury was to be supplied by the several states according to the value of the lands, with the houses and improvements thereon, within the respective states. From the difficulty in making this valuation, the old congress were unable to apportion the requisitions for the supply of the general treasury; and obliged to propose to the states an alteration of the articles of confederation—by which the whole number of free persons, with three fifths of the slaves, contained in the respective states, should become the rule of such apportionment of the taxes. A majority of the states approved of this alteration, but some of them disagreed to the same; and for want of a practicable rule of apportionment, the whole of the requisitions of taxes made by congress during the revolutionary war, and afterwards, up to the establishment of the constitution of the United States, were merely provisional, and subject to revision and correction as soon as such rules should be adopted. The several states were credited for their supplies, and charged for the advances made to them by congress; but no settlement of their accounts could be made, for the want of a rule of apportionment, until the establishment of the constitution.[20]

When the general convention that formed the constitution took this subject into their consideration, the whole question was once more examined; and while it was agreed that all contributions to the common treasury should be made according to the ability of the several states to furnish the same, the old difficulty recurred in agreeing upon a rule whereby such ability should be ascertained;—there being no simple standard by which the ability of individuals to pay taxes can be ascertained. A diversity in the selection of taxes has been deemed requisite to their equalization. Between communities, this difficulty is less considerable; and although the rule of relative numbers would not accurately measure the relative wealth of nations; in states in the circumstances of the United States, whose institutions, laws and employments are so much alike, the rule of number is probably as nearly equal, as any other simple and practicable rule can be expected to be;—(though between the old and new states its equity is defective.)—These considerations, added to the approbation which had already been given to the rule by a majority of the states, induced the convention to agree, that direct taxes should be apportioned among the states, according to the whole number of free persons, and three fifths of the slaves which they might respectively contain.

The rule for apportionment of taxes, is not necessarily the most equitable rule, for the apportionment of representatives among the states;—property must not be disregarded in the composition of the first rule; but frequently is overlooked in the establishment of the second:—a rule which might be approved in respect to taxes, would be disapproved in respect to representatives; one individual possessing twice as much property as another, might be required to pay double the taxes of such other; but no man has two votes to another's one; —rich or poor, each has but a single vote in the choice of representatives.

In the dispute between England and the colonies, the latter denied the right of the former to tax them, because they were not represented in the English Parliament. They contended, that according to the law of the land, taxation and representation were inseparable. The rule of taxation being agreed upon by the convention, it is possible that the maxim with which we successfully opposed the claim of England, may have had an influence in procuring the adoption of the same rule for the apportionment of representatives: the true meaning, however, of this principle of the English constitution, is, that a colony or district is not to be taxed which is not represented; not that its number or representatives shall be ascertained by its quota of taxes. If three fifths of the slaves are virtually represented, [21] or their owners obtain a disproportionate power in legislation, and in the appointment of the president of the United States, why should not other property be virtually represented, and its owner obtain a like power in legislation, and in the choice of the president—Property is not confined to slaves, but exists in houses, stores, ships, capital in trade and manufactures. To secure to the owners of property in slaves, greater political power than is allowed to the owners of other and equivalent property, seems to be contrary to our theory of the equality of personal rights; inasmuch as the citizens of some states thereby become entitled to other and greater political power, than the citizens of other states. The present house of representatives consists of one hundred and eighty-one members; which are apportioned among the states in a ratio of one representative for every thirty-five thousand federal numbers, which are ascertained by adding to the whole number of free persons, three fifths of the slaves. According to the last census,[22] the whole number of slaves within the United States was 1,191,364; which entitled the states possessing the same, to twenty representatives, and twenty presidential electors more than they would be entitled to, were the slaves excluded. By the last census, Virginia contained 582,104 free persons, and 392,518 slaves. In any of the states where slavery is excluded, 582,104 free persons would be entitled to elect only sixteen representatives; while in Virginia, 582,104 free persons, by the addition of three fifths of her slaves, becomes entitled to elect, and do in fact elect, twenty-three representatives;—being seven additional ones on account of her slaves. Thus, while 35,000 free persons are requisite to elect one representative in a state where slavery is prohibited, 25,559 free persons in Virginia, may and do elect a representative—so that five free persons in Virginia, have as much power in the choice of representatives to congress, and in the appointment of presidential electors, as seven free persons in any of the states in which slavery does not exist.

This inequality in the apportionment of representatives was not misunderstood at the adoption of the constitution—but as no one anticipated the fact that the whole of the revenue of the United States would be derived from indirect taxes, (which cannot be supposed to spread themselves over the several states according to the rule for the apportionment of direct taxes,) it was believed that a part of the contribution to the common treasury would be apportioned among the states by the rule for the apportionment of representatives. The states in which slavery is prohibited, ultimately, though with reluctance, acquiesced in the disproportionate number of representatives and electors that was secured to the slave holding states. The concession was, at the time, believed to be a great one; and has proved to have been the greatest which was made to secure the adoption of the constitution.

Great, however, as this concession was, it was definite; and its full extent was comprehended. It was a settlement between the original thirteen states. The considerations arising out of their actual condition, their past connection, and the obligation which all felt to promote a reformation in the federal government, were peculiar to the time and to the parties; and are not applicable to the new states, which congress may now be willing to admit into the union.

The equality of rights, which includes an equality of burdens, is a vital principle in our theory of government; and its jealous preservation is the best security of public and individual freedom: the departure from this principle in the disproportionate power and influence, allowed to the slave holding states, was a necessary sacrifice to the establishment of the constitution. The effect of this concession has been obvious in the preponderance which it has given to the slave holding states, over the other states. Nevertheless, it is an ancient settlement; and faith and honour stand pledged not to disturb it. But the extension of this disproportionate power to the new states would be unjust and odious. The states whose power would be abridged, and whose burdens would be increased by the measure, cannot be expected to consent to it; and we may hope that the other states are too magnanimous to insist on it.

The existence of slavery impairs the industry and the power of a nation; and it does so in proportion to the multiplication of its slaves: where the manual labour of a country is performed by slaves, labour dishonours the hands of freemen.

If her labourers are slaves, Missouri may be able to pay money taxes, but will be unable to raise soldiers, or to recruit seamen, and experience seems to have proved that manufactures do not prosper where the artificers are slaves. In case of foreign war, or domestic insurrection, misfortunes from which no states are exempt, and against which all should be seasonably prepared, slaves not only do not add to, but diminish the faculty of self defence: instead of increasing the public strength, they lessen it, by the whole number of free persons, whose place they occupy, increased by the number of free men that may be employed as guards over them.

The motives for the admission of new states into the union, are the extension of the principles of our free government, the equalizing of the public burdens, and the consolidation of the power of the confederated nation. Unless these objects be promoted by the admission of new states, no such admission can be expedient or justified.

342

The states in which slavery already exists are contiguous to each other: they are also the portion of the United States nearest to the European colonies in the West Indies; —colonies whose future condition can hardly be regarded as problematical. If Missouri and the other states that may be formed to the west of the river Mississippi are permitted to introduce and establish slavery, the repose, if not the security of the union may be endangered; all the states south of the river Ohio and west of Pennsylvania and Delaware will be peopled with slaves and the establishment of new states west of the river Mississippi will serve to extend slavery instead of freedom over that boundless region.

Such increase of the states, whatever other interest it may promote, will be sure to add nothing to the security of the public liberties; and can hardly fail hereafter to require and produce a change in our government.

On the other hand, if slavery be excluded from Missouri, and the other new states which may be formed in this quarter, not only will the slave markets be broken up, and the principles of freedom be extended and strengthened; but an exposed and important frontier will present a barrier, which will check and keep back foreign assailants, who may be as brave, and, as we hope, will be as free as ourselves. Surrounded in this manner by connected bodies of freemen, the states where slavery is allowed will be made more secure against domestic insurrection, and less liable to be affected by what may take place in the neighbouring colonies.

It ought not be forgotten, that the first and main object of the negotiation which led to the acquisition of Louisiana, was the free navigation of the Mississippi; a river that forms the sole passage from the western states to the ocean. This navigation, although of general benefit, has been always valued and desired, as of peculiar advantage to the western states; whose demands to obtain it, were neither equivocal nor unreasonable. But with the river Mississippi,—by a sort of coersion, we acquired by good or ill fortune, as our future measures shall determine, the whole province of Louisiana. As this acquisition was made at the common expense, it is very fairly urged, that the advantages to be derived from it should also be common. This it is said will not happen, if slavery be excluded from Missouri, as the citizens of states where slavery is permitted will be shut out, and none but citizens of states where slavery is prohibited can become inhabitants of Missouri.

But this consequence will not arise from the proposed exclusion of slavery: the citizens of states, in which slavery is allowed, like all other citizens, will be free to become inhabitants of the Missouri, in like manner as they have become inhabitants of Ohio, Indiana and Illinois, in which slavery is forbidden. The exclusion of slaves from Missouri, will not therefore operate unequally among the citizens of the United States. The constitution provides, "that the citizens of each state shall be entitled to enjoy all the rights and immunities of citizens of the several states"[23]—every citizen may therefore remove from one to another state, and there enjoy the rights and immunities of its citizens. The proposed provision excludes slaves, not citizens, whose rights it will not, and cannot impair.

Besides there is nothing new or peculiar in a provision for the exclusion of slavery: it has been established in the states north west of the river Ohio, and has existed from the beginning in the old states where slavery is forbidden. The citizens of states where slavery is allowed, may become inhabitants of Missouri, but cannot hold slaves there, nor in any other state where slavery is prohibited. As well might the laws prohibiting slavery in the old states become the subject of complaint, as the proposed exclusion of slavery in Missouri; but there is no foundation for such complaint in either case. It is further urged, that the admission of slaves into Missouri would be limited to the slaves who are already within the United States; that their health and comfort would be promoted by their dispersion; and that their numbers would be the same, whether they remain confined to the states where slavery exists, or are dispersed over the new states that may be admitted into the Union.

That none but domestic slaves would be introduced into Missouri, and the other new and frontier states, is most fully disproved by the thousands of fresh slaves, which, in violation of our laws, are annually imported into Alabama, Louisiana and Mississippi.[24]

We may renew our efforts and enact new laws with heavier penalties, against the importation of slaves: the revenue cutters[25] may more diligently watch our shores; and the naval force may be employed on the coast of

344

Africa, and on the ocean to break up the slave trade—but these means will not put an end to it: so long as markets are open for the purchase of slaves, so long they will be supplied: and so long as we permit the existence of slavery in our new and frontier states, so long slave markets will exist. The plea of humanity is equally inadmissible; since no one who has ever witnessed the experiment, will believe, that the condition of slaves is made better by the breaking up and separation of their families, nor by their removal from the old states to the new ones; and the objection to the provision of the bill excluding slavery from Missouri, is equally applicable to the like prohibitions of the old states: these should be revoked in order that the slaves, now confined to certain states, may, for their health, and comfort, and multiplication, be spread over the whole union.

That the condition of slaves within the United States has been improved, and the rigours of slavery mitigated, by the establishment and progress of our free governments, is a fact that imparts consolation to all who have taken pains to inquire concerning it. The disproportionate increase of free persons of colour, can be explained only by the supposition that the practice of emancipation is gaining ground;—a practice which there is reason to believe would become more general, if a plan could be devised by which the comfort and morals of the emancipated slaves could be satisfactorily provided for, for it is not to be doubted that public opinion every where, and especially in the oldest states of the union, is less favourable than formerly to the existence of slavery. Generous and enlightened men in the states where slavery exists, have discovered much solicitude on the subject: a desire has been manifested that emancipation might be encouraged by the establishment of a place, or colony without the United States, to which free persons of colour might be removed; and great efforts for that purpose are making, with a correspondent anxiety for their success. These persons, enlightened and humane as they are known to be, surely will be unwilling to promote the removal of the slaves from the old states, to the new ones; where their comforts will not be multiplied, and where their fetters may be riveted for ever.

Slavery cannot exist in Missouri without the consent of congress; the question may therefore be considered, in certain lights, as a new one,—it being the first instance in which an enquiry respecting slavery, in a case so free from the influence of the ancient laws, usages, and manners of the country, has come before the senate.

The territory of Missouri is beyond our ancient limits; and the inquiry whether slavery shall exist there, is open to many of the arguments that might be employed, had slavery never existed within the United States. It is a question of no ordinary importance. Freedom and slavery are the parties which stand this day before the senate; and upon its decision the empire of the one or the other will be established in the new state which we are about to admit into the union.

If slavery be permitted in Missouri, with the climate, and soil, and in the circumstances of this territory, what hope can be entertained that it will ever be prohibited in any of the new states that will be formed in the immense region west of the Mississippi? Will the co-extensive establishment of slavery and of new states throughout this region, lessen the danger of domestic insurrection, or of foreign aggression? Will this manner of executing the great trust of admitting new states into the union, contribute to assimilate our manners and usages; to increase our mutual affection and confidence; and to establish that equality of benefits and burthens which constitutes the true basis of our strength and union?— Will the militia of the nation, which must furnish our soldiers and seamen, increase as slaves increase? will the actual disproportion in the military service of the nation be thereby diminished? a disproportion that will be, as it has been, readily borne, as between the original states, because it arises out of their compact of union; but which may become a badge of inferiority, if required for the protection of those who, being free to choose, persist in the establishment of maxims, the inevitable effect of which will deprive them of the power to contribute to the common defence, and even of the ability to protect themselves. There are limits within which our federal system must stop; no one has supposed that it could be indefinitely extended—we are now about to pass our original boundary; if this can be done without affecting the principles of our free government, it can be accomplished only by the most vigilant attention to plant, cherish and sustain the principles of liberty in the new states that may be formed beyond our ancient limits: with our utmost caution in this respect, it may still be justly apprehended that the general government must be made stronger as we become more extended.

But if, instead of freedom, slavery is to prevail, and spread as we extend our dominion, can any reflecting man fail to see the necessity of giving to the general government greater powers, to enable it to afford the protection that will be demanded of it;—powers that will be difficult to controul, and which may prove fatal to the public liberties.

The following letter contains the opinion of that great Civilian John Jay, [26] *on the Constitutional authority of Congress in the premises.*

Bedford, West Chester County, N.Y.
17th November, 1819.

DEAR SIR,[27]

I have received the copy of a Circular Letter, which as Chairman of the committee appointed by the late public meeting at Trenton, respecting slavery, you was pleased to direct to me on the 5th instant.

Little can be added to what has been said and written on the subject of Slavery. I concur in the opinion that it ought not to be introduced nor permitted in any of the *new states*, and that it ought to be gradually diminished and finally abolished in all of them.

To me the constitutional authority of the Congress, to prohibit the migration and importation of slaves into any of the states, does not appear questionable.

The *first* article of the Constitution specifies the legislative powers committed to the Congress. The 9th section of that article has these words—"The *migration* or *importation* of such persons as any of the *now existing* states shall think proper to admit, shall not be prohibited by the Congress prior to the year 1808—but a tax or duty may be imposed on such importation not exceeding ten dollars for each person."

I understand the sense and meaning of this clause to be—That the power of the Congress, although competent to prohibit such migration and importation, was not to be exercised with respect to the *then* exiting states (and them only) until the year 1808—but that the Congress were at liberty to make such prohibition as to any *new* state which might in the *mean* time be established.—And further that from and after *that* period,

347

they were authorized to make such prohibition as to *all* the states, whether *new* or *old*.

It will I presume be admitted that Slaves were the Persons intended.— The word Slaves was avoided probably on account of the existing toleration of Slavery, and its discordancy with the principles of the Revolution; and from a consciousness of its being repugnant to the following positions in the Declaration of Independence—"We hold these truths to be self-evident—that *all* men are created Equal—that they are endowed by their Creator with certain unalienable rights—that among them are Life, Liberty and the pursuit of happiness."

As to my taking an *active* part in "organizing a plan of co-operation," the state of my health has long been such as not to admit of it.

Be pleased to assure the Committee of my best wishes for their success, and permit me to assure you of the esteem and regard with which

I am,

Dear Sir,

Your faithful and obedient Servant,

JOHN JAY.

The Honourable
ELIAS BOUDINOT, Esq.

Notes

[1] Rufus King (1755–1827), originally of Maine, served as senator from New York, was an anti-slavery activist, became a diplomat, and ran multiple times as a Federalist vice-presidential and presidential candidate. Reprinted here are King's speeches on the Missouri question, but not those of John Taylor or James Tallmadge, who were also anti-slavery, nor the report from the Abolition Society of Delaware. For Taylor's speech, see *Annals of Congress*, 15th Cong., 2nd sess., 1170–1179. For Tallmadge's speech, see *Annals of Congress*, 15th Cong., 2nd sess., 1203–1214. For further details see the introduction to this pamphlet.

[2] John W. Taylor (1784–1854): New York congressman from 1812 until 1832, who served twice as Speaker of the House, in 1820 and 1825.

[3] James Tallmadge Jr. (1778–1853) of New York served as a congressman from 1817 until 1819.

[4] Founded in 1788, the Delaware Society for Promoting the Abolition of Slavery and for the Relief and Protection of Free Blacks and People of Colour, Unlawfully Held in Bondage or Otherwise Oppressed sought to ameliorate the condition of freed slaves, and worked to further the abolitionist cause. The society was unique among early anti-slavery organizations in denying membership to slaveholders.

[5] Article 4, section 3 of the U.S. Constitution.

[6] In 1803, the United States purchased Louisiana from France for 15 million dollars. The territory was roughly bounded by the Gulf of Mexico, the Mississippi River, the present-day border with Canada, and the Rocky Mountains.

[7] Article 4, section 3 of the U.S. Constitution.

[8] In 1807, Congress enacted a bill that forbade the transatlantic slave trade, effective January 1, 1808.

[9] Article 1, section 9 of the U.S. Constitution.

[10] Article 6 of the Northwest Ordinance of 1787.

[11] North Carolina and Georgia ceded their western lands to the federal government in 1789 and 1802, respectively. Both states included provisions that protected the institution of slavery within the ceded territory.

[12] Tennessee, Mississippi, and Alabama were admitted to the union in 1796, 1817, and 1819, respectively.

[13] In 1804, Louisiana was divided into two parts: the Territory of Orleans, which corresponds to the present-day state of Louisiana, and the District of Louisiana, which included part or all of the present-day states of Arkansas, Oklahoma, Texas, New Mexico, Colorado, Kansas, Missouri, Iowa, Nebraska, Wyoming, Montana, North Dakota, South Dakota, and Minnesota.

[14] King uses rounded numbers derived from the 1810 census.

[15] Writ of Habeas Corpus: one of several common law written orders issued to free authorities to bring prisoners forward for a hearing.

[16] Article 3 of the 1803 Treaty for the Cession of Louisiana.

[17] Article 3 of the 1803 Treaty for the Cession of Louisiana.

[18] Slaves had first been introduced in the colony of Virginia at least as early as 1619, not 1620. In the early 1500s, the Spanish brought the first African slaves to the present-day United States.

[19] In 1772, the Virginia House of Burgesses unsuccessfully petitioned the Privy Council to prohibit the importation of slaves into the colony. The petition was partly economically motivated in that by restricting the supply of imported slaves, the petition would have insured that slaves already in the colony increased in value.

[20] See article 1, section 2 of the U.S. Constitution.

[21] Virtual representation: a theory of representation that holds that members of a polity may be represented in a legislative body without the ability to elect their representatives. Prior to the American Revolution, supporters of the Crown used the theory of virtual representation to justify parliamentary taxation and regulation of the American Colonies without colonial representation.

[22] King refers to the 1810 census.

[23] Article 4, section 2 of the U.S. Constitution.

[24] Between 1811 and 1820, approximately 10,000 Africans were illegally transported to the United States as slaves.

[25] The Revenue Cutter Service, also known as the Revenue Marine, was a law enforcement agency created in 1790, charged with overseeing customs regulations and duties, as well as the protection of United States fishing waters. In 1915, the Revenue Cutter Service was merged with several other agencies to form the U.S. Coast Guard. The term "cutter" is English in origin and originally denoted a specific type of small, decked, one-masted ship. It later came to define any vessel of Great Britain's Royal Customs Service and was adopted by what would become the Revenue Cutter Service. Today, a cutter refers to any Coast Guard vessel more than sixty-five feet in length.

[26] John Jay (1745–1829): A New Yorker who served as a member of the Continental Congress, a diplomat, governor of the State of New York, and the first chief justice of the U.S. Supreme Court. During the ratification of the U.S. Constitution, Jay joined James Madison and Alexander Hamilton in drafting the *Federalist Papers*.

[27] Jay addresses his letter to Elias Boudinot (1740–1821), a former president of

the Continental Congress, and, as an extension of the anti-slavery views that he shared with his friend John Jay, a chairman of the Trenton Committee for the Missouri Bill.

WORKS CONSULTED

Adams, Alice Dana. *The Neglected Period of Anti-Slavery in America, 1808–1831.* Gloucester, Mass.: Peter Smith, 1964.

"Albany, Feb. 20." *The Pennsylvania Gazette,* March 1975.

Allinson Family Papers, 1761–1812. Special Collections, Alexander Library, Rutgers University, New Brunswick, N.J.

American Convention for Promoting the Abolition of Slavery. *Minutes of the Proceedings of the Second Convention of Delegates from the Abolition Societies Established in Different Parts of the United States, Assembled at Philadelphia.* Philadelphia: Zachariah Poulson, 1795. Schomburg Center for Research in Black Culture. Manuscripts, Archives and Rare Books Division.

American Convention for Promoting the Abolition of Slavery, and Improving the Condition of the African Race. *Minutes of the Proceedings of a Special Meeting of the Fifteenth American Convention for Promoting the Abolition of Slavery, and Improving the Condition of the African Race, Assembled at Philadelphia, on the Tenth Day of December, 1818, and Continued by Adjournments until the Fifteenth of the Same Month, Inclusive.* Philadelphia: Printed for the Convention by Hall & Atkinson, 1818.

"The American Female Poets." *The North American Review* 68 (April 1849).

Annals of Congress of the United States 1789–1824. Vol. 33. Washington, D.C., 1855.

Aptheker, Herbert. "The Quakers and Negro Slavery." *The Journal of Negro History* 25 (July 1940).

Arbena, Joseph L. "Politics or Principle? Rufus King and the Opposition to Slavery, 1785–1825." *Essex Institute Historical Collections* 101, no. 1 (1965).

Astley, Thomas, ed. *A New General Collection of Voyages and Travels.* 4 vols. London: 1745.

Bacon, Jacqueline. *The Humblest May Stand Forth: Rhetoric, Empowerment, and Abolition.* Columbia: The University of South Carolina Press, 2002.

Bacon, Margaret Hope. *History of the Pennsylvania Society for Promoting the Abolition of Slavery: the Relief of Negroes Unlawfully Held in Bondage; and for Improving the Condition of the African Race.* Philadelphia: Pennsylvania Abolition Society, 1959.

Baepler, Paul, ed. *White Slaves, African Masters: An Anthology of American Barbary Captivity.* Chicago: University of Chicago Press, 1999.

Bailyn, Bernard. *Ideological Origins of the American Revolution.* Cambridge, Mass.: Harvard University Press, 1967.

Barbot, Jean. *Barbot on Guinea: The Writings of Jean Barbot on West Africa 1678–1712.* Edited by P.E.H. Hair et al. 2 vols. London: Hakluyt Society, 1992.

Basker, James G. *Amazing Grace: An Anthology of Poems About Slavery, 1660–1810.* New Haven: Yale University Press, 2002.

Bauman, Richard. "The Campaign Against the Slave Trade," *For the Reputation of Truth: Politics, Religion, and Conflict Among the Pennsylvania Quakers 1750–1800.* Baltimore and London: Johns Hopkins Press, 1971.

Bauman, Richard. *For the Reputation of Truth.* Baltimore: Johns Hopkins Press, 1971.

Benezet, Anthony. *A Short Account of That Part of Africa Inhabited by the Negroes.* Philadelphia: W. Dunlop, 1762.

———. *Some Historical Account of Guinea.* London: J. Phillips, 1788.

Bennett, Thomas. "Servile Conspiracy in S. Carolina." *Niles' Weekly Register,* September 7, 1822.

Berlin, Ira. *Many Thousands Gone: The First Two Centuries of Slavery in North America.* Cambridge, Mass.: Harvard University Press, 1998.

Biddle, Henry D. *Extracts from the Journal of Elizabeth Drinker, from 1759 to 1807, A.D.* Philadelphia: J.B. Lippincott Co., 1889.

Biography and Genealogy Master Index. Farmington Hills, Mich.: Gale Group, 1980–2001.

Boudinot, Elias to John Jay. November 5, 1819. Columbia University Rare Books Collection, The John Jay Papers.

Bowden, James. *The History of the Society of Friends in America.* Vols. 1 and 2. London: Charles Gilpin, 1850. Reprint, New York: Arno Press Inc., 1972.

Boyd, George Adams. *Elias Boudinot: Patriot and Statesman, 1740–1821.* Princeton: Princeton University Press, 1952.

Bridenbaugh, Carl and Jessica. *Rebels and Gentlemen: Philadelphia in the Age of Franklin.* New York: Oxford University Press, 1962.

Bridenbaugh, Carl. "The Press and the Book in Eighteenth Century Philadelphia." *The Pennsylvania Magazine of History and Biography* 65 (January 1941).

Brookes, George S. *Friend Anthony Benezet.* Philadelphia: University of Pennsylvania Press, 1937.

Brüe, André. "Voyages and Travels along the Western Coast of Africa, on Account of the French Commerce." *A New General Collection of Voyages and Travels.* Vol. 2. London: Astley, 1745.

Bruns, Roger A. "Anthony Benezet and the Natural Rights of the Negro." *The Pennsylvania Magazine of History and Biography* 96 (January 1972).

Bruns, Roger. *Am I Not a Man and a Brother: The Anti-Slavery Crusade of Revolutionary America, 1688–1788.* New York: Chelsea House Publishers, 1977.

Cadbury, Henry J. "Quaker Bibliographical Notes." *Bulletin of Friends' Historical Association.* Vol. 26. Swarthmore, Pa.: Friends' Historical Association, 1937.

Calvert, Monte A. "The Abolition Society of Delaware, 1801–1807." *Delaware History* 10, no. 4 (1963).

Carter, Clarence E., ed. *The Territory Northwest of the River Ohio, 1787–1803.* Vol. 2, *The Territorial Papers of the United States.* Washington: U.S. Government Printing Office, 1934.

"Christopher Sower, Pennsylvania-German Printer." *The Pennsylvania Magazine of History and Biography* 82 (July 1958).

Comley, John, ed. *Friends' Miscellany.* Philadelphia: William Sharpless, 1831.

Cover, Robert M. *Justice Accused: Antislavery and the Judicial Process.* New Haven: Yale University Press, 1975.

Curtin, Philip D. *The Atlantic Slave Trade.* Madison: University of Wisconsin Press, 1969.

David Cooper Letters, etc. Allinson Family Papers. The Quaker Collection. Haverford College, Haverford, Pa.

Davidson, Robert. "To the Editor." *Poems, on Various Subjects.* Carlisle, Pa.: A. Loudon (Whitehall), 1805.

Davis, David Brion. "New Sidelights on Early Antislavery Radicalism." *The William and Mary Quarterly* 28 (October 1971).

Davis, David Brion. *The Problem of Slavery in the Age of Revolution, 1770–1823.* Ithaca, N.Y.: Cornell University Press, 1975. Reprint, New York: Oxford University Press, 1999.

Debates and Proceedings in the Congress of the United States; with an Appendix, Containing Important State Papers and Public Documents, and All the Laws of a Public Nature; with a Copious Index. House of Representatives. Washington: Gales and Seaton, 15th Cong., 2nd sess., 1855.

Dodson, Howard, Christopher Moore, and Roberta Yancy. *The Black New Yorkers: The Schomburg Illustrated Chronology.* New York: John Wiley, 2000.

Eberly, Wayne J. "The Pennsylvania Abolition Society, 1775–1830." PhD diss., Pennsylvania State University, 1973.

Edwards, Tryon, ed. *The Works of Jonathan Edwards, D.D. Late President of Union College, with a Memoir of his Life and Character.* 2 vols. American Religious Thought of the 18th and 19th Centuries. New York: Garland Publishing, Inc., 1987.

Ellis, Joseph J. *Founding Brothers: The Revolutionary Generation.* New York: Alfred A. Knopf, 2000.

Ellis, Milton and Emily Pendleton. *Philenia: The Life and Works of Sarah Wentworth Morton, 1759–1846.* Orono: University Press of Maine, 1931.

Ernst, Robert. "Rufus King, Slavery, and the Missouri Crisis." *New York Historical Society Quarterly* 46, no. 4 (1962).

Ernst, Robert. *Rufus King, American Federalist.* Chapel Hill: Published for the Institute of Early American History and Culture at Williamsburg, Va., by University of North Carolina Press, 1968.

"Extract of a Letter from Alicant, to a House in this City, dated 23d November, 1793." *The Pennsylvania Gazette.*

Fehrenbacher, Don E. *The Slaveholding Republic: An Account of the United States Government's Relations to Slavery.* Edited by Ward M. McAfee. New York: Oxford University Press, 2001.

Fehrenbacher, Don E. "The Missouri Controversy and the Sources of Southern Separatism." *Southern Review* 14, no. 4 (1978).

Ferm, Robert L. *A Colonial Pastor, Jonathan Edwards the Younger: 1745–1801.* Grand Rapids: William B. Eerdmans Publishing Company, 1976.

Finkelman, Paul. *Slavery and the Founders: Race and Liberty in the Age of Jefferson.* New York: M.E. Sharpe, Inc., 1996.

Finnie, Gordon E. "The Antislavery Movement in the Upper South before 1840." *Journal of Southern History* 35, no. 3 (1969).

Franklin, John Hope and Alfred A. Moss Jr. *From Slavery to Freedom.* 3rd ed. New York: Knopf, 2000.

Fraser Jr., Walter J. *Charleston! Charleston! The History of a Southern City.* Columbia: University of South Carolina Press, 1989.

Frazier, E. Franklin. *The Negro Church in America.* New York: Schocken Books, 1963.

Freedom's Journal. New York, February 22, 1828. Reproduced in "Accessible Archives CD-ROM Edition: The African-American Newspapers: the 19th Century," item #839.

Freeman, Rhonda Golden. *The Free Negro in New York City in the Era before the Civil War.* New York: Garland Publishing, 1994.

Friends' Review (Philadelphia), January 1, 1862–October 26, 1862.

"From the Minerva." *Columbian Gazetteer,* October 1794.

Fucilla, Joseph G. "An American Diplomat in Settecento Italy." *Italica* 26 (March 1949).

Garraty, John A. and Mark C. Carnes. *American National Biography,* 24 vols. New York: Oxford University Press, 1999.

Gellman, David N. "Race, the Public Sphere, and Abolition in Late Eighteenth-Century New York." *Journal of the Early Republic* 20 (Winter 2000).

Gellman, David N. and David Quigley. *Jim Crow New York: A Documentary History of Race and Citizenship.* New York: New York University Press, 2003.

Hamilton, James. "Recollections of Men and Things in Penna, About 1800." *Two Hundred Years in Cumberland County.* Edited by D.W. Thompson et al. Carlisle, Pa.: The Hamilton Library and Historical Association of Cumberland County, 1951.

Harris, Leslie M. *In the Shadow of Slavery: African Americans in New York City, 1626–1863.* Chicago: University of Chicago Press, 2003.

Hazel, John. *Who's Who in the Roman World.* New York: Routledge, 2001.

Heffernan, William. "The Slave Trade and Abolition in Travel Literature." *Journal of the History of Ideas* 34 (April–June 1973).

Hirsch Jr., Leo H. "New York and the National Slavery Problem." *The Journal of Negro History* 16, no. 4 (1931).

Hixson, Richard. *Isaac Collins, A Quaker Printer in 18ᵗʰ Century America.* Trenton: New Jersey Historical Commission, 1968.

Hixson, Richard. *The Press in Revolutionary New Jersey.* Trenton: New Jersey Historical Commission, 1975.

Hockett, Homer C. "Rufus King and the Missouri Compromise." *Missouri Historical Review* 2 (1908).

Jackson, Kenneth. *The Encyclopedia of New York City.* New Haven: Yale University Press, 1995.

Jackson, Maurice. "The Social and Intellectual Origins of Anthony Benezet's Antislavery Radicalism." *Pennsylvania History* 66 (1999).

James, Janet Wilson. *Changing Ideas About Women in the United States, 1776–1825.* New York: Garland Publishing, Inc., 1981.

James, Sydney V. *A People Among Peoples: Quaker Benevolence in Eighteenth Century America.* Cambridge, Mass.: Harvard University Press, 1963.

Jefferson, Thomas. *Notes on the State of Virginia.* New York: Harper Torchbooks, 1964.

Jefferson, Thomas. *The Writings of Thomas Jefferson,* vol. 15. Edited by Albert Ellery Bergh. Washington, D.C.: The Thomas Jefferson Memorial Association of the United States, 1907.

Jennings, Judith. *The Business of Abolishing the British Slave Trade: 1783–1807.* London: Frank Cass & Co., Ltd., 1997.

Johnson, Michael P. "Denmark Vesey and His Co-Conspirators." *William and Mary Quarterly* 58, no. 4 (2001).

Jordan, Winthrop D. *White Over Black: American Attitudes Toward the Negro 1550–1812.* Baltimore: Penguin Books, 1968. Reprint, New York: Oxford University Press, 1974.

Journal of the Twenty Third House of Representatives of the Commonwealth of Pennsylvania. Harrisburg, Pa.: J. Peacock, Market Street, 1812 [1813].

Kaminski, John P., ed. *A Necessary Evil? Slavery and the Debate Over the Constitution.* Madison: Madison House, 1995.

Keane, John. *Tom Paine: A Political Life.* London: Bloomsbury, 1995.

Kennicott, Patrick C. "Black Persuaders in the Anti-Slavery Movement." *Journal of Black Studies* 1, no. 1 (September 1970).

Kerber, Linda. *Women of the Republic: Intellect and Ideology in Revolutionary America.* Chapel Hill: University of North Carolina Press, 1980.

King, Charles R. *Rufus King, Life and Correspondence: Comprising His Letters, Private and Official, His Public Documents, and His Speeches.* 4 vols. New York: G.P. Putnam's Sons, 1894–1900.

King, Rufus. *The True Advocate of Free Soil [the Substance of Two Speeches on the Missouri Bill Delivered in the Senate of the United States].* Newark: Steam Power Press, [1848?].

Klein, Herbert S. *The Atlantic Slave Trade.* New York: Cambridge University Press, 1999.

Lendrum, John. *A Concise and Impartial History of the American Revolution: to Which Is Prefixed, a General History of North and South America; Together with an Account of the Discovery and Settlement of North America, and a View of the Progress, Character, and Political State of the Colonies Previous to the Revolution.* Boston: Thomas and Andrews, 1795; repr. Trenton: James Oram, 1811.

Lincoln, Eric C. and Lawrence H. Mamiya. *The Black Church in the African American Experience.* Durham: Duke University Press, 1990.

Littlefield, Daniel C. "John Jay, the Revolutionary Generation, and Slavery." *New York History* 81, no. 1 (2000).

London Yearly Meeting. *Extracts from the Minutes and Advices of the Yearly Meeting of Friends Held in London, From its First Institution.* London: James Phillips, 1783.

Lowance Jr., Mason I. *A House Divided: The Antebellum Slavery Debates in North America, 1776–1865.* Princeton: Princeton University Press, 2003.

Marietta, Jack D. *The Reformation of American Quakerism, 1748–1783.* Philadelphia: University of Pennsylvania Press, 1984.

"Memoir of Ann Alexander." *Friends' Review: A Religious, Literary and Miscellaneous Journal* 3, no. 22 and 23 (1850).

"The Memorial of the Pennsylvania Society for Promoting the Abolition of Slavery, and the Relief of Free Negroes Unlawfully Held in Bondage." *The Pennsylvania Gazette*, June 1787.

Meyer, Duane. *The Heritage of Missouri—a History.* Saint Louis: State Publishing Company, Inc., 1967.

Miller, Randall M. and John David Smith, *Dictionary of Afro-American Slavery.* New York: Greenwood Press, 1988.

Minkema, Kenneth P. "Jonathan Edwards on Slavery and the Slave Trade." *The William and Mary Quarterly.* Third Series, Vol. 54, Issue 4 (Oct., 1997).

Mintz, Steven. *Moralists and Modernizers: America's Pre-Civil War Reformers.* Baltimore: Johns Hopkins University Press, 1995.

"Miscellany." *Columbian Centinel,* Saturday June 9, 1792.

Moore, Glover. *The Missouri Controversy 1819–1821.* Lexington: University of Kentucky Press, 1953.

Morton, Sarah Wentworth Apthorp. "The African Chief." *Columbian Centinel,* Saturday June 9, 1792.

Morton, Sarah Wentworth Apthorp. "Apology for the Poem." In *Beacon Hill.* Boston: Manning and Loring, 1797.

Morton, Sarah Wentworth Apthorp. "The Tears of Humanity." *Columbian Centinel,* August 6, 1791.

Nash, Gary B. "African Americans in the Early Republic." *Magazine of History* 14, no. 2 (2000).

Newman, Richard S. *The Transformation of American Abolitionism: Fighting Slavery in the New Republic.* Chapel Hill: University of North Carolina Press, 2002.

Newman, Richard, Patrick Rael, and Philip Lapansky, ed. *Pamphlets of Protest: An Anthology of Early African-American Protest Literature, 1790–1860.* New York: Routledge, 2001.

Oldfield, J. R. "The London Committee and Mobilization of Public Opinion against the Slave Trade." *The Historical Journal* 35, no. 2 (1992).

Oliver, Isabella. *Poems, on Various Subjects.* Carlisle, Pa.: A. Loudon (Whitehall), 1805.

Page, Willie F. *Encyclopedia of African History and Culture.* New York: Facts on File, 2001.

The Pennsylvania Gazette, April 27, 1791–January 4, 1792.

"A Poetical Epistle." *Universal Asylum and Columbian Magazine* 5 (December 1790).

Randall, Randolph C. "Authors of the Port Folio Revealed by the Hall Files." *American Literature* 11 (January 1940).

Rawley, James A. *The Transatlantic Slave Trade: A History.* New York: W.W. Norton & Co., 1981.

"Redemption of American Captives at Algiers." *Columbian Gazetteer,* October 1794.

Rothermund, Dietmar. "German Problem of Colonial Pennsylvania." *The Pennsylvania Magazine of History and Biography* 84 (January 1960).

Rury, John L. "Philanthropy, Self Help, and Social Control: The New York Manumission Society and Free Blacks, 1785–1810." *Phylon* 46, no. 3 (1985).

Rush, Benjamin. "Paradise of the Negro Slaves—A Dream." *Friend Anthony Benezet.* Edited by George S. Brookes. Philadelphia: University of Pennsylvania Press, 1937. First published in Benjamin Rush. *Essays, Literary, Moral, and Philosophical.* Philadelphia: Thomas and William Bradford, 1806.

Salzman, Jack, David Lionel Smith, and Cornel West. *African-American Culture and History.* New York: Simon and Schuster Macmillan, 1996.

Sansom, Joseph. "Outlines of the Life and Character of William Penn." *The Port Folio* 1 (March 1809).

Savery, William. *Two Sermons: Delivered at the Bank Meeting-House.* Burlington: Allinson, 1805.

Sellers, Charles Coleman. *Benjamin Franklin in Portraiture* New Haven: Yale University Press, 1962.

Sellers, Charles Coleman. "Joseph Sansom, Philadelphia Silhouettist." *Pennsylvania Magazine of History and Biography* 88 (October 1964).

Shoemaker, Ralph R. and Richard H. Shaw. *American Bibliography: A Preliminary Checklist for 1805, Items 7819–9785.* New York: Scarecrow Press, Inc., 1958.

Simpson, Albert F. "The Political Significance of Slave Representation, 1787–1821," *Journal of Southern History* 7 (1941).

Simpson, Albert F. *Sketches of Lower Canada*. New York: Harpers for Kirk & Mercein, 1817 and *The Portico, a Repository of Science* 4 (November 1817).

Soderlund, Jean R. *Quakers & Slavery: A Divided Spirit*. Princeton: Princeton University Press, 1985.

Spann, Edward Kenneth. "John W. Taylor, the Reluctant Partisan, 1784–1854." PhD diss., New York University, 1957.

Statutes at Large of the United States of America, 1789–1873, 17 vols. (Washington, D.C., 1850–1873).

Sweeney, Douglas A. *Nathaniel Taylor, New Haven Theology, and the Legacy of Jonathan Edwards*. Oxford and New York: Oxford University Press, 2003.

Tebbel, John. *Vol. I: The Creation of an Industry, 1630–1865, A History of Book Publishing in the United States*. New York: R.R. Bowker, 1972.

Thomas, Hugh. *The Slave Trade: The History of the Atlantic Slave Trade: 1440–1870*. New York: Simon & Schuster, 1997.

Thomas, Isaiah. *The History of Printing in America*. New York: Weathervane Books, 1970. First published, Worcester: The Press of Isaiah Thomas, 1810.

Thorpe, Francis Newton, ed. *Federal and State Constitutions, Colonial Charters, and Other Organic Laws of the States, Territories, and Colonies*. Vol. 5. St. Clair Shores, Mich.: Scholarly Press, Inc., 1977.

Tolles, Frederick B. *Meeting House and Counting House: The Quaker Merchants of Colonial Philadelphia, 1682–1763*. New York: Norton, 1948.

Trotter Jr., Joe William and Eric Ledell Smith, ed. *African Americans in Pennsylvania: Shifting Historical Perspectives*. University Park, Pa.: Pennsylvania State University Press, 1997.

Tully, Alan W. "Ethnicity, Religion, Politics—Early America." *The Pennsylvania Magazine of History and Biography* 107 (October 1983).

Turner, Lorenzo Dow. *Anti-Slavery Sentiment in American Literature Prior to 1865*. Port Washington, N.Y.: Kennikat Press, 1929.

Vaux, Roberts. *The Memoirs of the Life of Anthony Benezet*. New York: Burt Franklin, 1969.

Walker, George E. *The Afro-American in New York City, 1827–1860*. New York: Garland Publishing, 1993.

Ward, Townsend. "The Germantown Road and its Associations." *The Pennsylvania Magazine of History and Biography* 5 (1881).

Warner, Robert Austin. *New Haven Negroes: A Social History*. New Haven: Yale University Press, 1940.

Watts, Emily Stipes. *The Poetry of American Women from 1632 to 1945*. Austin: University of Texas Press, 1971.

Wesley, Charles H. "The Negroes of New York in the Emancipation Movement." *Journal of Negro History* 24, no. 1 (January 1939).

White, Shane. *Somewhat More Independent: The End of Slavery in New York City, 1770–1810*. Athens: The University of Georgia Press, 1991.

White, Shane. "'We Dwell in Safety and Pursue Our Honest Callings': Free Blacks in New York City, 1783–1810." *The Journal of American History* 75, no. 2 (September 1988).

Wiecek, William M. *The Sources of Antislavery Constitutionalism in America, 1760–1848*. Ithaca: Cornell University Press, 1977.

Williams, Oscar. *African Americans and Colonial Legislation in the Middle Colonies*. New York: Garland Publishing, Inc., 1998.

Winch, Julie. *A Gentleman of Color: The Life of James Forten*. New York: Oxford University Press, 2002.

Woodson, Carter G. *Negro Orators and their Orations*. New York: Russell and Russell, 1925.

The Works of Thomas Jefferson: The Anas 1791–1806.

World Book Atlas. Chicago: Field Enterprises Educational Corporation, 1972.

Wright, Donald R. *African Americans in the Early Republic 1789–1831*. Arlington Heights, Ill.: Harlan Davidson, 1993.

Wright, Esmond. *Franklin of Philadelphia*. Cambridge, Mass.: Harvard University Press, 1986.

Wright, Sheila. *Friends in York: The Dynamics of Quaker Revival, 1780–1860*. Keele, U.K.: Keele University Press, 1995.

Zeitz, Joshua Michael. "The Missouri Compromise Reconsidered: Rhetoric and the Emergence of the Free Labor Synthesis." *Journal of the Early Republic* 20, no. 3 (2000).

Zilversmit, Arthur. *The First Emancipation: The Abolition of Slavery in the North*. Chicago: University of Chicago Press, 1967.

INDEX

SET IN BASKERVILLE TYPE
PRINTED ON HAMMERMILL PAPER
DESIGNED BY JERRY KELLY